Consuming
Environments

Consuming Environments

Television and Commercial Culture

**MIKE BUDD, STEVE CRAIG,
and CLAY STEINMAN**

Rutgers University Press

New Brunswick, New Jersey,
and London

Library of Congress Cataloging-in-Publication Data

Budd, Mike, 1944–
    Consuming environments : television and commercial culture / Mike
Budd, Steve Craig, and Clay Steinman.
        p.   cm. — (Communications, media, and culture)
    Includes bibliographical references and index.
    ISBN 0-8135-2591-8 (hardcover : alk. paper). — ISBN 0-8135-2592-6
(pbk. : alk. paper)
    1. Television broadcasting—Social aspects.   2. Television
broadcasting—Influence.   3. Television broadcasting—Economic
aspects.   4. Television advertising—Social aspects.   I. Craig,
Steve, 1947–   .   II. Steinman, Clayton M.   III. Title.   IV. Series.
PN1992.6.B79   1999
302.23′45—dc21   98-22954
                                                                                    CIP

British Cataloging-in-Publication data for this book is available from the British Library

Manufactured in the United States of America

To our children,
Steve, Lisa, and Laura Budd
Amy, Ben, and Jeff Craig
and
Daniel Garrett-Steinman

Contents

CHAPTER FOUR

Signification, Discourse, and Ideology

82

CHAPTER FIVE

Television Realisms

108

CHAPTER SIX

The Flow of Commodities

138

CHAPTER SEVEN

From Consumers to Activitists

169

Notes

Index

Telling All the Stories

Andrew Fletcher of Saltoun (1653–1716) wrote in a letter to the marquis of Montrose, the earl of Rothes, "I knew a very wise man that believed that if a man were permitted to make all the ballads, he need not care who should make the laws of a nation."

Today it's television that makes "all the ballads." It comes into the home where the child is born. The stories it tells socialize us into roles of gender, age, class, vocation, and lifestyle and offer models of conformity or targets for rebellion. They weave the seamless web of the cultural environment that cultivates most of what we think, what we do, and how we conduct our affairs.

This is the most profound historic change with far-reaching consequences. The storytelling process used to be handcrafted, homemade, community-inspired. Now it is mostly mass-produced and policy-driven. It is the end result of a complex manufacturing and marketing process. The situation calls for a new diagnosis and a new prescription.

The stories that animate our cultural environment have three distinct but related functions. These functions are (1) to reveal how things work; (2) to describe what things are; and (3) to tell us what to do about them.

Stories of the first kind, revealing how things work, illuminate the all-important but invisible relationships and hidden dynamics of life. Fairy tales, novels, plays, comics, cartoons, and other forms of creative imagination and imagery are the basic building blocks of human understanding. They show complex causality by presenting imaginary action in total situations, coming to some conclusion that has a moral purpose and a social function. You don't have to believe the "facts" of Little Red Riding Hood to grasp the notion that big bad "wolves" victimize old women and trick little girls—a lesson in gender roles, fear, and power.

Stories of the first kind build, from infancy on, the fantasy we call reality. I do not suggest that the revelations are false, which they may or may not be, but that they are synthetic, selective, often mythical, and always socially constructed.

Stories of the second kind depict what things are. These are descriptions, depictions, expositions, reports abstracted from total situations and filling in with "facts" the fantasies conjured up by stories of the first kind. They are the presumably factual accounts, the chronicles of the past and the news of today.

Stories of what things are may confirm or deny some conception of how things work. Their high "facticity" (i.e., correspondence to actual events presumed to exist independently of the story) gives them special status in political theory and often in law. They give emphasis and credibility to selected parts of each society's fantasies of reality. They convey information about finance, weddings, crime, lotteries, terrorists, and so on. They alert us to certain interests, threats, opportunities, and challenges.

Stories of the third kind tell us what to do. These are stories of value and choice. They present things, behaviors, or styles of life as desirable (or undesirable), propose ways to obtain (or avoid) them, and explain the price to be paid for attainment (or failure). They are the instructions, laws, regulations, cautionary tales, commands, slogans, sermons, and exhortations. Today most of them are called commercials and other advertising messages and images we see and hear every day.

Stories of the third kind clinch the lessons of the first two and turn them into action. They typically present an objective to be sought or to be avoided and offer a product, service, candidate, institution, or action purported to help attain or avoid it. The lessons of fictitious Little Red Riding Hoods and their more realistic sequels prominent in everyday news and entertainment not only teach lessons of vulnerability, mistrust, and dependence but also help sell burglar alarms, more jails and executions promised to enhance security (which they rarely do), and other ways to adjust to a structure of power.

Ideally, the three kinds of stories check and balance each other. But in a commercially driven culture, stories of the third kind pay for most of the first two. That creates a coherent cultural environment whose overall function is to provide a hospitable and effective context for stories that sell. With the coming of the electronic age, that cultural environment is increasingly monopolized, homogenized, and globalized. We must then look at the historic course of our journey to see what this new age means for us and our children.

For the longest time in human history, stories were told only face to face. A community was defined by the rituals, mythologies, and imageries held in common. All useful knowledge was encapsulated in aphorisms and legends, proverbs and tales, incantations and ceremonies. Writing was rare and holy, forbidden for slaves. Laboriously inscribed manuscripts conferred sacred power on their interpreters, the priests and ministers. As a sixteenth-century scribe put it:

> Those who observe the codices,
>   those who recite them.
> Those who noisily turn the pages of
>   illustrated manuscripts.
> Those who have possession of the
>   black and red ink and that which is pictured;
> they lead us, they guide us, they tell us the way.

State and church ruled in a symbiotic relationship of mutual dependence and tension. State, composed of feudal nobles, was the economic, military, and political order; church, its cultural arm.

The industrial revolution changed all that. One of the first machines stamping out standardized artifacts was the printing press. Its product, the book, was a prerequisite for all the other upheavals to come. Printing begins the industrialization of storytelling, arguably the most profound transformation in the humanization process.

The book could be given to all who could read, requiring education and creating a new literate class of people. Readers could now interpret the book (at first the Bible) for themselves, breaking the monopoly of priestly interpreters and ushering in the Reformation.

When the printing press was hooked up to the steam engine, the industrialization of storytelling shifted into high gear. Rapid publication and mass transport created a new form of consciousness: modern mass publics. Publics are loose aggregations of people who share some common consciousness of how things work, what things are, and what ought to be done—but never meet face to face. That was never before possible.

Stories could now be sent—often smuggled—across hitherto impenetrable or closely guarded boundaries of time, space, and status. The book lifts people from their traditional moorings as the industrial revolution uproots them from their local communities and cultures. They can now get off the land and go to work in faraway ports, factories, and continents and have with them a packet of common consciousness—the book or journal, and later the motion picture (silent at first)—wherever they go.

Publics, created by such publication, are necessary for the formation of individual and group identities in the new urban environment, as the different classes and regional, religious, and ethnic groups try to maintain some sense of distinct integrity and also to live together with some degree of cooperation with other groups.

Publics are the basic units of self-government. They make it possible to elect or select representatives to an assembly trying to reconcile diverse interests. The maintenance and integrity of multiple publics makes self-government feasible for large, complex, and diverse national communities. People engage in long and costly struggles to be free to create and share stories that fit the reality of competing and often conflicting values and interests. Most of our assumptions about human development and political plurality and choice are rooted in the print era.

One of the most vital provisions of the print era was the creation of the only large-scale folk institution of industrial society, public education. Public education is the community institution where face-to-face learning and interpreting could, ideally, liberate the individual from both tribal and medieval dependencies and all cultural monopolies.

The second great transformation, the electronic revolution, ushers in the telecommunications era. Its mainstream, television, is superimposed upon and reorganizes print-based culture. Unlike the industrial revolution, the new upheaval does not uproot people from their homes but transports them in their homes. It retribalizes modern society. It challenges and changes the role of both church and education in the new culture.

For the first time in human history, children are born into homes where mass-produced stories can reach them on the average more than seven hours a day. Most waking hours, and often dreams, are filled with these stories. The stories do not come from their families, schools, churches, neighborhoods, and often not even from their native countries or, in fact, from anyone with anything relevant to tell. They come from a small group of distant conglomerates with something to sell.

The cultural environment in which we live becomes the by-product of marketing. The historic nexus of state and church is replaced by the new symbiotic relationship of state and television. The "state" itself is the twin institution of elected public government and selected private corporate government, ruling in the legal, military, and economic domains. The media, its cultural arm, are dominated by the private establishment, despite their use of the public airways.

Giant industries discharge their messages into the mainstream of common consciousness. Channels proliferate and new technologies pervade home and office while mergers and bottom-line pressures shrink creative alternatives and reduce diversity of content.

These changes may appear to be broadening local, parochial horizons, but they also mean a homogenization of outlooks and limitation of alternatives. For media professionals, the changes mean fewer opportunities and greater compulsions to present life in salable packages. Creative artists, scientists, humanists can still explore and enlighten and occasionally even challenge, but, increasingly, their stories must fit marketing strategies and priorities.

Viewing commercials is "work" performed by audiences in exchange for "free" news and entertainment. But, in fact, we pay dearly through a surcharge added to the price of every advertised product that goes to subsidize commercial media and through allowing advertising expenditures to be a tax-deductible business expense. These giveaways of public moneys for private purposes further erode the diversity of the cultural mainstream.

Broadcasting is the most concentrated, homogenized, and globalized medium. The top 100 U.S. advertisers pay for two-thirds of all network television. Four networks, allied to giant transnational corporations—our private "Ministry of Culture"—control the bulk of production and distribution and shape the cultural mainstream. Other interests, religious or educational, minority views, and the potential of any challenge to dominant perspectives, lose ground with every merger.

Formula-driven assembly-line–produced programs increasingly dominate the airways. The formulas themselves reflect the structure of power that produces them and function to preserve and enhance that structure of power. Perhaps the leading example of such story functions is violence. It is a good example of how the system works; it is also an indication of the magnitude and nature of the challenge before us.

Humankind may have had more bloodthirsty eras, but none as filled with images of crime and violence as the present. While violent crime rates remain essentially flat or decline, news of crime surges to new highs.

A study by Robert Entman for the Chicago Council on Urban Affairs found not only that local news shows are dominated by vivid images of violence but that "a high percentage of African-Americans and Latinos are shown as victimizers of society, and few as social helpers," contributing to a sense of fear and distrust (that our own research diagnosed as the "mean world syndrome") and to the notion that "the inner city is dominated by dangerous and irresponsible minorities."

Another study of homicide news reporting found that only one of three actual homicides was reported and that the most likely to be selected were those in which the victims were white rather than black or Latino, contrary to the actual crime statistics. University of Pennsylvania sociologist Elijah Anderson also noted that media portrayals of crime and violence involving blacks and the resulting demonization of black males become a major reason for "white flight." In fact, however, African American men, not whites, are the most likely to be the victims of violence.

Our Cultural Indicators study of local news on Philadelphia television found that crime and/or violence items usually lead the newscast and preempt any balanced coverage of the city. Furthermore, 80 percent of crime and violence reported on Philadelphia local news was not even local to the city. It is as if a quota were imposed on the editorial staff to fill from wherever they can. It is also the cheapest way to fill the time. We also found that whites are more likely to be reported when they are the victims and African Americans are more likely to be reported when they are the perpetrators. Black-on-white crime is less frequent but more newsworthy than any other combination.

Violence is, of course, a legitimate and even necessary news and dramatic feature to show the tragic costs of deadly compulsions. However, such tragic sense of violence has been swamped by "happy violence" produced on the television dramatic assembly line. "Happy violence" is cool, swift, and painless and always leads to a happy ending. Far from Shakespeare or the Bible, it occurs five times per hour, designed to deliver the audience to the next commercial in a receptive mood.

Violence is a demonstration of power. Its principal lesson is to show quickly and dramatically who can get away with what against whom. That exercise defines majority might and minority risk. It shows one's place in the societal "pecking order."

The role of violence in the media mainstream of television emerges from our analysis of prime-time network programs monitored since 1967. Women play one out of three characters in drama, one out of six in the news. Young people constitute one-third and old persons one-fifth of their actual proportions of the population. Most other minorities are even more underrepresented. Most of the groups that are underrepresented are also those who suffer the worst fate.

The typical viewer of prime-time television drama sees, every week, an average of 21 criminals arrayed against an army of 41 public and private law enforcers. Crime and violence engage more characters than all other occupations combined. About one out of three speaking parts, and more than half of all major characters, are involved in violence either as victims or as victimizers, or both.

We calculated the violence "pecking order" by counting the number of victims for every 10 perpetrators of violence. That "risk ratio" expresses the "price" groups of characters pay for committing violence. We found that overall average risk ratio (the number of victims per 10 perpetrators) is 12. But the ratio for women is 17, for lower-class characters 19, for elderly characters 20, and for women of color 22. In other words, minority groups tend to pay a higher price for their show of force than do the majorities.

Our surveys show that heavy viewers express a greater sense of apprehension and vulnerability than do light viewers in the same groups. Heavy viewers are more likely than comparable groups of light viewers to overestimate their chances of involvement in violence; to believe that their neighborhoods are unsafe; to state that fear of crime is a very serious personal problem; and to assume that crime is rising, regardless of the facts of the case. Heavy viewers are also more likely to buy new locks, watchdogs, and guns "for protection" (thus becoming the major cause of handgun violence).

Moreover, viewers who see members of their own group underrepresented but overvictimized develop an even greater sense of apprehension and mistrust. Insecure, angry, mistrustful people may be prone to violence but are even more likely to be dependent on authority and susceptible to deceptively simple, strong, hard-line postures and appeals.

What drives media violence? The usual rationalization that media violence "gives the public what it wants" is disingenuous. The public rarely gets a fair choice in which all elements but violence, including placement, headline, promotion, airtime, celebrity value, treatment, and so on, are equal. There is no evidence that, cost and other factors being equal, violence per se gives audiences "what they want." As the trade paper *Broadcasting & Cable* editorialized on

September 20, 1993 (p. 66), "the most popular programming is hardly violent as anyone with a passing knowledge of Nielsen ratings will tell you."

We compared the ratings of more than 100 violent and the same number of nonviolent shows aired at the same time on network television. The average Nielsen rating of the violent sample was 11.1; the rating for the nonviolent sample was 13.8. The share of viewing households in the violent and nonviolent samples, respectively, was 18.9 and 22.5. The nonviolent sample was more highly rated than the violent sample for each of the five seasons studied. The amount and consistency of violence further increased the unpopularity gap.

Concentration of ownership denies access to new entries and to alternative perspectives. Having fewer buyers for their products forces the remaining "content providers" deeper into deficit financing. As a consequence, most television and movie producers cannot break even on the U.S. domestic market. They are forced into video and foreign sales to make a profit. Therefore, they need a dramatic ingredient that requires no translation, "speaks action" in any language, and fits any culture. That ingredient is violence.

Syndicators demand "action" (the code word for violence) because it "travels well around the world," said the producer of *Die Hard 2*. "Everyone understands an action movie. If I tell a joke, you may not get it but if a bullet goes through the window, we all know how to hit the floor, no matter the language."

Our analysis shows that violence dominates U.S. exports. We compared 250 U.S. programs exported to 10 countries with 111 programs shown in the United States during the same year. Violence was the main theme of 40 percent of home-shown and 49 percent of exported programs. Crime/action series constituted 17 percent of home-shown and 46 percent of exported programs.

People suffer the media violence inflicted on them with diminishing tolerance. A March 1985 Harris survey showed that 78 percent disapprove of violence they see on television. In a Times-Mirror national poll in 1993, 80 percent said entertainment violence was "harmful" to society, compared with 64 percent in 1983.

Local broadcasters, legally responsible for what goes on the air, also oppose the overkill and complain about loss of control. *Electronic Media* reported on August 2, 1993, that in its own survey of 100 general managers, three out of four said there is too much needless violence on television and 57 percent would like to have "more input on program content decisions." A *U.S. News & World Report* survey published on April 30, 1994, found that 59 percent of media workers saw entertainment violence as a serious problem.

Formula-driven media violence is not an expression of freedom, popularity, or crime statistics. It is a de facto censorship that chills originality and extends the dynamics of domination, intimidation, and repression domestically and globally. The media violence overkill is an ingredient in a global marketing formula imposed on media professionals and foisted on the children of the world.

This is but the tip of the iceberg that, as Budd, Craig, and Steinman document in this book, confronts us with "an ecological and social crisis of major proportions." It is high time that the full extent of this, well, titanic prospect is exposed and explored in a way that turns apathy and cynicism into action.

George Gerbner
Philadelphia
February 1998

Preface and Acknowledgments

Whether they love it, hate it, or use it just to pass the time, average adults in the United States are watching more television than ever, up to four hours a day by some estimates. This gives commercial TV unprecedented power in the construction of the mental environments of our lives and makes it a major reason we lack time for families, friends, and ourselves.

Advertisers and TV executives want us to spend as much time as we can in front of our sets, for it is access to our brains that they buy and sell. Yet the most important effect of TV may be one that no one intends—accelerated destruction of the natural environment, caused by the overconsumption commercial television fosters.

Consuming Environments explores how much TV people watch, why they watch so much, and what they see. It argues that while people may have good reasons for watching television habitually, they seem to do so unaware that their activity might be harmful to their environmental health. It examines the advertising and media companies that have shaped the commercial character of most television, tracing their motives and operations and their increasing concentration in fewer hands. And it looks at the way commercial priorities affect the content and form of television shows.

Intended for readers concerned about the impact of media on the environment as well as for those interested in critical studies of television, *Consuming Environments* combines methods of close analysis with attention to television as an industry and includes perspectives drawn from environmentalist, feminist, and multicultural studies. The book shows how advertisements and programs are put together in complex ways normally invisible to viewers. It argues that television's appeal indeed requires its methods to be hidden from view, so that viewers can feel in control of the meanings they make of television and the ways they respond to its attractions.

Although it concentrates on contemporary television, *Consuming Environments* also looks at commercial TV's roots in department store windows and its future in a new media environment. It considers the impact of cable, satellites, and the Internet on TV. It offers specific ways citizens can get involved in joining those who seek to turn back TV and overconsumption's assault on the environment. Commercial television overall does harm to our world in ways and for reasons still beyond democratic reach. If there is light at the end of the tunnel of these times, we can find it only in the cares and struggles of each other, not in the flickering of screens.

Joint Acknowledgments: This book in significant part responds to the concerns, needs, questions, and values of our many students over the years, who thus have shaped it in important ways. The three coauthors of this book have been talking, teaching, and writing together since the mid-1970s, when we found ourselves beginning our academic careers in the Department of Communication at Florida Atlantic University in Boca Raton, Florida. By the mid-1980s, with the support of a sympathetic dean, Jack Suberman, the department's media studies program had grown enough to attract an eclectic but inspiring group of junior faculty, including Fred Fejes, Betsy Holdsworth Nielsen, Harriet Margolis, Mike Nielsen, Andrea Press, and Ramona (then Cathy) Schwichtenberg, who kept each other abreast of what the *Journal of Communication* in a 1983 special issue called a paradigm-shifting "ferment in the field." We learned from one another, from colleagues in other fields (such as Lynn Appleton, Carlos Nelson, and Bruce Williams), and from an extraordinary group of students (Al Berman, Rose D'Agostino, Richard Garrett, Gabriel Gomez, Shannon Kratz, Margaret Montalbano, Diana Saco, and Mauricio Trapper, to name only a few) in ways that continue to inform our teaching and our writing. And we developed a collaborative method in which we share authorship of every word and list our names as we do only in a nod to alphabetic chance. Since then, there have been other ferments, in the field, at Florida Atlantic, and in our lives. They have made writing collaboratively more difficult, and we are grateful to Leslie Mitchner at Rutgers University Press for her support and patience as we worked to bring our efforts together. We also want to thank our series editors at Rutgers (George Custen of the City University of New York, Larry Gross of the University of Pennsylvania, Ellen Seiter of the University of California, San Diego, and Virginia Wright Wexman of the University of Illinois, Chicago) and the anonymous reviewers whose suggestions were so useful at a crucial time in the book's development, and Marilyn Campbell, managing editor at the press, who helped us finish even with our idiosyncratic formats.

We are especially grateful to George Gerbner for agreeing to write the foreword and for his insights and actions on behalf of a democratic and sustainable cultural environment.

Of the more than two dozen people we contacted for chapter 6, most generous were Al Berman of CBS News, Joan Bogin of MasterCard International, Paul Schwartz of Clean Water Action in Washington, D.C., and especially Lorraine Antoniello of Advertising Information Services.

Mike Budd: For key ideas and paradigms, political and intellectual inspiration, and valuable support over the many years of the development of this book, I thank Lynn Appleton, David Bordwell, Stuart Ewen, Fred Fejes, Eric Freedman, Bruce Gagnon, Jane Gaines, Todd Gitlin, Sut Jhally, Mark Crispin Miller, Bill McKibben, Bill Nichols, Eleanor Schuster, Chris Scodari, Kristin Thompson, Barbara Trent, Mimi White, and Raymond Williams. Above all, though, I am grateful to Suzanne Sheber, my friend and my love, to whose green values I hope this book is true.

Steve Craig: My appreciation goes to the University of Maine, whose sabbatical program supported some of the research for chapters 2 and 3, and to the Department of Radio, Television, and Film at the University of North Texas. My special thanks to Gretchen Craig for her patient help as consultant, adviser, and copy editor.

Clay Steinman: Thanks to Tom Banks, Daniel Garrett-Steinman, Richard Garrett, Steve Hecker, Hsueh Yeh, Allan Steinman, Florence Steinman, Deborah Whitworth, and especially Bob Entman for counsel and ideas, and to them and to Sallie Brown, Peter Clark, Daniel del Castillo, Kate Kane, Evelyn Orr, Mark Pinsky, Ryan Schram, and Adam Tressler for attentive readings of parts of the manuscript. Evelyn Orr also shared her research on detergents and their effect on water quality, conducted at Macalester College in 1988. At Macalester, Carol Horton, David Itzkowitz, Julia Kirt, Anna Meigs, Phil Mikosz, Charles Norman, Anthony Pinn, Peter Rachleff, Ahmed Samatar, Sandy Schram, Paul Solon, Doug Stone, Anne Sutherland, Matthew Weinstein, and members of the Interdisciplinary Writing Group—especially Beth Cleary, Ruthann Godollei, Michal McCall, Leslie Vaughan, and Joëlle Vitiello—read drafts of one or two chapters and offered suggestions and support, and Norm Rosenberg and Linda Schulte-Sasse contributed more than one has any right to expect from colleagues; Eric Hausken, Rebecca Moskow, Jen Neuber, and Chris Teske provided research assistance, as did Sarah Johnson, Nathan Munson, and Sarah Zeller—these three helped so much I consider them collaborators. At the Macalester Library, Terry Fishel and Dave Collins provided research assistance; and Tom Browne and the Media Services Department made possible early versions of the illustrations. Ben Archibald, Betty Garrett, André LaFosse, John Pavlovich, and Hayden Shumsky contributed ideas and observations. Gratitude also to participants in the Macalester Seminar in Budapest, July 1995, organized by Anne Sutherland, for their insights into environmental issues in central eastern Europe and worldwide. Earlier versions of the arguments about capitalism and the environment and about advertising and multiculturalism were presented at the December 1993 and March 1995 conferences of the Union for Democratic Communications, whose members made comments that led to revision. Colleagues at Macalester in Communication Studies—Sally Caudill, Adrienne Christiansen, Dick Lesicko, Stevie Rawn, and especially Roger Mosvick—and Media Services—Brian Longley, Dave Reynolds, and Kristi Wheeler—provided the supportive environment that enabled me to complete my portion of this work. And most of all, Lynn Garrett helped refine every idea and contributed her intelligence, political sense, and knowledge of prose to every page I managed to draft, and her patience and support to every year it took to get this project done.

None but us should be held responsible for our use of what they shared.

Consuming Environments

CHAPTER ONE

Television and the Environment: An Introduction

Welcome in our homes for the entertainment it provides, television works for multinational corporations that do environmental harm. Television beams at us, entices us to watch as much as we can. It slices and dices us demographically, sells advertisers access to our brains. Indeed, more than 1 billion TVs occupy the households of the world, and their number grows every day. As each new child is born, somewhere on the planet another television set goes on-line.

Television does not turn people into zombies. Viewers do not absorb its images as if by hypodermic injection. Yet television continues to be influential because it remains part of so many hours, more than any other activity except sleep and work.[1] Of course, not all of its forms function like commercial TV. Public television occasionally offers alternative art (*Alive from Off Center*) and information (*Frontline,* sometimes), no matter how influenced most of it is by corporate power and local elites; individual Public Broadcasting Service (PBS) stations, especially those in cities with two public channels, sporadically brave the unexpected. Pay channels such as HBO and noncommercial networks such as C-SPAN eschew advertiser control for viewers affluent enough to afford them. Videotapes and local special interest and cable access programs offer still more choices.[2] So do computer Web sites, as commercialized as they threaten to become.

In a generation or two, advertising-supported broadcast television as we know it may disappear. Computers and TVs may converge, as Microsoft and other titans combine on-line operations with network television, and high-definition television (HDTV) diffuses and requires all-digital programming. Yet for years to come, as long as we allow it, commercial TV will remain the mental environment in which people in the United States and elsewhere spend much, if not most, of their screen time. This environment has its own ways of representing the world, and these shape experience away from the set. By promoting concentration on the individual self and wasteful consumption, commercial television damages the physical environment of which we are a part.

How does commercial television matter to the health of the environment? What does it tell us about our relation to the social and natural worlds, to each other, and to ourselves? What can we do about it? These questions constitute the focus of this book.

Television cannot be understood solely as a set of technologies, or as a group of programs, genres, or even business institutions. It exists as many things at once: a machine, a piece of furniture, an industry, programming, ads, the experience of viewing, and effects on viewers and the world. In this book, we view television not as a technology, a purposeful application of science, but as an *apparatus,* an ensemble of operations designed to accomplish a task. This term has been used to analyze film, but here we use this idea to specify four levels of the apparatus of television:[3]

- The "technical base"—cameras, lights, microphones, transmitters, satellites, receivers, and so forth.
- The "conditions of spectatorship"—its primary placement in the home, the positioning of bodies in the path of picture screens and speakers.
- The cultural material broadcast through or played on the set. These constitute television's "texts," texts designed to appear in the aggregate as a translucent window on the world rather than as an opaque screen.
- The "mental machinery" that enables viewers to turn images and sounds, phosphors glowing and speakers vibrating, into meaningful advertisements, amusements, reports, and stories.

In addition, we consider television an *institutional apparatus,* and so we add a fifth level. This level includes:

- The institution created by powerful organizations, particularly economic ones such as national advertisers, and the ways in which television itself systematically affects the natural and social environment of which it is a part.

As an institutional apparatus, television will vary across cultures and time, as will its effects. As an institution, it can be changed, although not easily.

Television's Influence

In part, television has become so difficult to change because it plays such an important role in people's lives. Newton Minow in 1991 said daily viewing, presumably by household, had grown from 2.175 to 7.3 hours since he had called television a "vast wasteland" while chair of the Federal Communications Commission 30 years before.[4] Less clear, however, is how much time individuals spend watching. Some say less than 2.25 hours a day.[5] Others say 3.[6] Still others 4.27.[7] The numbers vary depending on who has been asked, when they have been asked, and how they have been counted.[8] Older people watch more, as during the week do those who work at home, mostly women still in the 1990s. Adolescents watch less than adults or children between the ages of 2 and 11.[9] (Nielsen starts counting people as viewers when they are 2 years old.) Those with more income tend to watch less, probably because they have more paid work or have more resources to take advantage of disposable time.[10] Attempts at more precise passive measures such as people meters, which register who is watching, ignore variations in attention and the conversations, household tasks, catnaps, and so forth that reduce the significance of sitting in front of the set.[11] The Nielsen and most other ratings are produced for use within the television business; the "audience" they quantify as marketing data is not identical to the thinking beings within reach of their sets. Ratings say nothing about what different groups of viewers consciously or unconsciously *do* with what they see, phenomena difficult to define.[12]

Just why people spend so much time watching television is also difficult to know. According to one survey, nearly two-thirds of U.S. residents in the early 1980s found it "dull and repetitive."[13] Yet some 55 percent of those surveyed at the end of the decade said it would be "very difficult" for their family to give up television for six months. More than one-quarter said they would not give up watching television permanently, even for a million dollars or more, a finding *TV Guide* replicated in 1992.[14]

Measuring television's effects, like measuring its audience, is difficult. Even ratings data are slippery, as we show in chapter 2. Human behavior is neither uniform, neatly categorized, nor easily observed outside the laboratory. Therefore, isolating "an effect" is difficult, and singling out television, let alone a single show, as "a cause" is perhaps impossible. The most thorough social science research about television tends to be cautious and limited in its claims.[15] This does not necessarily mean television has limited effects, only that social scientists may be limited in their capacity to capture these effects with certainty. It may be that the major effect of advertiser-supported television, as Michael Schudson says of advertising generally, is that it provides people with terms for thinking about their lives, terms generated not to help people get along but to facilitate commercial ends.[16] Along with other institutions like school and the state, advertising and its media provide each of us with a wardrobe of resources outfitted with such markers of identity as speech, diet, posture, clothes, information, entertainment, and modes of transportation. These allow us to signal—even better, to *construct*—who we "are" (and are not) to others, which in turn allows a sense, however imaginary it might be, that each of us is indeed some*one*. One definition of identity seems particularly applicable here: "an active set of performances which show to others and to [oneself] the kind of person [one] desires to be taken to be."[17] Identity in this sense functions especially well for corporations when its pursuit means buying and showing off marketed products or experiences. Too often what makes these seem special is that they are priced just out of range for what their buyers normally can afford. Many people have come to define their individuality, their personal uniqueness, in terms of mass-produced commodities available to anyone with the ability somehow to pay. Both cause and effect of this synthetic individuality have been hyperinflated wants and needs that further divide people along lines of economic inequity. Yet while advertisers do want to move goods, they have little professional interest in the social discrimination and psychological stress such consumption causes. What TV does, then, may be a by-product unintended by anyone who works in the business: channeling *noneconomic* desire along paths designed to sell commodities. Economists would call this an "externality," an effect unrelated to any firm's specific goals, just as they call a steel mill's pollution of air and water an externality to its goal of making steel to sell. Nevertheless, just as industry's physical pollution affects us intended or not, so, too, television's environmental impact costs everyone. This is true for all of us no matter what we individually watch, or whether we watch at all. Even those without a TV must live in a world touched by what it promotes.[18]

Many of us would describe the experience of television as entertainment, as an escape and diversion from the stress of the world and its work. Noticed or not, the experience of television is also one of simulated abundance. Through the TV screen pours a cornucopia of images and sounds, of situation comedies, ads, police shows, ads, soaps, ads, game shows, ads, promotions and ads, movies, news, ads, talk shows, and more ads. A new immigrant from a developing country might well identify the United States more with commercial abundance, overflowing supermarkets, and cable channels by the dozen than with values of democracy and freedom. Or abundance and democracy might seem intrinsically associated.

Indeed, companies such as 7–11 and Burger King have campaigned on "freedom of choice," equating the diversity of similar products to the political franchise. Internationally and at home, the television screen has become the vanguard of commercial culture, a socioeconomic form that encourages more people to become consumers every year. Every year, too, experienced consumers find themselves shopping to meet more needs, or what seem to be needs, and spending more time working to pay for them. This is good for everyone, according to the values of commercial culture. The leading financial and political forces in the West have argued for the last century that the expansion of this culture at home and in less industrialized parts of the world improves the lot of humankind. It "develops" the planet, transforming what is not human to human ends, radically altering the environment in the process.

An Environment Endangered

At the same time, as more of us spend more time in a world of screens, the body of the earth, its inhabitants, and its cultures accumulate scars of disregard.[19] Soil, air, and water suffer increasing pollution, diversity of plant and animal life becomes threatened, too many overcrowded people go hungry and homeless. Too few feel at home. Industrialized countries, especially the United States, use far more than their share of natural resources in terms of population, generating monstrous quantities of waste. The average person in the United States—rich, middle, and poor combined—consumes more than twice the grain and 10 times the oil of one in Brazil or Indonesia; indeed, each child born here will command between 7 and 8 times the planetary resources of one in born in India.[20] According to the World Resources Institute, the United States by the late 1980s had lost—developed or polluted—95 percent of what were once its forest habitats, 99 percent of what were once its savanna grasslands, and 53 percent of what were once its wetlands.[21] In 1996, the United States alone produced more than 208 million metric tons of solid waste, even with a 27 percent recycling rate.[22] Much of this had to be burned or buried in landfills.

In less industrialized countries, people suffer while their resources, their wealth, their space are commandeered to support comfortable lifestyles in richer nations. Pressing their right to pollute as much as local law will allow, multinational corporations ignore professed environmental commitments made at home when they venture abroad for profit.[23] Agencies such as the World Bank encourage consumption of environments and labor time in poorer nations to serve the needs of those higher on the human food chain, although at times residents of poorer countries may benefit economically, as in parts of South Korea and Taiwan. These changes accelerate as corporations and governments seek to accumulate capital at intensified rates worldwide. For example, in 1991 Nike paid its workers in Indonesia $1.03 *a day*, even as it earned $3 billion in annual profit.[24] As Neil Smith argues in *Uneven Development*, investors think of space on earth as a site of potential profit rather than as a locale in which people live.[25] The results: degradation of nature, failure to develop sustainable economies, global polarization of rich and poor, and grotesquely inflated military budgets even as the Cold War recedes in memory.

Green social movements have sounded an additional alarm: the development of the world, carried through under the flag of human enhancement, has become its overdevelopment. Continued development unchecked would bring more misery for the many and risk eventual extinction for all. Researchers at the Worldwatch Institute put it succinctly: the international economy may be expanding at record pace, "but the ecosystem on which it depends is not expanding at all."[26] In its 1997 report, the institute predicted increased hunger and starvation for millions in developing countries and conflict throughout the world over food.[27] Production of meat has grown fourfold since 1950, in response to increased demand by those who can afford it, disproportionately robbing those who cannot of access to grain, which rises in price as it is commandeered as feed.[28] Consensus grows among scientists that higher levels of carbon dioxide and methane in the air produce a greenhouse effect, the result of industrialization, forest burning, and, again, vastly enlarged herds of animals raised to become Big Macs and other meat. This long-term warming of the planet's entire atmosphere by several degrees Fahrenheit will have potentially catastrophic effects—droughts, heat waves, and rising ocean levels from melting polar ice caps. Already the weather has become so volatile, its storms so severe, that the insurance industry has joined the fight against global warming and for reduction in use of fossil fuels. Since 1979, the planet has seen the 14 hottest years since records were first kept in 1866, including 1997, the warmest year yet.[29]

We face an ecological and social crisis of major proportions, a crisis for which individualist market culture has not prepared its habitants. The crisis threatens us as individuals, to be sure, and as individuals we can try to delay its arrival. Yet these trends cannot be undone by changes in personal behavior. Their perpetuation is *institutional*. Certainly, one might want to protest environmental waste by consuming less, and the act of trying to live lightly has moral significance. But the problems are so severe, the forces that drive them in corporations and governments so relentless, that biking more, eating vegan, recycling, buying cottons and keeping them longer, even taking the pledge against sport utility vehicles—individual acts such as these make little substantive difference. We cannot avert this crisis as individuals, only as engaged participants in an interdependent world, only if there are many of us, well organized in favor of community survival. Orienting personal environmentalism around consumer choice, around style, may as much as anything perpetuate the antiactivist thinking on which the system depends.

No wonder optimism about the future can seem naive. Bill McKibben argues in *The End of Nature* that overdevelopment has ended nature itself, ended our human relation to a larger, distinct domain apart from human control yet containing human life and culture.[30] However, views such as this may not be the most helpful in generating more enthusiasm for the political fight for the environment, as McKibben himself seems to have recognized when he wrote his subsequent *Hope, Human and Wild*.[31] In *A Moment on the Earth*, Gregg Easterbrook argues that "environmental commentary is so fog bound in woe that few people realize measurable improvements have already been made in almost every area," at least in the United States, and so the fight for more substantial improvements and for less wasteful consumption continues to have genuine possibilities for measurable success.[32] Worldwide, the manufacture of CFCs, the main culprit damaging the ozone layer, continues its decade-long decline.[33] While use in 1996 of the most common fossil fuels—coal, gas, and oil—continued slowly to rise (by 1.8, 4.5, and 2.3 percent, respectively), producing a record 6.25 billion tons of carbon emissions, wind power grew by an encouraging 26 percent and solar battery use increased 16 percent, even if together these sources remain proportionately small.[34] Although the United States, source of nearly one-quarter of the world's carbon emissions, continues slowly to increase the burning of fossil fuels, "air pollution, water pollution, ocean pollution, toxic discharges, acid rain emissions, soil loss, radiation exposure, species protection, and recycling are areas where the trend lines have been consistently positive for many years," thanks in large part to government intervention.[35] Environmentalists have questioned Easterbrook's data and his motives, just as antienvironmentalists have questioned theirs. And indeed this argument could seem conservative and apologist if a more radical environmental movement were already amassed. In the present, however, with the main struggle against antienvironmentalists rather than moderate ones, Easterbrook's and similar ideas might be useful indeed. That pro-environment regulation and action, including consumption taxes, have worked, and can be both progressive and to everyone's long-term benefit, is important to recognize as conservative corporate forces try to roll them back in Congress and in the states. While it may lack a sustainable vision for the future, thinking such as Easterbrook's may prove better able to win people to environmentalist movements than predictions of an inevitable apocalypse. Small victories can be precious sources of renewable energy.

Such energy might well be linked to a reorientation away from commercial culture's virtual environment and toward reconnection with people and the natural environment in which we live. In this the critique of commercial television would play only one part. Advertising alone does not cause societal overdevelopment or individual preoccupation with commodities, although it works on their behalf. It is part of a cultural-economic system. Still, advertising does tend to be the most visible partner in an overall marketing mix that also includes packaging, wholesale selling, promotion, pricing, and distribution.[36] Tracking its effects is notoriously difficult. Yet however difficult it might be to measure its effects on consumption, advertising has defined television as a commercial form.[37] As television systems increasingly fall into private hands worldwide, advertisers have more power to promote consumption. Regardless of the values anyone in business might personally hold, capitalist enterprises need to grow or they die, requiring more consumption, and so overall they tend to encourage profligate use of scarce resources, thus threatening the health of the planet.[38] Think of the lobbying for highways and other facilities for automobiles and against mass transit by corporate forces in this century. Environmental issues, however, go beyond economics, into cultural forms and the timbre of life. Television programs, cultural products made as vehicles for ads, tend to stress individual desires and goals. This individualism does not derive from any willful advertiser conspiracy. The belief that individual choice and action are the best levers for democratic change has been a fundamental U.S. value. But for at least a century, this individualism has increasingly centered on the obsessive possession of products.

On the History of Commercial Culture

How did these desires develop as they did in the United States during the last century? In *Captains of Consciousness,* Stuart Ewen surveyed corporate efforts to consolidate commodity culture, mainly in the 1920s.[39] More recently, William

Leach in *Land of Desire* has traced this culture back to the development of department stores beginning in the 1890s.[40] He shows that consumerist habits of thought and activity taken for granted today were systematically cultivated by merchants and others (media, banks, government, the transportation and tourism industries) who prospered with the growth of manufacture and marketing. Consumerist culture was an effect, an effect that in retrospect says more about specific historical forces and strategies than it does about any universal human nature. Driven not by preexisting consumer demand but by businesspeople interested in immediate gain, this creation may have given some people much greater access to material goods than ever before, but it foreclosed other options for historical development such as democratizing access to political or economic power.[41] Its "cardinal features . . . were acquisition and consumption as the means of achieving happiness; the cult of the new; the democratization of desire; and money value as the predominant measure of all value in society."[42] These qualities were new to the world in the late 19th century, although they had antecedents in earlier cultural forms. Their success was no doubt in part due to ways they rode (and shaped) the cultural revolution that came in modernity's wake.

Increasingly, dreams and norms were cast more by capital than by church, community, or country, shaped as by-products of the imperative to produce, sell, and reinvest, to produce and sell more, to turn over money with intensified speed. "A commercial aesthetic of desire and longing took shape to meet the needs of business."[43] Corporate interests used psychological technologies to capitalize on the very alienation their transformation of society had produced, engendering the first major power shift brokered by desire. As manufacturers focused more on making money than on making goods, they learned to emphasize meanings over materials for customers at large. They did so at a moment when regimented factory and office systems were attacking what remained of people's sense of self, when industrialization and urbanization were fragmenting people's sense of place and wreaking havoc on the environment.[44] Lacking traditional forms of identity, people used what was available. Anxious shoppers were given what Georg Simmel called a "sham individualism" to mark them off from others in cities where few knew their name.[45] Throughout the century, social identity would come increasingly to draw more on differentiated preferences for goods and store-bought experiences and less on what one did on the job.[46] Workers and farmers would become consumers, easing the task of retailers and their suppliers but making class-based organizing Sisyphean. Corporations increasingly offered a dematerialized lifeworld of images, a *"this*-worldly paradise that was stress free and 'happy'" (emphasis in original).[47]

Facilitating this process was the development in the early 1900s of show windows, department store promotions whose primary elements were color, light, and glass. Before the 1890s, most selling occurred face to face. Within 10 years, however, illustrated ads, posters, billboards, and electrical signs began systematically presenting goods to consumers separate from personal contact. Between 1880 and 1910, annual corporate advertising grew from $30 million to $600 million, in the process making economically possible such mass-market magazines as *Cosmopolitan,* the *Saturday Evening Post,* and the *Ladies' Home Journal* and providing the lifeblood of many a daily newspaper.[48] Advertising began to control the ostensibly noncommercial parts of media, the news and the fiction, tailoring the information and entertainment people received to its goal of creating a favorable environment for moving goods and consequently shaping more of what people thought in terms favorable to market society.[49]

The abstraction of the printed ad, its separation from the explicit personal sale, reached its zenith in show windows, some as large as household rooms. By the 1910s, merchants had learned that show windows could wed products with meanings with which they had no inherent connection—shoes with grace, clothes with a taste for travel, jewels and perfume with romance, furniture with royalty. By the mid-teens, merchandisers were arranging products in tableaux, drawing on knowledge of staging from parlor performance as well as from professional theater to create, for example, a ballroom scene ostensibly set on the Riviera.[50] The royal road to sales was understanding and manipulating—*fooling*, to put it plainly—the minds of potential customers. In Anne Friedberg's words, "The shop window was the proscenium for visual intoxication, the site of seduction for consumer desire."[51] As one of the most successful designers of department-store display, Arthur Fraser of Marshall Field's, described his task: "I hoped to create in the mind of the viewer a psychological harmony, a sort of 'glimpse into the interior of the temple.'"[52]

Color, light, and glass. Leach argues that the incorporation of glass into marketing established a distance crucial to the mystification of commodities. Glass "closed off smell and touch, diminishing the consumer's relationship with the goods. At the same time, it amplified the visual . . . permitting everything to be seen yet rendering it all beyond touch."[53] It "served to bring light to the dank interior selling space of the store."[54] The "interior of the temple" had to be inaccessible—yet visible—for it to seem a higher realm. It had to be distant enough to motivate the *want to have* as skeleton key for the *want to be* in a "mingling of refusal and desire that must have greatly intensified desire."[55]

This desire for possession followed on the 19th-century development of what Friedberg calls the "mobilized gaze," *sightseeing* moments of shopping and tourism in which spectators sense their calling as masters of, connoisseurs of, or potential customers for what they have the power and right to see. In cities generally, making available this new, modern mode of life were "architectural forms . . . which facilitated and encouraged a pedestrian mobilized gaze—exhibition halls, winter-gardens, department stores, museums."[56] Addition of the "virtual gaze of photography" in the cinema, newspaper, magazine, window display, and the like allowed an even more modern form, what Friedberg calls the "mobilized virtual gaze." This gaze, cultivated especially in connection with shopping, created a physical and psychological space formerly closed to women but now newly open to them, that of the urban wanderer/observer.[57] Indeed, the consumer gaze was the legitimate public position most frequently offered to women by civil society, especially in the years before suffrage.

Entering the Home

What moved increasingly common encounters with commodity tableaux into a full-blown environment of commercial images was their entrance into the home, their occupation of domestic space. Until the turn of the century, few homes beyond those of the affluent contained more than scattered examples of corporate efforts to link products with images. Only with the rise of national brands and display advertising in the early 20th century, and their entrance into the home through newspapers and magazines, did the family become a site in which idealized commodities occasionally mattered. With the explosion of radio, color advertising in magazines, and an industry of advertising researchers and copy-writers in the 1920s, the promotion of goods, previously public, became routine in private family ritual. Newspapers in the morning and evening, designated times for listening to specific radio programs throughout the week, discussions about shopping, and shopping itself. For advertisers, this invasion allowed increasing control over family time. As Edwin L. Artzt, until recently board chair and chief executive officer of Procter & Gamble, once told an audience of advertising insiders:

> Advertising started in print. When radio came along and we all had to buy time as well as space—and sell with words and music and no pictures—we, the advertising industry, took control of our environment.
>
> We created programming. We molded the environment to fit our needs. We were no longer dealing just with newspapers and magazines that people bought and read every day. We had to create listener loyalty to programming we sponsored. We created soaps, comedy shows, variety shows, and mysteries. We made listening to radio every Sunday night a family institution.[58]

According to Artzt, radio was the "greatest selling tool ever conceived." But powerful as radio was, it was TV that conquered the living space of families.

> Then along came television and everything changed again—back to pictures, the era of visual demonstration, a boom time for the advertising industry. With television, we could do more than describe the benefits of our products. We could show those benefits. . . . And again, the advertising industry grabbed the technology in its teeth and turned it into a bonanza for advertisers. The first 40 years of television could be called the "Big Brand Era," a period in which advertising could create Tides and Tylenols, Pampers and Pepsis—almost overnight, by harnessing the dynamic power of mass audience reach, the drama of moving pictures, and the repetitive force of immense audience loyalty to programming.

The addition of color behind the gleaming glass of the screen made television the show window of the second half of the 20th century, bringing the store home, surpassing even the most audacious vision of early merchants' dreams. First centered in the living room, then scattered across family rooms and bedrooms, increasingly omnipresent in kitchens and other workspaces, television offers a continuing parade of showrooms, glimpses into what Leach calls a "separate world of consumption as the domain of freedom, self-expression, and self-fulfillment."[59] Through its glass shines an insistent series of associations between products and meanings, intensified by Artzt's "drama of moving pictures and the repetitive force" of viewer loyalty.

The addition of remotes, VCRs, and soon instant access and retrieval by computer can only enhance Friedberg's "mobilized virtual gaze," conceivably breaking that loyalty apart. Contemporary society may be producing new forms of identity in flux, postmodern subjectivities of oscillating, contradictory positions—aficionado of world music in the morning, business professional in the afternoon, reserve soldier in the evening, sexual being after dinner, without ever becoming one identity entirely. Optimists argue that these technological and social changes will combine to limit or even end mass-market, commercial control. As far as advertisers and their supporters are concerned, however, wherever the desiring gaze goes, that's where they'll be. To the extent that corporate forces succeed in this, an exploding number of media choices can only enhance diversity superficially, or enhance it only for moments that themselves go on sale. Market niches may become more pointedly designed. Subscription channels and prerecorded programming may offer some respite for those who can afford it. Public television can offer alternatives to different degrees. In general, however, televisions will remain sales showrooms, their programming designed to draw audiences large enough to sell to advertisers for more than they cost to attract.

No one can know in advance the precise contours of these new forms, or their consequences, including whether they will allow for spaces that remain commercial-free. Yet without such knowledge it should be impossible to say decades from now that these consequences were *invited* by the public.[60] New media technologies do not come packaged with a list of potential side effects. Certainly television did not, and this was crucial for it to have seemed so attractive. Lynn Spigel writes in *Make Room for TV* that the set in the postwar United States was as much invited into the home as it was positioned there by external forces. The public's early enchantment with TV was not orchestrated by big-business promotion but instead "rooted in modern American culture and its long-standing obsession with communication technologies."[61] Not stressed at the time in any widely available medium, however, was that TV was, as Artzt says, a "bonanza" for private companies, with its incorporation of that temple's glimpse into living room shrines nationwide. The specific quality of early U.S. television, more commercial by far than its counterparts worldwide, was driven by business priorities. These priorities required a commercial aesthetic that would appeal widely enough to those who could afford to participate in the national marketplace, offend few, and provide a hospitable environment for the selling that paid its way. We shall argue that this aesthetic has changed, as marketing strategies have become more carefully defined. Broadcasters do risk offending many if they can capture enough of the audience they seek. And they do offend many: there is wide discontent about sex and violence on television, just as many people find much of the local news and many of the shows and ads stupid. But what matters about television extends beyond what people feel.

Commercial Culture and the Environment

The resources of the planet cannot long sustain a culture that in its commercials and its programs sells wasteful models of affluence, style, and value. Again, the problem is not just television. Desires for single-family homes with lawns and for private, gasoline-fueled personal vehicles, especially ever new ones, are arguably the most environmentally wasteful aspects of this culture, and they have existed in the absence of television. Nor is the issue one of equally shared responsibility. Consuming takes different forms with different effects across cultures and historical situations and across economic groups within a culture. Discretionary spending on unneeded commodities rises with income; the poor consume far less than their share.[62]

Moreover, commercial culture can be environmentally sensitive, or at least can seem so.[63] Since Earth Day in 1970 some Green values have become part of common sense. News stories treat environmental problems as disorders, showing an underlying commitment to an ideal order without them.[64] Along with occasional commercial comedies or dramas, they might well function to increase environmental awareness. Documentaries on the Discovery Channel and elsewhere might spectacularize nature, making it seem Other rather than part of what we are, but they also would seem to heighten awareness among those who see them. Cartoons for children make villains of polluters. However, connections remain unexplored between environmental change and a market economy, or patriarchal, heterosexist culture, or new forms of old racist traditions. TV viewers continue to get more environmental information from corporate advertisements than they do from news reports.[65] Rarely do the media relate the benefits of consumption to their environmental costs, as if the drive to satisfy cultural desires had as its consequence only the creation of more human happiness.

Green and allied theorists argue that culture and nature *are* interrelated, a belief acted on intellectually by "expanding the moral vision beyond human life to all life processes."[66] Most environmentalists would agree that thoughtless assaults on the ecosystem have their roots in market economies, patriarchal cultures, and old racist traditions that justify one group's dominion over others. But the determination runs both ways. Culture affects nature, to be sure, but we also want to argue that *culture is a part of nature's dance.* That is, even at its most obsessively artificial, culture is an element of nature.

A look at a related idea might make this clearer. The modern sense of individuality, privately experienced as a state of nature, is paradoxically a cultural product. It is shared. It links people as much as it divides them. In the same way, believing that culture is separate from nature, we argue, is certainly cultural. It bespeaks an underlying fear that each of us may, at last, be nature, as mortal and ultimately *untamed* as are nature's living parts. This fear of succumbing to nature has in this century fueled the industries that encouraged anxiety over body smells, over smelling "like an animal." It fuels certain forms of tourism (and book, film, magazine, and television consumption) as well, appealing to those who seek comfort in seeing other parts of the world as a wild kingdom.

Modernity, with its accelerated development of methods of social and environmental domination, has played out the legacy of the Enlightenment, the 18th-century movement that privileged human reason over religious superstition, seeking to illuminate the world through scientific mapping and then control of the nature it surveyed *from outside.*[67] Commercialized Enlightenment culture reifies conceptual distinctions between culture and nature, making them seem palpable.[68] Reification helps those who want to serve their culture by ransacking what they conceive of as separate nature, including other peoples and their cultures. Aggressors carry it with them like a lunch pail, allowing them to feed off its assurances that they are right to plunder Others because Others seem *really* separate from, different from, and inferior to the aggressors' truly human life. Reification can be found wherever people use nature as an alibi for oppression, as when claiming that human "nature" is aggressive or territorial or heterosexual or that women are "naturally" passive or docile or made for the dominion of men. It can be found wherever nature is altered without thought to general consequences, wherever people seek advantage over others while envisioning them as objects for their enrichment, pleasure, or power. Reification of the environment, of women, of the "undeveloped" world by colonial and imperial powers, of workers by employers in systems of slave and wage labor—these carry interrelated traces of the arrogance of domination. Indeed, reification can itself be pleasurable, compensating for uncertainty, offering aggressors a sense of unity.[69] Yet just as the reified can suffer from internalization of others' demeaning views of them, those who reify others suffer as well, if to very different degrees, diminishing their own subjectivity as they lose ability to recognize how others are like themselves. Those who reify nature, who think of the environment as the human environment, who separate themselves from the nonhuman, in turn reduce what it means to be a person in this world.[70]

Commercials may propose that logging companies are one with the nature they cut down, but those who sponsor them limit their holistic environmental consciousness to the screen, obscuring what falls outside. Corporations have no interest in diversity they cannot sell, and so globally they tend to attack cultural and biological diversity with equal ferociousness if either gets in their way, making the world increasingly unlivable. Denying its interconnection with all else, commercial culture contributes to the maldistribution of resources in the world, as it seeks to pay its workers as little as it can, charge its customers whatever the market will bear, and pocket the difference.

Occupying Time

Because its main weapon is entertainment rather than violence, commercial television may prove to be the most effective colonial agent the world has ever known. What other colonizer has been so welcome in people's homes? In the United States, for example, not even organized religion has been able to get so many adults to do the same thing at the same moment as television has with the Super Bowl, the last episodes of *Cheers, M*A*S*H,* and *Seinfeld,* or the live broadcast of *ER* (although the Reverends Billy Graham and Pat Robertson have certainly tried). TV occupies so much of people's time—whether they are actively viewing or not—that it has exceeded its origin as a medium. It has expanded into an environment itself, in which human identity seems disconnected from its roots in community and nature. Frequent mergers and acquisitions put control of this environment into fewer but more powerful hands.[71] In the early 1990s, George Gerbner and others founded the Cultural Environment Movement, a coalition whose goal is to democratize control over the media and its images, seeing an urgent need for change to halt the increasing commercialization of life. This can only be done from below, by a new social movement it seeks to help form. The CEM opposes both government censorship and concentrated private control. As Gerbner wrote in the organization's prospectus: "For the first time in human history, most children are born into homes where most of the stories [they are told] do not come from their parents, schools, churches, communities, and in many places even from their native countries, but from a handful of conglomerates who have something to sell. . . . Media are coalescing into an integrated cultural environment that constrains life's choices as the natural environment defines life's chances."[72]

Television's representation of the world does matter. In Gerbner's words, it "cultivates a sense of opportunities and life chances. It contributes to our conception of who we are and how we relate to others and the world. It helps define our strengths and vulnerabilities, our powers and our risks."[73] Television has become the "mainstream of the cultural environment in which most children grow up and learn."[74] Absent voices offer stories through screens; unlike friends, parents, relatives, or teachers, they cannot respond to young listeners' concerns and needs.[75] In the words of Captain Kangaroo (Bob Keeshan), "Television is not a tool for nurturing. It is a tool for selling."[76]

Others have said this before. Jerry Mander observed two decades ago (following on arguments by Gerbner and others) that the United States was the "first culture to have substituted secondary, mediated versions of experience for direct experience of the world."[77] Already in the 1970s, most adults—indeed, nearly as many adults as children—had come to use television to learn how to deal with problems of life.[78] People had come to think they could experience someone or someplace else through their screens. In some ways this was similar to the relation that moviegoers had felt with stars since decades before.[79] Yet in watching TV there was an immediacy, a sense of presence, that movies had never had.[80] Television seems to be more of a "real" environment; taped sitcoms and other material appear no different from broadcasts that are "live." Perhaps this explains why television spawns ersatz *Cheers* bars nationwide, where drinkers can hang out in street clothes in a space virtually the same as TV's, while movies were more likely to produce changes in fashion, allowing consumers to model themselves after stars in a space that did not change.[81] Still, in the end, Mander said, viewers were wrong to believe they were savoring life via television: "It was only the experience of sitting in a darkened room, staring at flickering light, ingesting images which had been edited, cut, rearranged, sped up, slowed down, and confined in hundreds of ways. Were people aware of the difference?"[82] We derive our sense of where we live from the "information flow" provided by our environment.[83] As that environment becomes more electronic, *where* we live becomes less an issue of physical space and more an electronic production. Our access to other forms of environmental information declines accordingly, and dangerously.

Voracious for profit, this project of commercialized Enlightenment seeks control over all that lives on the planet, including those who otherwise profit most from its expansion. Even well-paid individuals carry effects of the commercial system, ingesting at least some of its poisons, experiencing at least moments of its disembodied ways of life. Relentlessly, the corporate media appropriate and articulate identities and differences of class, ethnicity, gender, nation, and sexual orientation in terms that serve its needs, taking increasing amounts of people's time, further alienating culture from its basis in nature. Still, these processes are not totalitarian but hegemonic. Ordinarily *hegemony* means the rule of one group over another. Some 20th-century political thinkers, however, have followed Antonio Gramsci in narrowing the definition to domination based more on acquiescence or consent than on violence or its threat.[84] Crucial is that consent here is not just formal (as in obeying the law or voting) but also involves sharing systems of meaning "not only in political and economic institutions and relationships but also in active forms of experience and consciousness."[85] This usage connects ideology to power. The disadvantaged live "within an ideological space that does not seem at all 'ideological': which appears instead to be permanent and 'natural,' to lie outside history, to be beyond particular interests."[86] Hegemony moves through contested terrain as leading economic and political interests, in Stuart Hall's words, try to "articulate and disseminate ways of understanding the world" in forms appealing to people at large. Elite blocs define reality, shape common sense to "win the consent of subordinated classes to their continuing sway."[87] This partly explains how television can be so appealing, in its confirming of viewers' understandings of themselves in the world, even as, all told, it helps take so much—in time, in sense of self, in resources, in quality of life.

Because hegemony needs consent to survive, it must at least appear to address the concerns of its potential opponents, to speak in a voice that these potential opponents can recognize as their own. The Environmental Defense Fund has successfully exploited this need in its negotiations with McDonald's, resulting in less wasteful and damaging packaging, so that McDonald's can avoid seeming an alienating environment to customers who think of themselves as people who care about what happens to the containers they buy. Sometimes, however, hegemony fails to incorporate and lull opposition, as it did briefly in such instances as the Three Mile Island nuclear accident, which jeopardized the nuclear power industry, or the transformations from Communism in the Soviet Union and Eastern Europe, which threatened weapons manufacturers in North America and Western Europe. Such rearticulation of anticapitalist ideas (that the throwaway economy is wrong, that nuclear power is contrary to the public interest, that arms expenditures are mostly handouts to manufacturers) revises them into mainstream culture (that small measures help the environment, that nuclear power needs to be better controlled, that weapons budgets can trimmed after the Cold War has been won). Yet faced with movements strong enough, corporate hegemony could suffer more than temporary setbacks—it might indeed be *lost*.[88] This keeps the future open, at least in theory. In moments of political opening, social movements articulate new ways of understanding the world. Television at those times could also serve to spread the word about new ideas and images, however mediated they might be by the commercial networks' tendency to marginalize movements for radical change, their insistence on *"framing* all competing definitions of reality within their range, bringing all alternatives within their horizon of thought" (emphasis in original).[89] Discontent, opposition, resistance, refusal, revolt, all may develop—from each of us, from groups and organizations with which we might identify, from political forces that may yet be able to align social policy more harmoniously to heal the planet.

Violence and Television

One encouraging example may be the movement against television violence, which argues against the logic of market interest in violence and has included grassroots organizations like the National Parent Teacher Association. If it does not settle for the new ratings system most networks accepted in 1997, which kept the ratings in network hands and may have no effect on programming, this movement might lead to discussion of cultural policy in general, discussion that has been "center stage . . . in other democracies for some time."[90] This broad discussion has been muted since the Reagan era, yet criticizing market control of television would not be a radical idea in U.S. political discourse. Such a critique would follow the same logic in the 1990s as the New Deal critique of market allocation of electricity in the 1930s: since corporations owe it to their stockholders to provide only service that is profitable, service driven by broader imperatives requires either public subsidy or capital investment in nonprofit institutions, including public agencies.

Instead, mainstream journalists tend to frame TV violence in terms of Washington politics or scientific findings of television's effects on violent behavior offscreen. Certainly these findings need to be taken seriously. They may be indicators of specific problems, such as the inordinate effect of TV violence on children in violent households. However, since effects on general behavior tend to be unproven and are perhaps unprovable,[91] focus on the "facts" of effects may obscure more politically difficult but urgent arguments about economic causes of violent behavior and crime. Yet the critique of TV violence does highlight ways in which the TV set is not just a means for personal escapism but is indeed an institutional apparatus, with causes and implications. Decades of research by Gerbner and his colleagues demonstrate that whatever other impact it might have, watching violent television regularly for years tends to *cultivate* a sense that the world is more violent and dangerous, more "mean and gloomy," than it otherwise might seem, particularly for those who watch more than average amounts of TV.[92] This process is not simple—television is not a ray gun that sends messages to viewers who identically understand and absorb them, and it does not function identically across demographic groups.[93] No one knows with certainty the effects on the average 18-year-old viewer of a childhood spent witnessing 25,000 dramatized murders.[94] Peer and family relations affect TV's power; children with strong peer or family connections seem less engaged by television's world.[95] The signs television broadcasts are available elsewhere in the culture; they would have to be in order for them to make sense. Some may watch above average amounts of television because they are fearful about the world rather than vice versa.

Yet cultivation patterns have been so widely observed that they are difficult to deny. As Minow has said, "More people learn more each day, each year, each lifetime from television than from any other source. All of television is education; the question is, what are we teaching and what are we learning?"[96] Researchers have been able to show, for example, that viewers who watch more television than average are more likely to buy new locks, watchdogs, and guns "for protection" than those who watch less, even after other variables (education, age, gender, place of residence, newspaper reading, and so on) have been taken into account.[97] The apologist position, which argues that TV only responds to what viewers want, founders on this issue. Violent shows tend to have lower ratings in the United States than nonviolent ones. Yet producers continue to manufacture them for first run on the domestic market because, with their generic plots, they sell better overseas than situation comedy or drama, and export revenues more than supplant revenue loss caused by lower ratings in the United States. The contours of market systems are decisive here—not viewer democracy.[98] Abroad, licenses for imported shows cost less than local productions, so again audience size is not as decisive as it might otherwise be in determining what is on the air. This illustrates an important point about commercial broadcasting: its programming strategies respond to profitability, not popularity, and they respond to popularity only when it coincides with profitability. Violent programming spreads in commercial broadcasting systems because it is profitable. As far as we know, there is no nonprofit television station or network that has the amount and degree of violence of U.S. commercial television.

This violence seems to have political consequences—more externalities of the industry's drive for profit—especially when attached to nonfiction TV. This was evident in 1993 and 1994 when several commentators saw a connection between rising public fear of violent crime *as it was declining* and increased media attention to it, especially on television. In 1993, poll taker Peter Hart found that 13 percent of people in the United States named crime as the number one problem facing the nation. One year later, that number had jumped to 43 percent. During that year, according to one survey, the evening news shows on ABC, CBS, and NBC devoted double the amount of time to crime that they had in 1990, and about a quarter more than they had in 1992. The networks were not alone in featuring crime: the airwaves were filled with fear dished out on syndicated "reality" shows like *Cops,* sensational news show like *A Current Affair,* and a growing number of daytime talk shows. Politicians seized on and seemingly exacerbated crime fears to push their own agendas. All of this no doubt helped passage of repressive crime legislation at the time. It may be impossible to trace precise causes and effects, but for many viewers it seems the world had become more mean and gloomy, at least as far as they could see it through their sets.[99] Between 1993 and 1996, the murder rate dropped 20 percent in the United States. At the same time, coverage of murders on network TV news soared 721 percent to reach 1 of every 20 stories.[100]

An Imaginary Voice

Commercial culture saturates identity in the United States, sometimes in ways not normally in view. As it has at least since the 1920s, this culture asks people to think of themselves as individuals in need who require commodities to become who they are, as private competitors for plenitude in interpersonal and economic markets. Although other social forces continue to define identity, the entertainments of commercial culture model this individuality. To do so effectively, as Lynn Spigel suggests, advertising early on adopted the "voice of an imaginary consumer."[101] It learned to speak in terms meaningful to those it would target for sales. This has been key to commercialism's hegemonic power. Not surprisingly in an individualist culture, advertising on television and elsewhere has tended to adopt a voice that feels like an individual motivated not by a commercial system but by personal desire, for a sense of generosity in oneself as well as for accumulation. Advertisers conceive this voice in the image of a shopper whose personal choices shape private life experience as well as the operations of the market. This is the imaginary voice television viewers are invited to assume for hours a day, so much so that it can seem like second nature, especially in combination with the print ads, billboards, and radio pitches that have survived earlier eras.

Some ignore this voice. Others turn it to their own purposes, finding ironic pleasure in it or using it to think critically about the culture. Moreover, other less commercial currents structure identity in the United States (communities of place and work along with age, ancestry, gender, hobbies, politics, sexual orientation, religious and other institutions, sports). Yet commercial culture has gained hegemony by what to many must seem its responsiveness to human desire. It rearticulates other currents of identity in commercial terms. In that context, Fredric Jameson's warning that "everyone reproduces the market system" internally, "like a conscience" that constantly gives advice about what is best, would explain why more citizens of industrial society have not revolted against commercial culture despite its costs.[102]

Not that prospects for revolt have been entirely evacuated. Change may come from the more disadvantaged zones of the world, where residents may yet lack the "conscience" Jameson names. Commercial culture's emphasis on identity begins to reach the limit of psychic space, crowding out other conceptions of self, identity becoming increasingly visible as a *thing*. Identity for contemporary consumers combines an Enlightenment sense of self as an object with postmodernity's fragmentation. It has become externalized, susceptible to manipulation by others and, in a process of self-reification, by consumers themselves. This signals new forms of alienation but also opportunities for new visions of change. As capital investment in new communication technologies intensifies, profitability becomes more difficult and requires that new ways be found to stretch and secure the time people spend in the new screen environment. Credit expands consumer money, mortgaging future labor to pay for goods in the present. The day cannot expand. Although we can do more than one thing at a time, our time is limited.

Increasingly, the contests of the future will be over "leisure" time between, on the one hand, time spent in noncommercial activity and institutions and, on the other, time spent in front of a screen that alternately elicits work and promises new commercial identities. This is an argument we develop in our concluding chapter. As video capabilities grow and techniques of screen seduction become even more subtle, it will become increasingly difficult to retreat to, or even imagine, a world of primarily noncommercial, local communication. Yet within areas of such communication, enhanced no doubt by new forms of noncommercial e-mail and cybernetic interaction, possibilities for what Ynestra King and others have called the "rational reenchantment of the world" will survive.[103] They could do so not as nostalgia but as the ground for a new subjectivity that draws on the fragmentation of the traditional self to develop a new sense of unlimited interconnection and a new radical politics free from the tyranny of the mythic binary oppositions that divide us (to name just a few: black/white, culture/nature, cultured/wild, feminine/masculine, heterosexual/homosexual). This new self would begin to recover the environmental knowledge Bill McKibben shows has been left aside in *The Age of Missing Information,* knowledge necessary for humans to adapt their practices to the changing status of an injured planet. It may discover a new geography, reconstructed in terms developed within and against the Enlightenment mappings of the past. Part of the struggle against these mappings will be a growing sense of the consequences of overdevelopment and deprivation across borders of want.

Others prefer this vision of "nature-as-self" over conceptualizing humans as the eye of a separate, surrounding environment and see such a vision as necessary to renewed conversation regarding major social change in the overdeveloped world.[104] Such organizing might stress building coalitions in common cause against inequalities and environmental degradation without denigrating diversity. It might stress commonalities in the different identities each of us articulates, including commonality in difference. The goal is not to attack shopping or to proselytize for asceticism. Against preaching for a Green "neopuritanism," the task is to begin to figure out how to reclaim pleasures of life in ways that break with corporate and acquisitive priorities, that eschew desires for scraps of identity accumulated by harming others, to substitute communal values sensitive to the consequences of what we do, to "work for the creation of a sensuous environment."[105]

In the chapters that follow, we flesh out the argument that audiences' immersion in television connects them to a world that only seems to be the one in which they live. As a result, people increasingly live as if they were not part of the natural world. The following coordinates help us map this changing environment:

• *Political economy explains why television seeks to occupy people.* Economics traditionally begins its analysis with an individual entity (a person or firm) that confronts a field of production, distribution, and sales. Taking individualist Western culture as its model, it assumes an autonomous rational actor who makes rational choices based on self-interest. It sees the individual as a cause. Critical political economy sees the individual and the economic terrain as effects as well. "Where economics begins with the individual, naturalized across time and space, political economy starts with the socially constituted individual, engaged in socially constituted production."[106] In this analysis, relations between viewers and television are determined not only but crucially by the prevailing context of state and economic system, of which both viewers and television as an institution are products.[107] It refuses to see television as inherently commercial. Rather, it sees it as having been historically constituted as such by specifiable forces. Indeed, in most of the world, television was not initially a commercial medium, and its configuration in the United States was not preordained.[108] Yet public policy in this country, responsive to commercial interests, has guaranteed television's commercial structure. That viewers think the purpose of television programs is information or fun even as they are aware that TV, after all, is commercial indicates not that they are stupid but how well the purpose behind TV's images has been obscured. As Schudson says of advertising, "People do not necessarily 'believe' in the values that advertisements present. Nor need they believe for a market economy to survive and prosper. People need simply to get used to, or get used to not getting used to, the institutional structures that govern their lives."[109] That people think of advertiser-supported television's effects as psychological or ideological and are blind to its economic operations, a position many scholars and critics share, shows how TV's contribution to the wasting of the environment has been mystified.

• *Textual analysis explains the pleasure and comfort people get from television and the complementary relationships between programs and advertisements.* Critics of commercial television must account for one irrefutable fact: people choose to watch it for hours and hours. Television appeals to their desires, even if it does not satisfy them. It does so in part by trading on what Hall calls the "reality effect," the sense that each of us can know the facts of the world through the television screen. Again, this effect occurs not because viewers are "cultural dupes" but because TV's images are so familiar that "they appear to involve no intervention of coding, selection or arrangement.[110] To the extent that they remain familiar, "they appear to reproduce the actual trace of reality."[111] In doing so, they deflect attention from television's partiality, its selection of certain representations over others. Viewers to whom television, especially the news, seems partial tend to talk of bias or to bemoan cultural workers with axes to grind. But because television (like any form of representation) cannot help but be selective, "bias" is a red herring, and its use only reinforces belief in the possibility of impartial representations. This belief is crucial to television's success as an environment, especially one that promises escape from the annoyances of everyday life. Critics such as McKibben in *The Age of Missing Information,* who rightly fear television's effects, offer no explanation for why it is so popular. To take television's popularity seriously, we need closely to analyze how its productions are put together and ask what it is *in the details* that attracts so many to its screen.

The look of television is crucial in this regard. Although the medium has its distinctive forms (such as "live" programming and its simulations, game shows, news, soap operas, and sports), its staple remains series shows whose visual designs imitate those developed by the film industry in the late teens, although since *Miami Vice* in the 1980s there have been dramatic shows like *Homicide* and *ER* that strive for a look that may appear more realist in its congruence with current familiar stylizations, a look that hybridizes conventions from other television genres (music video, news, documentary, commercials).[112] Yet whether classically realist or postmodern, these designs can be shown by close analysis to anticipate and cue viewer response. As we shall demonstrate, TV cameras tend to picture the world from gendered perspectives that influence composition, lighting, and editing.

At the same time, creating quilts of combinations, advertisers select certain types of shows in which to embed their commercials, making possible what Raymond Williams called "flows" between program and ad.[113] Such flows are familiar from magazines and newspapers, but we usually do not notice them. They may enhance advertising's effects, but they may also engender situations in which viewers construct unanticipated meanings.[114]

• *Audience studies indicate the complexities and contradictions of viewer response, particularly along lines of wealth, ethnicity, and gender.* Much scholarship in television and cultural studies since the mid-1980s has sought to describe viewer response and to contest the power of media in making meanings. While social-scientific research has yet to produce an adequate account of what particular bits of television mean to their audiences, neither political-economic nor textual analysis can tell us how people respond to texts. Depending on their cultural identities, including educational levels, different viewers might well find different meanings in identical material. These meanings may be so different that for practical purposes diverse viewers watching the same channel at the same time might encounter different texts. In other cases, responses may be more alike. Differential responses of this order raise questions about our earlier comment that relations between viewers and television are shaped by political-economic forces. What about other influences on viewers, particularly those of identity, that fracture audience response? What about changing historical situations that may change the context in which audiences make meaning of a particular image on television? That make a generalized notion of "audience response" seem inadequate?

Perhaps the answer is not to choose between political economy, textual analysis, and audience studies but to envision multiple sets of operations involved in television watching, each one "mutually constituted" by another.[115] If we define discourses as particular ways of thinking and representing the world, then we can see how both textual and audience discourses are shaped by multiple experiences and constraints that are fashioned prior to but also during the moment in front of the screen. Because audience discourses do vary, both linkages and disconnects operate between them and the television texts. Examination of these relations can illuminate the uneven power of advertiser-supported television. How much this unevenness matters in terms of television's environmental effects needs to be explored, with attention to the specifics of any situation that might be analyzed.

  • *Issues of identity and difference show the audience to be increasingly fragmented into groups seeking distinction and recognition, but commercial television takes this up only in structurally limited ways.* Television does not produce this fragmentation. Indeed, it offers surprisingly little diversity given the growing number of channels.[116] But advertiser-supported programming is called on to respond to diversity by corporations seeking to target specific audiences with their products. At the same time, offending even portions of audiences becomes risky behavior, at times giving religious right-wingers disproportionate power. As a result, television tends to present identity and difference moderately, or as issues involving Others not targeted for commercial appeal. It acknowledges difference, perhaps, but it fails to allow a hearing for the more radical position some identity-based social movements take: that the majority categories assume norms that wrongly marginalize those thought to be different. This marginalization works against diversity, causing pain to people of color as well as to bisexual, gay, or lesbian people and to the socially disadvantaged, including those who live against their designated roles. It homogenizes the cultural environment to the detriment of everyone. This becomes evident when it is compared with the commercial music industry, whose economics allows for much greater, if still limited, diversity, or cable access, where ratings matter little economically. Even radio is more diverse, despite recent lurches toward concentration of control.

Programs that do speak to the marginalized, like *The Cosby Show* or *In Living Color* or *Ellen* (especially since the April 1997 coming out show and attendant publicity), to succeed handily must not do so in a way that puts off large audiences that might find their main characters alien offscreen. As William Julius Wilson writes in another context, "If a political message is tailored to a white audience, racial minorities draw back, just as whites draw back when a message is tailored to minority audiences."[117] To ensure against this in a range of contexts of which race is only one, television has made itself into a voice not just of blandness but of comfort. As the networks lose audience share and jackpot shows on the scale of *The Cosby Show* become impossible, this voice no longer has to be quite as soothing to quite as many people (hence, for example, the possibility of *Murphy Brown*'s 1992 flouting of religious right morality). Yet programming in the unalloyed voice of the marginalized remains structurally impossible, except on cable access or on Comedy Central (think of *South Park*) or other venue with a comparatively small, self-selected audience. In this regard, what is crucial about *Ellen,* for example, is not that its main character (and performer) is presented as lesbian, although that remains an invaluable achievement, but that its presentation of the title character's sexuality is limited by the taboo against seeming contentious for any economically significant portion of its target audience.[118] As ABC's vice president for broadcast standards and practices acknowledges, "I don't think we put things on that are patently offensive to a *large* number of people. That's what will protect us from a backlash" (emphasis in original).[119] Hence the absence of same-sex physical contact comparable to that in a heterosexual show. Hence the lack of critique of heterosexual practices one might see in a sitcom designed for gay or lesbian or bisexual audiences. Commercialism both restricted and sparked *Ellen's* innovations. Even the decision to represent *Ellen's* main character as lesbian, according to Ellen DeGeneres, was a commercial decision. It stemmed from a sense that to survive the show "desperately needed a point of view"[120]—but not too much, not too soon.

• *Watching television, whatever its other effects, steals time from what might be our relations with each other, in friendships and in families, and by ourselves.* Of course, not every moment watching television is a waste of time. Of course, there are times when television can enhance communication between people, providing a source of common reference or pleasure shared.[121] Of course, people talk while watching television. Still, because so many people find watching television entertaining, its critique depends on alternative values that see time spent in front of the set as, in general, time better spent elsewhere. One form this critique takes is a vision of life based on human connection, as opposed to connection with or through things or with or through images of humans on a screen, of a nonindividualist identification of oneself with others and as a part of the natural world. From this perspective, advertiser-supported television's major offense would be that it persuades us to take on a new, alienated nature, spending ever more time engaged by a screen and by commodities. This distances us from our existence as active, conscious agents in the environment. True, prospects for new media, such as the Internet or new cable or telephone boxes with hundreds of choices, include the promise of reempowering audiences who can afford them and are educated in their use. But in doing so they also threaten to reinscribe power differentials in new forms, further preoccupying people with a screen-mediated world as they sit in front of their terminals or theaters at home.[122] Current debates among elites in the United States over the future of new media at best include minimal guarantees of public access. At worst they make admission to the new media marketplace dependent on private wealth, restricting admission to those who qualify as potential buyers, the group Eileen Meehan calls the "commodity audience."[123] Even the best elite proposals place control over new media in private hands, rather than seeing them as public resources that could facilitate new generations of democratic interconnection. Some proposals would leave noncommercial concerns out of the planning entirely.

By conservative estimates, residents of the United States spend between six and seven hours a day exposed to media including television, nearly all of it commercial.[124] To the extent that commercial media play the role of community space, connecting viewers virtually, they may offer nearly everyone a more expansive sense of the world and its people, but at the same time they contribute to the loss of what Robert Putnam and others, after Jane Jacobs, call "social capital."[125] Putnam defines this as the "networks, norms, and social trust that facilitate coordination and cooperation for mutual benefit."[126] These are necessary both for democracy to work and for social trust to develop to the point where egalitarian values could replace opportunism as the basis of social interaction. Moreover, while we shall argue that commercial television cultivates a solipsistic self, Putnam argues that "dense networks of social interaction probably broaden the participants' sense of self, developing the 'I' into the 'we,' . . . enhancing the participants' 'taste' for collective benefits."[127] These networks have been in decline for decades. In 1993, for example, only 13 percent attended a meeting of a public body, government, or school, down from 22 percent in 1973. Similar declines have been reported for participation in election campaigns. "Every year over the last decade or two, millions more have withdrawn from the affairs of their communities." PTA membership declined from more than 12 million in 1964 to 7 million now. Membership in women's and men's civic and social organizations has dropped similarly.[128] And—in the example that led Putnam to title his research "Bowling Alone"—league bowling decreased 40 percent between 1980 and 1993, while the total number of bowlers rose by 10 percent.[129]

Though there may be a variety of causes, Putnam finds most persuasive the theory that technological trends are "radically 'privatizing' or 'individualizing' our use of leisure time and thus disrupting many opportunities for social-capital formation." He explains, "The most obvious and probably the most powerful instrument of this revolution is television. Time-budget studies in the 1960s showed that the growth in time spent watching television dwarfed all other changes in the way Americans passed their days and nights. Television has made our communities (or, rather, what we experience as our communities) wider and shallower."[130] As Putnam himself recognizes, television has no monopoly on blame. Participation is voluntary, after all; people willingly, if not willfully, slight other aspects of their lives for television. Yet they do so in the United States as nowhere else. Perhaps it is no coincidence that this was the country where television was first thoroughly commercialized, the first seeking hours unlimited of people's time. Putnam finds historical connections worldwide between the creation of social capital and economic development and representative government. On the other side of this phenomenon, it may also be that when economic development becomes overdevelopment, social capital will begin to fall, as corporations and their economic policies press more to work more hours, intensifying the double shift for women in traditional households, and persuade consumers to spend more of their declining unpaid time in commercialized experience. This is precisely what seems to have happened in the United States. Indeed, at a certain point in economic growth, there may be an inverse relation between dissipation of social capital and accumulation and concentration of private wealth.[131]

Forming new social capital, then, would seem urgent for anyone interested in moving from the "I" to the "we," an effort synonymous with ecological thinking. The situation is neither fixed nor one sided. Unanticipated social developments could ignite successful political struggle. New media could involve public resources, resources that might at last facilitate new generations of democratic, environmentally sensitive connection. By facilitating connection, such media could work against reification, allowing for the flowering of new forms of intersubjectivity.

Television in a Different World

People concerned about the environment are showing increasing sympathy for a radical reorientation of our culture away from commercialized individualism toward sensitivity to environmental harm. They point toward a new environmental consciousness that sees each of our fates interwoven, each of our identities elements of a global being that takes nature as ourselves.

The argument of this book is more specific: to consider the place of television in healing the environment, it is vital to keep television's commercial imperatives in mind—and to imagine what television might be like if it were free from its commercial base yet not monopolized by any political power. That imagining television in a different world is so difficult and may seem pointless shows how much our current political atmosphere has robbed us of our ability to dream. One way to dissolve our reification of television as it is might be to see it first as a technology that has been and continues to be shaped with specific interests and purposes in mind. In that sense as a technology it has hardly been neutral.

Yet Mander's critique of television, one of the most influential, argues that TV has certain medium-specific forms that make it irredeemable. These include TV's distribution costs, its one-way communication, its reduction of sensory information to the visual and aural, and its low definition and size. This is why television favors the isolation of individuals in the frame to the exclusion of social movements or swatches of the environment. So serious is this for us and the planet, Mander says, that television should be banished from the earth. Certainly, some of TV's characteristics could change with its technology (interactive and high-definition television, for example, or perhaps 3-D or even a new form of Smell-O-Vision), but for Mander new gizmos are not the issue: television's rap sheet is too long for rehabilitation. Even foreseeable interactive programs would restrict choices to a menu not of viewers' design. Indeed, high-definition television, with its more attractive picture, and home theaters, with their more attractive sound, could offer even more seductive worlds in which to pass the time. That would make them more dangerous. And danger here is no exaggeration, for Mander finds television's sin to be a crime against nature: "Since 'natural' was all we had for virtually the entire course of human evolution, that is what our bodies are attuned to. *Anything* that intervenes in this arrangement is potentially dangerous" (emphasis in original).[132]

A more productive notion of "nature" would include what it is that humans do, activities that can enhance the planet's well-being as well as bringing harm. Against Mander, we argue that the limits on television in the future will be economic, cultural, and political—not technological. Uncontested, television's determination by these forces would restrict its ability to help us redefine ourselves within the world and to construct a world in which such redefinition might take place. In that sense, the struggle to change television is as much as anything a struggle to change the larger forces that give it its shape. Joining movements to change those forces can enhance interconnection, a sense of being at home in the world, even as it can produce livable spaces and make the world a better place in which to live. For those whose lives include hours a day in front of the set, our proposal is simple to articulate yet difficult to realize, given TV's power: Use television, don't let it use you. Live more in the space of the world, less in the imaginary one of TV-land. Get involved with people to give more than you take. Watch selectively. When in doubt, turn it off.

FURTHER READING

Bagdikian, Ben H. *The Media Monopoly.* 5th ed. Boston: Beacon Press, 1997.

Brown, Lester R., Christopher Flavin, and Hilary F. French. *State of the World 1997: A Worldwatch Institute Report on Progress toward a Sustainable Society.* New York: Norton, 1997.

Ewen, Stuart. *All Consuming Images: The Politics of Style in Contemporary Culture.* New York: Basic Books, 1988.

Gerbner, George. "Television Violence: The Power and the Peril." In *Gender, Race, and Class in Media: A Text-Reader,* edited by Gail Dines and Jean M. Humez, 547–557. Thousand Oaks, Calif.: Sage, 1995.

Hall, Stuart. "The Rediscovery of 'Ideology': Return of the Repressed in Media Studies." In *Culture, Society, and the Media,* edited by Michael Gurevitch, Tony Bennett, James Curran, and Janet Woollacott, 56–90. London: Methuen, 1982.

Huston, Althea C., et al. *Big World, Small Screen: The Role of Television in American Society.* Child, Youth, and Family Services. Lincoln: University of Nebraska Press, 1992.

Kinder, Marsha. *Playing with Power in Movies, Television, and Video Games: From Muppet Babies to Teenage Mutant Ninja Turtles.* Berkeley: University of California Press, 1991.

King, Ynestra. "Healing the Wounds: Feminism, Ecology, and the Nature/Culture Dualism." In *Reweaving the World: The Emergence of Ecofeminism,* edited by Irene Diamond and Gloria Orenstein, 106–121. San Francisco: Sierra Club Books, 1990.

Leach, William. *Land of Desire: Merchants, Power, and the Rise of a New American Culture.* New York: Pantheon, 1993.

McKibben, Bill. *The Age of Missing Information.* New York: Random House, 1992.

Meehan, Eileen. "Why We Don't Count: The Commodity Audience." In *Logics of Television: Essays in Cultural Criticism,* edited by Patricia Mellencamp, 117–137. Bloomington: Indiana University Press–British Film Institute Publishing, 1990.

CHAPTER TWO

An Overview of
Television Economics

The television industry is changing so fast that sometimes it seems that each day brings reports of new technologies, new corporate mergers, and even new networks. Much of this change has been brought about by trends that have shaped international business generally, such as downsizing, merging, globalization, and diversification. In the television business, however, these tendencies have been accelerated both by the introduction of new technologies and by the lessening of government regulation. These transitions affect who owns the television industry, how they spend their money, how the business is financed, and, ultimately, what television programs and ads appear on our home sets each day.

Such questions are of more than passing interest, since, as we have said, many in the United States spend a good portion of their lives watching television. Nearly everyone has a TV. In addition, 92 percent of U.S. homes are equipped with VCRs, and 66.1 percent have cable.[1] Further, the personal lives of many people are deeply intertwined with the television programs they watch.[2] This chapter provides an overview of television economics in this era of radical industrial change. Although studying the television industry today is like shooting at a moving target, some knowledge of industry economics is essential if we are to understand who controls U.S. television and why.

Television in a Changing World

The television industry has always been tied to technological change, but in the past two decades, those new technologies that have encouraged the growth of cable TV stand out as the most significant. The development of more sophisticated space satellites in the 1970s made it relatively inexpensive to interconnect cable television systems around the country. This, in turn, made it profitable for new services such as HBO and CNN to distribute their programs to viewers without using expensive land lines. This new networking technique vastly increased the choice of programs for cable audiences and resulted in explosive growth for cable TV companies as more homes eagerly subscribed, agreeing to pay extra for these new channels. The growth in cable homes affected other segments of the industry as well. It extended the signal reach of many low-profit UHF channels, expanding their audience and increasing advertiser revenues. This, in turn, encouraged the construction of new UHF broadcast stations, making even more new channels available to cable systems.

The result of these changes has been nothing less than a realignment of the industry. During the 1950s, 1960s, and well into the 1970s, the three major broadcast networks (ABC, CBS, and NBC) dominated the national television business. Along with their advertisers, they determined which TV shows were produced and when and if those shows would be scheduled for broadcast. Most local TV stations were affiliates of one of the three networks (the most profitable tended to be owned by them) but had small say in network programming decisions. Since the number of desirable television frequencies available in an area was severely limited, so was the number of stations that could compete for business and audience. Under this form of shared monopoly, profits in the television industry were some of the highest among U.S. businesses.

The spectacular growth of cable and UHF television since the 1970s brought with it new channels and new program types—all eager for a share of the pie. Yet it is important to realize that more and more channels did not produce more and more television viewers. In fact, the size of the U.S. television audience and the amount of time viewers spend watching TV have increased very little over the past few years. The new channels did not make the overall audience pie larger; they just sliced it into more (and smaller) pieces. New forms of entertainment such as home VCRs, video games, and computers also began to compete for the time viewers spend watching traditional TV.

The big three broadcast networks had traditionally relied on attracting a large and diverse audience for their programs. Television shows were designed to have broad audience appeal, and programs that did not draw a large share of the audience generally did not stay on the air. Successful network programs were given big budgets because they drew large and profitable audiences. The new cable channels, on the other hand, were unable to compete for the massive audiences the networks attracted, so they aimed their programs at particular audience segments. Some have termed this approach "narrowcasting" or "niche broadcasting." Specialty channels, such as the all-music Music Television (MTV), the all-news CNN, and the all-sports Entertainment and Sports Programming Network (ESPN), were developed to appeal to slices of the audience.

Narrowcasting proved attractive to advertisers. Although most cable channels attract only a tiny fraction of the number of viewers watching network broadcasts, cable viewers are more homogeneous in terms of age, class and income, ethnicity, sex, and other demographic factors that interest advertisers. These specifics are useful for advertisers, making their commercial time purchases much more efficient. For example, an automobile tire company might find it more economical to buy commercial time on ESPN rather than on a broadcast network because men buy more tires and dominate the audience for telecast sports.

As a result, the big three broadcast networks have seen substantial declines both in numbers of viewers and in advertiser interest. In the 1979–1980 television season, the average combined prime-time rating for the three major networks (ABC, CBS, and NBC) was 56.5. This means that on the average, 56.5 percent of all U.S. television households were tuned to one of the three networks during the prime-time hours. A decade later, this percentage had fallen to 39.7. As the 1990s progressed, viewing of the big three continued to slip, so that by the end of the 1997–1998 season, the rating stood at 28.2. To put it another way, by the 1997–1998 season, 53 percent of the homes watching TV during prime time were tuned in to something besides one of the big three networks. While the big three continue to attract large numbers of prime-time viewers, the ever growing number of alternatives will doubtlessly continue to erode their share of the audience.[3]

Some of the big three's lost viewers switched to new and sometimes innovative programming offered by the Fox network and, to a lesser extent, by the emerging networks, UPN and WB. These new networks are not cable networks, since they make use of broadcasting affiliates to distribute their programs. However, they were made possible by cable because cable extended the potential audience of many independent broadcast stations and so made these new networks economically viable. By the end of the 1997–1998 season, Fox's average prime-time rating stood at 7.1, just below that of ABC. Especially significant is the fact that Fox was successfully programmed to attract the younger demographics most desirable to many advertisers. The newer networks, UPN and WB, had far fewer hours of programming a week, and their shows drew less than one-half of the audience of Fox programs.[4] Should audience numbers for the big three networks continue to decline, and those for cable and the smaller networks climb, the big three networks may one day find it economically advantageous to eliminate the present structure of local broadcasting affiliates and themselves convert to cable or satellite delivery. Such a move would leave local television stations hard pressed to find programs and audience in an ever more competitive marketplace.[5]

But even as new channels erode the viewing audience of the big three networks, newer technologies are bringing even more change. Digital compression, for example, greatly reduces the amount of frequency bandwidth required to send a television signal and so makes possible more or higher-definition channels. Fiber optic cable multiplies this capacity even more. Such innovations make it technologically feasible for cable systems that once could carry "only" 50 channels to be able to offer 500 (whether or not this is economically feasible is discussed below). Yet traditional cable delivery itself may be threatened by Direct Broadcasting from Satellite (DBS) (also marketed under the name Digital Satellite Service, or "DSS"), or it may find a new future as a carrier for digital television via the World Wide Web.

DBS offers cablelike program services beamed directly to the home from a space satellite in a so-called fixed orbit.[6] The dish for DBS is much smaller and less expensive than old-style home satellite antennas, making DBS a viable alternative to cable, even in urban areas where the size of older satellite dishes made their use impractical. Although public response to DBS in the United States has been favorable so far, its long-term economic impact on the television industry remains unclear. In many areas, it offers local cable systems their first real direct competition, not only for subscribers but for programming and advertising as well.[7] Indeed, DBS offers the United States its first national television distribution services. That is, DBS has the potential of reaching the entire country without the current networks' need for intermediary broadcasters or cable systems to sell and distribute programming at the local level. This boosts the profit potential of DBS but could devastate local operators—especially those in smaller markets. Yet at least some of the cable companies have hedged their bets. Primestar, the country's second-largest DBS company (after DirecTV), is a joint venture of several firms, including eight of the nation's largest cable companies.[8] (DirecTV itself is owned by a subsidiary of General Motors.) Rather than being hurt by the growth of DBS, program services such as HBO have seen large profit increases as new DBS subscribers add to the network's paid viewership.[9]

Still another element in this television revolution has been the home VCR and the attendant new market in home video sales and rentals. Not only does tape rental offer viewers access to programs not otherwise available, but it also allows them to schedule viewing at their leisure. VCRs give viewers the power to program their own viewing, though still only within the options provided by program marketers. Yet here too, new technologies, driven by prospects for new markets and greater profits, threaten the existence of the older video rental business. Cable and DBS systems increasingly offer pay per view (PPV) services whereby viewers select the program they wish to watch from a large on-line inventory. The program is descrambled to those homes choosing to pay for it, and the charge is simply added to the monthly cable statement. Still, technology in the industry is changing so fast that many companies have been cautious about investing large amounts of capital in even newer systems that would allow subscribers instantaneous tapelike access to programming.

The country's conversion to high-definition digital television (HDTV; or, sometimes, DTV) promises to add even more complexity to the picture of technological change. By the time you read these words, HDTV may have been introduced by broadcasters in the largest U.S. markets. According to the Federal Communication Commission's plan for introducing the new system, all U.S. television stations are scheduled to be converted to HDTV transmission by 2006, although some observers doubt whether this goal is practical.[10] HDTV offers sharper pictures, clearer sound, and better reception of over-the-air signals, and its introduction means a multibillion-dollar bonanza for equipment manufacturers who will sell new HDTV equipment to consumers. It may also mean a major boost for digital DBS. At this writing, the three major networks and HBO planned to begin HDTV transmission by the end of 1998, but some local broadcasters and cable companies are reluctant to invest the capital required for conversion to HDTV.[11] There may also be shortages of equipment and technicians that delay full implementation.

Economic Convergence: Megamergers and Synergy

Today, the term *convergence* is being used to describe rapid movement toward newer technological and economic structures in the media industries. As table 2.1 illustrates, the television industry's recent history has involved nothing less than a total economic reorganization. Most changes have occurred after companies sought economic advantage from new technologies in an environment of weakening government regulation. The realignments began in 1985 and 1986, when within a few months all big three networks changed hands. In the ensuing 12 years, CBS and ABC changed hands a second time (and NBC's owner, General Electric, has been trying to sell it as well). Table 2.1 describes many of the major economic events of this period, and the trends are apparent. Through multiple purchases, takeovers, and mergers, companies in the television industry have begun to converge, with global megacorporations increasing their control over all aspects of television, from program production through distribution to the audience. At the same time, these giants are also consolidating their hold on other sectors of the media such as theatrical film production, book and magazine publishing, and the recorded music industry. In addition, they have acquired new interests in emerging technologies such as computers and DBS.

Other corporate players are also on the horizon. Telephone companies (TELCOS), which have long provided video and data connections to commercial users, now plan to offer these services to the home, while cable TV companies wish to

TABLE 2.1. TV'S MAJOR ECONOMIC EVENTS, 1985–1997

Year	Event
1985	• Capital Cities Communication takes over ABC for $3.5 billion. • News Corp. purchases Twentieth Century Fox studios. • Ted Turner fails in attempt to take over CBS. CBS falls under control of Lawrence Tisch.
1986	• Turner Broadcasting System buys MGM/UA Communications. • News Corp. purchases six U.S. television stations and launches Fox, a new fourth network. • General Electric takes over RCA for $6.4 billion and gets NBC in the bargain. In the decade that follows, GE makes several unsuccessful attempts to sell off the network.
1988	• Sony purchases CBS Records from CBS for $2 billion.
1989	• Time, Inc., agrees to merge with Warner Brothers at a cost of $14 billion to form the world's largest media conglomerate. • Time Warner acquires Lorimar Telepictures, Inc., a major Hollywood TV studio. • Sony buys Columbia Pictures from Coca-Cola for $4.9 billion.
1990	• Primestar Partners begins to provide limited DBS service. A joint venture of several major corporations, including 8 of the 15 largest cable companies, the move fuels charges that the cable industry is attempting to stifle DBS competition and spurs antitrust investigations at both state and federal levels.
1992	• In response to consumer complaints about rising cable rates, Congress passes the Cable Television Act of 1992, a section of which forces the big companies to make the cable networks they own available at fair prices to competing distributors such as DBS.
1993	• Disney purchases Miramax Film Corporation and an NHL expansion team, later named the Mighty Ducks.
1994	• New Corp. invests $500 million in New World Communications Group, Inc. As part of the deal, 12 of New World's TV stations switch network affiliation to Fox. This, coupled with Fox's $1.56 billion bid for four years of NFL football, sets off a national chain reaction of station affiliation realignment. • Viacom acquires Paramount Communications, Inc., and Blockbuster Entertainment for a combined $17.4 billion. • Cap Cities/ABC invests $100 million in a joint partnership with Dreamworks SKG. • DirecTV and USSB roll out 18-inch DBS systems and sell 1 million units in 12 months—the most successful first year of any consumer-electronics product.
1995	• FCC abolishes fin-syn and prime-time access rule. • Westinghouse purchases CBS for $5.4 billion. • Canadian distiller Seagram purchases 80% of MCA for $5.7 billion. • Disney enters joint venture with BellSouth, SBC Communications, and Ameritech to develop, market, and deliver video programming.
1996	• Congress passes Telecommunication Act, further deregulating the industry. • Disney purchases Capital Cities/ABC for $19 billion, temporarily making it the largest media company in the world. • DirecTV announces it will begin selling 18-inch home DBS reception systems for $200.
1997	• Time Warner acquires Turner Broadcasting System for $7.5 billion in stock, reclaiming the title of largest media company in the world. • News Corp. enters partnership with Primestar for DBS service. • Microsoft purchases WebTV Networks for $425 million. The company makes set-top boxes that connect TVs to the World Wide Web. • Microsoft invests $1 billion in Comcast Corporation, the nation's fourth-largest cable systems owner. In the week following the announcement, cable industry shares on the stock market jump 13%.

provide telephone service and high-speed Internet links using their existing network of cable. News publications, TV stations, film studios, and even large advertisers have already begun marketing via the World Wide Web—a step that may eventually lead to video transmission. The result has been additional impetus toward corporate mergers and buyouts as companies find diversification into new technologies essential for continued profits.

Economists use the term *synergy* to describe the potential economic advantages that come from a single corporation's ownership of different aspects of a single industry. The idea is that products made by one branch of a company may be distributed and sold by other branches, leading (at least in theory) to more efficient operation and higher profits. One of the most important aspects of the television industry's recent megamergers has been the potentially synergistic combinations of production studios with television networks.

Until the 1980s, most prime-time television programs were produced by subsidiaries of the major Hollywood theatrical studios or one of a handful of independent production companies. But beginning in 1985, these studios became part of the economic realignment of the industry. As table 2.2 shows, each of the seven big studios that dominated theatrical film production in the 1980s has become part of a television megacorporation of the 1990s. Three of the studios became cornerstones for new networks, Fox, UPN, and WB. Disney bought an existing network, ABC, and Time Warner's acquisition of Turner effectively combined two studios under one corporate umbrella.

The motivation for such acquisitions is largely synergy. For example, Disney's acquisition of ABC gave it an outlet for its live and animated movies and television shows and enabled it to promote its theme park and motion pictures through coverage on the network's other programs. A good example of how synergy can work can be seen in Disney's relationship with the hit TV sitcom *Home Improvement.* "Disney produces the show, distributes it through its Disney Television division and broadcasts it on Disney-owned ABC. Moreover, it has used this leverage to coax star Tim Allen to take roles in Disney movies and write bestsellers for Disney's book-publishing arm."[12]

But experience has shown that developing synergy in the television industry can sometimes cause difficulties.[13] In 1997, Wind Dancer Production Group, a partner in *Home Improvement,* sued Disney, claiming that the company allowed ABC (its newly acquired network) to renew the show's contract for a smaller licensing fee than the program was worth, effectively cutting into Wind Dancer's profits. As the *Wall Street Journal* put it, "Call it the dark side of synergy: the not-unanticipated consequence of having both the suppliers and the distributors of TV programs and movies under one single roof. In today's Hollywood, deal-makers are increasingly wrestling with a tricky question: How hard a bargain can you drive when, in essence, you're negotiating with yourself?"[14]

Industry executives have also found that maximizing synergy does not always mean maximizing profits. Corporations have sometimes found it in their interest to continue relationships with outside companies or even competitors. For example, in 1996, cable giant TCI decided to streamline operations and dropped the MTV network, owned by major competitor Viacom, from many of its cable systems. After waves of subscriber protest, TCI restored MTV to its systems.

But despite the limitations of synergy, many in the industry are fearful that the industry's future may lie in studios that produce shows only for their own

TABLE 2.2. THE ECONOMIC REALIGNMENT
OF HOLLYWOOD'S MAJOR STUDIOS

Studio	Rank*	Year: Purchase	TV Network
Paramount	1	1994: Paramount acquired by Viacom	UPN
Warner Brothers	2	1989: Warner Brothers becomes part of Time Warner	WB
MCA/Universal	3	1995: MCA/Universal purchased by Seagram	
Twentieth Century Fox	4	1985: Fox purchased by News Corp.	Fox
Columbia Pictures	5	1989: Columbia purchased by Sony	
Walt Disney	6	1995: Disney buys Cap Cities/ABC	ABC
MGM/UA	7	1986: MGM/UA bought by Turner Broadcasting 1997: Turner merges with Time Warner	

*Studio rank is based on theatrical film rental revenues from North America as reported in Justin Wyatt, *High Concept* (Austin: University of Texas Press, 1994), 86.

company's networks, thus further reducing competition and all but eliminating small independent producers. Others fear that the creative power of producers, writers, directors, and actors will be reduced.[15]

A major factor in limiting the chances for such a scenario, however, is the possibility of reregulation. Government officials, fresh from rounds of economic deregulation based on increased competition (see below) and spurred on by fears articulated by the industry's smaller competitors, may more critically question the fine line between synergy and antitrust violations.[16] On the other hand, media conglomerates may be wise enough to avoid such problems by allowing their studios to continue their still profitable practice of producing and selling programs to all comers.

Technical Convergence: TV as Computer
or Computer as TV?

With digital electronics, computers and television sets are becoming more and more alike. As early as 1997, computer dealers began marketing "multimedia" big-screen units that contained a full Pentium computer, a TV tuner, and a 30-inch computer screen capable of displaying the new high-definition TV pictures. Such units are the prototypes for the HDTV receivers that will receive and display high-definition digital broadcasts as well as function as computer browsers for the World Wide Web, thus allowing for interactive as well as passive viewing. A number of computer companies are experimenting with "video streaming" technologies capable of sending real-time video over a computer connection. In fact, the technology and software for sending real-time video over the Web has already been developed.[17] What is now lacking are the technical refinements and broadband circuits to the home that would allow the signals to be improved and make them easily receivable. Such circuits may soon be made readily available from existing local cable TV operators, who, if they smell profits large enough to merit the capital outlay, will install the fiber optic lines necessary for such a system. The implications of such a new technology for television are immense. Just as the World Wide Web of today makes every computer user a potential worldwide publisher, the technology of the not-too-distant future may make every computer a potential television station. In such a world, the question of 500 channels delivered by a local cable system would become moot as computer-television combinations would allow viewers to surf a virtually infinite number of channels.

Some in the industry are pursuing just such ideas. In early 1996, Microsoft's Bill Gates held a video press conference on the Web using streaming technology. The next year, Microsoft purchased WebTV, a company that makes set-top boxes that convert a home TV set into a Web browser, and a few months later, Gates invested $1 billion in ComCast, the nation's fourth-largest cable system operator, with 3.5 million subscribers. Gates announced plans to use Comcast's cable systems to experiment with the new high-speed data connections that would allow quality video over the Internet.[18] In the week following the announcement, the price of cable industry shares on the stock market jumped 13 percent.[19] In mid-1997, Microsoft purchased interests in several companies developing video streaming computer software, including Progressive Networks, Inc., and by September of that year introduced (along with Intel and Adobe) a new streaming video format.[20] In the same month, Microsoft also introduced an updated version of the set-top WebTV box that would deliver a high-bandwidth data stream over existing cable systems.[21] The $300 converter allows TV viewers to browse the Web and receive streaming video. One of the first things they saw when they visited the new WebTV site? Commercials!

Technology and Television Economics

Clearly, new technologies are crucial to the changes taking place in the television industry. But as Raymond Williams argued two decades ago, the *invention* of a new technology does not determine its *use*, and invention itself is as much the product of social priorities as it is the isolated development of scientific knowledge.[22] The invention and diffusion of any new technology requires the right combination of social forces. There must be a technical basis for a new technology. That is, the society must be at a stage of scientific and technical advancement to enable invention to take place. A practical television system, for example, was invented only after countless other developments in chemistry and physics made the electronic picture tube and other components conceivable and workable. On the other hand, just because an invention is technologically feasible does not mean that it will be successfully developed. It must also have a sound economic basis; that is to say, the society (or, rather, those who control its resources) must want this new technology enough to sacrifice some of its wealth to obtain it. In a capitalist country like the United States, this means that the technology must attract investors—those already rich in capital—to finance its development and integration into society. Since investors seek a return greater than bank rates, they must believe that there will be enough customers willing to pay enough money for the new technology for it to be worth their investment.

But even this may not be enough to ensure the introduction of the new technology. DirecTV and its partner USSB had both the technology and the money to launch new high-powered DBS services that required only an 18-inch reception dish. However, they were initially unable to get access to programming. The most popular cable channels such as HBO, ESPN, and CNN are owned by large corporations that also own major cable systems (see table 2.3), and, as mentioned earlier, many of these companies have also invested in Primestar, DirecTV's major DBS competitor. These corporations had little economic incentive to provide DirecTV access to the programming it needed, and it was only after antitrust investigations led Congress to pass legislation barring the big companies from withholding their channels that the new services became viable. This illustrates that unless the government or other nonprofit institution intervenes, new technologies—no matter their potential *social implications*—will be limited to those desired by the financiers for their own *private* purposes.[23]

Consider, for example, the new technologies that can make 500 channels of television available over cable systems (or even more in the future via the World Wide Web). We have already discussed how the advent of new cable channels in the 1980s did not result in more viewers or a significant amount of added time spent viewing. Adding more channels, therefore, poses several economic questions: If the audience can't grow, how can these new channels attract enough viewers to be profitable for investors? Will the money generated by these new channels take away from other, already established segments of the industry, or would they be new revenues, plumbed more deeply than ever from the pockets of the viewers? If that's the case, how much are consumers willing and able to pay for these new channels? How will new competition from DBS or the need to invest in new HDTV equipment affect this willingness? Will new interactive computer services be developed that will favor the expansion of broadband cable systems? These are all questions on which the economic development and survival of a 500-channel cable system will depend.

This example illustrates one of the major difficulties for today's television industry—the economic uncertainties that accompany rapid technological change, which in capitalist economics is itself driven by the ceaseless search for greater profits. If a corporation involved in television does not invest in new technologies, it is almost certain to lose out financially—maybe to the point of being driven out of business. Yet investing too heavily in the wrong technology could be equally disastrous. Today, some of the world's most financially successful corporations grew from small companies that backed the right technologies a few years ago. In any case, absent popular intervention, the private investment priorities of corporations will determine the shape of television technology, regardless of environmental or other effects.

Scenarios such as these ensure that the turmoil and uncertainty caused by innovative new technologies and the drive for profits will continue well into the future. However, unlike distribution, production is one segment of the industry that seems relatively secure. Virtually all of the new television technologies of the past two decades have brought changes to the way programs are distributed, but relatively little to the way they are produced.

Although the introduction of such innovations as digital special effects and editing has expanded what can be made for given budgets, it has not changed the fundamental organization of program production. Even with the new technological efficiencies, highly skilled producers, writers, directors, actors, and technicians must still invest countless hours of time to produce a single 30-minute program in a process that is both costly and time consuming.

So the industry must confront a dilemma. The proliferation of new channels has heightened the demand for new television programs, but at the same time it has reduced the potential audience size for each show. The result has been both a scaling back of production budgets for traditional network series and a need for new shows that can be produced quickly and at lower costs than traditional prime-time sitcoms or dramas.[24] As a result, the 1990s have seen major increases in sports programming, talk, and other "reality" shows, all relatively cheap to produce.[25] While budgets for traditional news programs have plummeted (especially at the big three networks), with more conglomeration, demands on news shows to produce a profitable audience for advertisers have increased. The result has been a proliferation of entertaining "soft" news both in traditional newscasts and in prime-time newsmagazine programs. No matter the technology used for delivery, there will always be a market for television programs that can attract viewers, especially those viewers advertisers most want to affect.

The Products of the Television Industry?

The television industry in the United States is unique. While in most countries the electronic media are government-owned, or at least publicly controlled, here television is mostly treated as just another business—a capital enterprise through which profits are to be made. Much of the government regulation of television that does exist in the United States is economic; that is, it is usually designed to protect the economic interests of one or another segment of the industry, rather than those of the public. The capitalist economic structure determines, of course, who controls television in the United States—who decides what is to be seen on our TV sets and why. Only the channels of public television are not part of this profit-making system, but even they must raise money to operate and often find it economically expedient to adopt commercial priorities, including corporate sponsorship and a limited form of advertising. In addition, they must often compete with profit-making corporations in deals for the buying and selling of programs.

It is helpful to think of the U.S. television industry as producing two major products. One segment of the industry is familiar to most people: it manufactures television programs. As we have seen, most of this manufacturing is done by a handful of Hollywood studios owned by large media conglomerates. Rights to show the television programs are sold to wholesalers (mainly the broadcast and cable networks), who distribute them, along with some commercials, to local retailers (the TV stations and cable systems). Another comparatively new source of profit for the industry is the distribution of programs, especially theatrical films, through the sale and rental of video tapes directly to consumers.

A second product produced by the television industry is not so obvious. It is *audience,* or, to put it another way, the attention of millions of television viewers. By using television programs as apparently free entertainment, television outlets can attract viewers for whom advertisers are willing to pay. In a real sense, then, the audience itself becomes the commodity to be sold. The value of this audience to the advertiser varies greatly with its size and also with its composition, principally the age and sex of the viewers, because these factors indicate the viewers' potential value as buyers of advertisers' products. Those viewers who belong to categories that spend more money on certain products are more valuable to advertisers of those products, so producers design their programs especially to attract and hold them. This is the "commodity audience" Eileen Meehan has described.[26]

So the products of the industry can be seen as both programs and audiences, with the production of programs having the production of audiences as its main goal. But the question of who constitutes the buyers of these products deserves further consideration.

Paying for Television: Two Models

When the U.S. television industry began to flourish in the late 1940s, it was built upon the foundation of an already vibrant, advertising-supported industry—radio. In most countries radio in its prime was funded by direct government grant or by listener license fees. In the United States, commercial advertising had become entrenched as the economic mechanism for paying for radio, even more than it had for most newspapers and magazines. This model was adopted and closely followed by television until the 1970s, when commercial-free pay cable channels such as HBO began to appear, introducing a new way of paying for television programs. The home VCR brought with it the tape rental business, in which consumers pay directly only for programs they watch. Today, then, the television industry is best thought of as having two complementary economic systems. The first is the traditional advertising-supported model. The second is the increasingly important subscription-supported model.

The Advertising-Supported Model

In the traditional advertising-supported model (see fig. 2.1), television programs are produced or manufactured by production companies. As with all capitalist enterprises, the programs are produced in response to expectations of sale and profit. The production companies sell the rights to use their programs to wholesalers. In this model, the "wholesaler" is usually one of the broadcast or advertising-supported cable networks, or it may be a program syndicator (a broker who sells program rights to local stations). The wholesaler will frequently sell some advertising time in the program directly to national advertisers, resulting in revenues directly from the advertiser to the wholesaler. The wholesaler then distributes the program—complete with some commercials—to the "retailer," a local television station or cable outlet. Retailers and wholesalers usually enter into complex agreements for program delivery that cover such details as scheduling, cost, exclusivity of rights, and so on. Depending on the specific arrangements and the size of the potential audience, money can flow either way. That is, the retailer may pay the wholesaler for the right to show the programs, or the wholesaler may pay the retailer for running the show plus the national ads they contain. Retailers will also sell additional advertising time in the programs either to local businesses or to national advertisers. In the traditional advertising-supported model, money flows from the advertiser to the retailer and wholesaler to the producer. It is important to note that television viewers themselves are not the direct "buyers" of

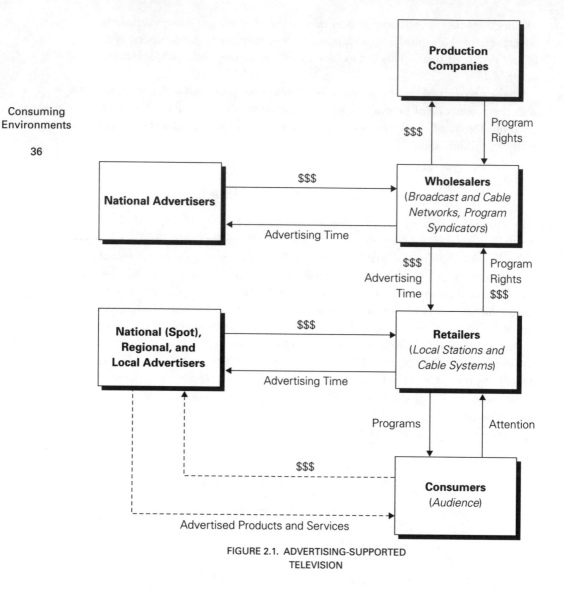

FIGURE 2.1. ADVERTISING-SUPPORTED
TELEVISION

the programs. That is, the programming is supplied to the audience without any direct payment. Instead, the advertisers are the economic consumers. Why is this important? It is because money talks: those who pay the bills have the most influence over which television programs will be produced and scheduled. But note that in this model, the advertiser is not buying the programs themselves but rather the attention of the audiences that view them. Yet it is the advertiser's dollars that finance the purchase and distribution of the programs. This means that the industry must produce programs that advertisers want to buy—and not *necessarily* those programs that viewers might want to watch, let alone those designed to serve the public good.

Many people who work in the industry like to call advertising-supported television "free TV." But it is, of course, far from being free. Although it is the advertisers who pay for the television programs directly, the viewers do so indirectly—and in several ways. First, of course, viewers must invest money in equipment simply to be able to watch TV programs. The sale of TVs and VCRs is a multibillion-dollar industry in the United States, almost solely financed by viewers. The introduction of new technologies such as DBS and HDTV will ultimately cost consumers far more in the purchase of new equipment than it will the industry itself.

More important, viewers pay increased prices for goods and services that are advertised. While it can be argued that mass advertising can increase demand for a product and thus lower its per-unit cost, the proper question to ask is, "Did consumers really need to purchase that product to begin with?" That is, advertising entices us to spend money on products we might otherwise not buy or that have few or no advantages over less costly unadvertised products.

Children are especially susceptible to advertising's effects. A visitor to a toy or grocery store will inevitably find small children begging their parents for some name-brand item or another. Our young have been recruited by Saturday morning ads to act as corporate sales agents for overpriced toys and sugar-laden breakfast foods. Some parents have expressed such concerns over advertising's influence that in recent years Congress and the Federal Communications Commission have been moved to regulate the worst abuses of commercials aimed at kids.

For many consumer items, advertising constitutes a substantial percentage of the cost of producing and selling the item. Compare the price of a bottle of a heavily advertised "name" brand of aspirin with its generic equivalent to see how this works. The aspirin is pharmaceutically the same in both bottles—only the brand name and price are different. Considering that television and other advertising costs more than $160 billion each year, this constitutes a hidden "tax" averaging several hundred dollars on everyone who buys advertised products.[27] Then there are the billions of dollars a year consumers pay in interest on unsecured loans needed to finance purchases they otherwise could not afford. This, too, must be considered a way in which consumers pay for television.

We even pay what must be considered an indirect taxpayer subsidy of the advertising industry. Since advertising costs are considered to be business expenses, companies pay no federal taxes on that part of their corporate income that they spend on advertising. In addition, most states exempt advertising sales from state and local taxes, and when businesses pay less in taxes, it means a heavier tax burden on the average citizen. Thus consumers' dollars ultimately pay the bills for "free" commercial television, even though the economic organization of the industry makes program (and ad) producers primarily responsible not to consumers or the public but to advertisers.

But perhaps the biggest cost of all to viewers is to their physical and psychological well-being. In promoting products and ideas that encourage waste and pollution—or even those that are just plain bad for our health—television advertisers invite us to participate in our own demise. Automobile commercials promoting overpriced, air-polluting gas guzzlers as the epitome of taste, refinement, and success are only one notorious example.

So, if there is anything "free" about "free TV," it is the free ride we give to the television advertisers by watching their programs and commercials. In a real sense, it is the viewer who is providing something for nothing. By watching television, we create a commodity (audience attention) that the retailer can sell to advertisers. This commodity has value because advertisers know that those who are watching are also learning to consume products and services they might not otherwise desire or buy.

The Subscription-Supported Model

In the early 1970s, an economic revolution in the television industry quietly began. It was during that time that cable operators discovered that viewers would pay extra to receive new program services not available from over-the-air broadcasters and that they would pay even more to see uncut, recently released theatrical films without any commercials. About the same time, practical home VCRs were introduced, making cable TV even more attractive, since programs could be recorded for later viewing or collection. Home VCRs also spurred the development of a new distribution system—rentals and sales of television on tape. But what made these distribution innovations possible was the evolution of a new system of paying for television directly by the viewer—the *subscription-supported model* (see fig. 2.2).

In it, production companies still sell rights to programs to wholesalers. In this case, however, the wholesalers are pay-TV cable channels or videotape movie wholesalers. The wholesalers distribute the programs to local retailers such as local cable systems or video rental outlets. Television viewers then choose which programs or channels they want and pay for them directly. The money flow in this model is directly from the viewer through the retailer and wholesaler to the production company.

Yet movies on cable and at rental stores are only apparently commercial-free. Many contain advertisements—so-called product placements—embedded within them for which corporations have paid hefty sums. Some examples include "the appearances of a new BMW Z3 roadster in *Goldeneye* (1995), a prehistoric McDonald's restaurant in *The Flintstones* (1994) and a futuristic Oldsmobile showroom in *Demolition Man* (1993). A Domino's pizza was delivered to the heroes in *Teenage Mutant Ninja Turtles* (1990), Michael J. Fox drank Pepsi-Cola in *Back to the Future II* (1989) and Rocky Balboa ate his Wheaties in *Rocky III* (1982). Before Coca-Cola sold the Columbia and Tristar studios to Sony, films like *The Big Chill* (1983) were awash in a sea of soft drinks."[28]

Placement firms assist client companies in spending an estimated $50 million each year for product placement in films.[29] Product placement has also enabled tobacco companies, forbidden from advertising directly on television, to secure a presence on the screen nevertheless: Philip Morris paid $350,000 to have Timothy Dalton as James Bond smoke Larks in the 1989 British film *License to Kill*.[30] Philip Morris was paying not only for access to the eyes of theater audiences but to the no doubt many more who would be exposed to the pitch on broadcast television, cable, and home video.

Another issue that subscription support raises is that of equity of access. At first, subscription may appear to be a democratic way to finance the television industry, and it is true that subscription makes available additional, less conventional programs not available under the advertising-supported system (just check out some of the more obscure titles in a large video store). Yet with the subscription-supported system, those who are wealthiest have the most access. A lower-income viewer may not be able to afford to subscribe to cable or to rent as many video tapes and therefore has diminished access to programs and a reduced eco-

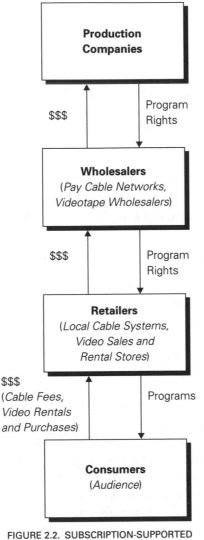

FIGURE 2.2. SUBSCRIPTION-SUPPORTED
TELEVISION

nomic say in what programs get produced and scheduled. With the development of the World Wide Web and its ever closer association with television, this question of equal access for the economically disadvantaged becomes increasingly critical.

Most cable television and DBS systems offer a service that is actually a hybrid of the advertiser and subscription models. Viewers must pay a monthly fee for a basic service that consists largely of advertising-supported channels. Viewers who want access to non-advertising-supported channels generally pay an additional premium. Cable and DBS systems must, in turn, pay a per-viewer fee to wholesalers for the right to carry non-advertising-supported channels (the systems pay a much lower per-viewer fee for the right to carry most advertising-supported channels).

Today, subscription-supported television is just beginning to make an impact on program production decisions. The advertising-supported model is still overwhelmingly dominant, yet the industry has shown remarkable ingenuity in finding new ways to make money from television. Two examples especially stand out.

The first is pay-per-view (PPV). With PPV, viewers pay a fee for a program only if they watch it. Video rental stores, of course, operate this way, but it has only been through the development of sophisticated addressable converters and broadband delivery systems that cable companies have been able to move successfully into PPV. For the increasing number of properly equipped cable systems, viewers can choose whether or not a particular program will appear on their home television. Computers at the cable company track orders, direct program feeds, and bill customers on their monthly statements. So far, most systems have only been able to offer a limited number of PPV programs, largely because of technical limitations. Technological developments such as broadband cable systems and DBS will result in a substantial expansion of PPV offerings, and it may not be too far in the future that live telecasts of major sporting events such as the Olympics, the Super Bowl, Wimbledon, and the World Series will be available only on PPV.[31]

A Third Model: Home Shopping Channels

While advertising and subscription account for almost all of television's economic support, we cannot ignore the success of what must be considered a third economic model—home shopping channels, one of the fastest growing components of the business.[32] These channels provide a continuous flow of telephone-order products hawked by fast-talking salespeople and celebrities. Home shopping represents what must be the ultimate corporate dream—a television channel that consists of nothing but advertising. (Yet some viewers have said they prefer the shopping channels because they have *no* commercials!) Economically, these channels represent a whole new way of generating revenue—a marriage of television advertising with the retail store by way of the street vendor, explicitly bringing the store window home. Rather than selling viewers to advertisers, the home shopping channel eliminates the intermediary (and, consequently, the need for programs) and sells products directly to viewers.

For many viewers, home shopping seems to offer a genuine advantage over retail shopping: one does not leave home to shop, so the salesperson may offer companionship and help but cannot press you to make a purchase as she or he might in a store. In any case, you need not respond—and changing the channel is certainly easier than walking out of the store. The cost for this isolation is the inability to comparison shop, or to pick up an item, hold it, walk around with it, and then turn around and put it back, without having to pay.

But home shopping seems to offer at least some of the audience far more than just convenience. Many home shopping "programs" are hosted by gregarious and conventionally attractive men and women who not only pitch the merchandise but also exploit what researchers have called "parasocial interactions," the seemingly personal relationships viewers develop with some television performers.[33] Salespeople frequently invite viewers to dial in and discuss not only their product purchases but also their personal lives, and many callers respond, conversing with on-air salespeople as if they were personal friends. Research suggests that many in the home shopping audience find companionship from the program's sales force in a sort of interactive version of a soap opera. Some researchers have speculated that such relationships may even contribute to compulsive buying—an overwhelming and deep-seated urge to buy things, psychologically akin to compulsive gambling and other addictive behaviors. Certainly many of the products offered on home shopping channels, such as cosmetics, clothing, "collectibles," jewelry, and electronic equipment, are the same products that compulsive buyers have been found to purchase with especially high frequency.[34]

By all accounts, home shopping channels are successful economically. Some vendors have had truly phenomenal results. For example, former television cooking show star Julia Child sold 10,000 copies of her new cookbook during a 35-minute appearance on QVC.[35]

In the future, home shopping may well be expanded to include higher-priced items such as automobiles. With technological advances such as integration of video and computers, it may become even easier to make impulse purchases— you'll need only point and click. This is another point at which television and the Internet are becoming more alike.

The ABC's of Television Economics

Regardless of which economic model best describes a particular part of the television industry, economists point out that there are certain inherent characteristics in the business that influence its structure. The three main ones are high fixed costs, high risk, and static revenues.[36] These characteristics favor large corporations with easier access to capital and more diverse enterprises that can make multiple use of their products and thereby disperse risk. This in turn makes smaller corporations in the television industry prime candidates for buyout and merger. Let's take a look at each of these characteristics in turn.

Entertainment businesses have high fixed costs because they generally must invest a great deal of money up front, before any return on investment can be realized. In addition, operation costs are mostly fixed, meaning that it will cost about the same amount to operate no matter how successful or unsuccessful the corporation. For example, investors must spend a good deal of money in production costs before a new television series can go on the air. Once on the air, the week-to-week cost of producing new episodes will be virtually the same no matter the number of advertisers or viewers.

There is, of course, some variation in just how "fixed" costs must be and in how much must be invested up front for different projects. For example, while the cable industry had to borrow billions of dollars to lay wire into homes, the DBS business, since it only leased the necessary satellite space, needs fewer customers to break even. Then, too, both cable and DBS pay for many channels on a per-subscriber basis, so their program costs are closely related to the number of their subscribers. Fixed costs are also high at the television production and wholesale level.

High fixed costs contribute to the second major economic characteristic of the industry, high risk. Since costs are fixed, the industry is often unable to respond rapidly to economic downturn or technological change. Then, too, television audiences are notoriously unpredictable; shows industry observers think are sure hits routinely flop while other new shows unexpectedly draw large audiences (*Dr. Quinn, Medicine Woman* was one of the latter). One result is that a painstaking process has been developed for choosing what new shows to produce. Every year, each of the major networks spends about $40 million buying about 30 pilots culled from 100 scripts to find the 10 new TV shows that reach the air.[37] Yet one need only note the high percentage of those new fall shows that are canceled before January to realize the high risk involved.

Each network invests about $1 billion annually for prime-time series, but these payments usually cover only about 80 percent of the production costs. In fact, few series make money for their producers until they have entered syndication.[38] Until relatively recently, regulations effectively restricted the amount of prime-time programming the big three networks could produce. This also meant they could not share in the potential profits reaped on domestic syndication. With deregulation, however, prime-time production is becoming a major area of network activity and, as we have seen, an important consideration in the merging of studios and networks.

One way the industry tries to reduce risk in producing new shows is by imitating its successes. Programs are spun off from successful shows or movies in the hope that they are more likely to be hits. Producers, writers, and actors with a history of success are highly sought after for the same reason. Whole show genres come and go based on the belief that imitation reduces risk.

Another way risk can be reduced is by economies of scale. A large studio can produce several shows. Some of them may be hits while others will be flops. Small studios, on the other hand, can be (and are) easily driven out of business by just one or two failures. Still another strategy is for the industry to share the risk at all levels of the economic chain. Producers frequently enter into partnerships with other investors and try to get networks financially committed to programming as early in the process as possible; in turn, the networks try to sign up advertisers for the fall season during the spring—long before the shows actually hit the airwaves, and sometimes even before production is completed. For their part, advertisers realize they must commit to a new show early or risk missing out on a hit. On the other hand, they also frequently demand contracts that specify financial penalties for programs that fall below a certain level of viewership.

Finally, the television industry is currently beset by fairly static revenues. The number of television viewers in the United States is growing only by the relatively small annual increase in population. Almost everyone who wants it has access to a television set, and the time spent with the TV on in the average U.S. household has leveled off in recent years at about 50 hours per week.[39] For that major portion of the industry financed according to the advertising-supported model, a static viewing level means static revenues. Advertisers will only pay more if they perceive themselves getting more. In addition, the growth of advertising-supported channels on cable has drained not only viewers from the big three broadcast networks but also revenues, since advertising income is directly related to viewing levels. The pie is only so big, and it is not getting any bigger.

One result has been the increased emphasis by programmers and advertisers on small, specialized "niche" audiences mentioned earlier. For example, if an advertising-supported cable network can program in such a way as to attract a group of viewers that can be narrowly defined by demographic characteristics (say, women from 18 to 49 years old), it can sell that audience at a premium to advertisers who aim to sell their product to that particular group. By charging more for this premium audience, the network can economically survive on fewer viewers. We'll discuss this strategy more fully in the next chapter.

Static revenues point up the importance to the industry of developing what economists call "new revenue streams." That is, if viewing levels—and advertising revenues—are fairly static, the industry can only increase revenues by generating new sources of income. The subscription-supported model gives the industry the opportunity of tapping consumer pocketbooks directly. New television marketing strategies such as pay-per-view and home shopping are examples of the potential for this approach.

Yet another strategy, already enormously profitable for decades, is globalization—increased selling of television programs overseas. The U.S. entertainment industry as a whole has always been successful exporting its product. Yet many people around the world see U.S. television programs and other entertainment as a kind of cultural imperialism, and foreign governments often impose tough import restrictions on U.S. entertainment products to protect their own culture's popular arts. This has been a major issue in U.S. trade relations with Europe, especially France. Even so, *Baywatch,* with 18 million European viewers, was one of 1994's most-watched television shows in the five largest European countries.[40]

These characteristics—high fixed costs, high risk, and domestic, industrywide, static revenues—have shaped the still enormously profitable U.S. television industry. All three favor large, well-capitalized, diversified, global corporations while discouraging the independent innovator with new ideas, let alone the small, nonprofit organization. From a corporate standpoint, risk is much reduced if the company can control all three levels of the business—production, wholesaling, and retailing—and this is the motivation for many of the mergers and acquisitions discussed earlier. Table 2.3 presents a summary of the major corporate players in the U.S. television industry today.[41] Most are involved in all three levels of the industry—production, wholesaling, and retailing—and most have other media interests as well. Several are involved in complex cross-ownership and joint venture arrangements that allow them to share risk and profits across companies. For example, Viacom jointly owns the cable network Comedy Central with Time Warner, while CBS has partnered with otherwise rival Fox to sell home videos.[42]

The Economics of Television Deregulation

Public policy and the government regulation that follows it have shaped U.S. broadcasting and cable since their beginnings. Corporations engaged in producing and distributing television programs must, of course, abide by the same laws as other businesses, governing such areas as taxes, labor, antitrust, copyright, and so on. But the television industry has historically been encumbered with an extensive and complex set of its own special laws and regulations.

It is helpful to consider government regulation of television as having three fairly distinct functions. Technical regulation seeks to set equipment and signal standards, minimize electronic interference, and so on. Program regulation polices television content for "indecency," truthfulness in advertising claims, political "fairness," and the like. Economic regulation includes government restrictions on industry ownership of television and cable outlets, investment in the production and distribution of programs, and so on. It is a wave of economic deregulation that has contributed to many of the important recent changes in the industry and on which we shall focus.

Historically, much of the economic regulation of the television industry has been based on the rationale that since broadcasting frequencies are severely

TABLE 2.3. MAJOR CORPORATE PLAYERS IN THE U.S. TELEVISION INDUSTRY

Parent Company	Television Interests*	Other Major Interests*
Time Warner	Owns and operates cable networks, cable television systems (over 12 million subscribers). Produces and distributes television programs for broadcast and cable networks, syndication, and home video. Warner Brothers, Time Warner Cable, Lorimar, Time-Telepictures, Castle Rock Entertainment, H-B Production Co., WB network, Home Box Office, Cinemax, Time/Warner Sports, Cartoon Network, E!, Comedy Central, Court TV, TBS Superstation, CNN, Headline News, Turner Program Services. Partner in Primestar DBS. Foreign program sales of 20,000 hours of TV programming in more than 40 languages to broadcasters in over 150 countries.	Music (38 record labels, music publishing, Columbia House music club [50%]); books (Warner Books, Little Brown, Time-Life, Turner Publishing, others); magazines (*People, Time, Sports Illustrated*, others); motion pictures (Warner Brothers, New Line); theme parks (Six Flags); sports franchises: Atlanta Braves (baseball), Atlanta Hawks (basketball).
Disney	Owns and operates broadcast and cable networks, television and radio stations. Produces and distributes television programming. ABC Television Network, ESPN, A&E, Lifetime Television, Disney Channel, several foreign television networks. ABC News, ABC Productions, Walt Disney Studios, Touchstone TV.	Theme parks (Disneyland, Disney World); retail stores (The Disney Store); books (Hyperion, Chilton); music (Hollywood Records, Wonderland Music); motion pictures (Walt Disney Pictures, Touchstone, Hollywood Pictures, Miramax); sports franchises: Mighty Ducks (hockey), Anaheim Angels (baseball).
Viacom	Produces and distributes television programs for domestic and international broadcast and cable networks, syndication, and home video. Owns and operates television and radio stations and foreign and domestic cable systems. Owns interest in television network (UPN). Produces interactive software. Owns video rental outlets. Paramount, Viacom Entertainment, Viacom Broadcasting, Viacom Productions, Showtime, The Movie Channel, MTV Networks (VH-1, Nickelodeon, MTV), Lifetime, Comedy Central, Viacom Enterprises (syndication). Spelling Entertainment Group, Inc., Blockbuster Entertainment. Programming licensing arrangements with Universal (Seagram).	Motion pictures (Paramount Studios).
The News Corporation, Limited	Produces and distributes television programs for domestic and international broadcast and cable networks, syndication, and home video. Owns and operates television and foreign and domestic cable and DBS systems. Owns Fox television network. Fox Broadcasting Co., Fox Network. New World Communications Group Inc., Twentieth Century Fox Television, Family Entertainment, Inc.	Newspapers (*Boston Herald*); books (HarperCollins, Basic Books, Scott, Foresman); magazines (*TV Guide*); motion pictures (Twentieth Century Fox); sports franchise: LA Dodgers (baseball). Large media holdings in Britain, Australia, and other countries.

Parent Company	Television Interests*	Other Major Interests*
Sony	Giant Japanese electronics equipment manufacturer moved into U.S. TV industry largely through 1989 purchase of Columbia Pictures. Owns new satellite channels in overseas markets such as Germany, Latin America, and Asia. Columbia TriStar Television, Game Show Network, Embassy Communications, Inc., Merv Griffin Enterprises.	Music (Columbia, Sony Music, other labels; music publishing, Columbia Music Club [50%]); motion pictures (Columbia Pictures, Sony Pictures); motion picture theaters (Loews, Sony, & Star Theaters).
TCI (Tele-Communications, Inc.)	Owns and operates cable television systems (largest U.S. cable operator with 10.2 million subscribers). Owns part interest in several foreign and domestic cable programming services (Discovery Channel, Black Entertainment Television, QVC, CourtRoom Television, Encore, The Family Channel, Video Jukebox Network). Owns Liberty Media Corp. Partner in Primestar DBS.	Motion picture theaters (United Artists Communications).
Seagram Co., Ltd.	Canadian liquor company entered U.S. television largely through purchase of most of MCA-Universal in 1995 for $5.7 billion. Major distribution agreement with DreamWorks SKG. Programming licensing arrangements with Viacom. USA Network, Sci-Fi channel. USA also has channels in South America, Europe, and Africa.	Music (MCA, Geffen, many other labels; music publishing); theme parks and concert halls (Universal Studios Theme Parks, Universal Amphitheatre LA, others); motion pictures (Universal, Jersey Films, Parkway, others); motion picture theaters (Cineplex, Odeon); retail stores (Spencer Gifts, DAPY). Seagram also owns 27 million shares of Time Warner.
Westinghouse-CBS, Inc.	Owns and operates broadcast and cable networks, television stations. Owns 175 radio stations. Produces and distributes television programming. Group W, CBS Broadcast Group, CBS Television Network, CBS Entertainment, CBS News, CBS Sports, The Nashville Network (TNN), Country Music Television (CMT), Midwest Sports Channel (cable).	Westinghouse is a large and diversified company involved in such areas as refrigeration, power generation (conventional and nuclear), waste disposal (including hazardous and radioactive), financial services, telephone and security equipment, satellite communications.
General Electric	Owns and operates broadcast and cable networks and television stations. Produces and distributes news, sports, and public affairs programming. NBC Television Network, NBC Productions, NBC News, NBC Sports, Consumer News & Business Channel (CNBC), Court TV, Bravo, American Movie Classics, MSNBC, A&E, History Channel, Independent Film Channel, Romance Classics.	In 1996, GE was listed as the world's largest public corporation with diverse interests in such areas as weapons, nuclear power, electrical generation, and appliances. The company also builds and launches, and owns, communication satellites and leases transponders to a myriad of users, including TV networks and DBS.

SOURCES: Compiled from various sources including *Hoover's Handbook of American Business*, the *Wall Street Journal*, and the *Nation*. *Not all interests are listed. Includes partially owned and minority interests as well as partnerships and joint ventures. For this reason, some interests (e.g., USA Network, Court TV, A&E, Primestar DBS) are listed more than once.

limited, free-market economics with open entry cannot operate normally, and so government regulation must intervene to level the playing field. In the early days of television, only a few VHF channels were allocated to each geographic area, and when successful applicants for these frequencies were awarded licenses, they were virtually guaranteed high profits and minimal competition.[43]

These limits on the number of television stations meant, in turn, a limited industry demand for programs. Thus, there were severe economic constraints on the number of program producers and wholesalers (such as TV networks) that could survive. Evolving from such a regulatory history, the economic structure of television in the United States is best described as an oligopoly—that is, the industry was (and, to a lesser extent, still is) dominated by relatively few program suppliers and distributors, and it was difficult, if not impossible, for new suppliers and distributors to enter the marketplace.[44]

A similar situation evolved among local cable operators, resulting in few communities in the United States having access to more than one local cable system. This came about because most local governments tend to treat cable operators as utilities and have granted them exclusive franchises to operate in much the same way. That is, most local governments are convinced that it would be physically and economically impractical to offer their communities competing cable systems in the same way that it has been considered impractical to offer competing local power, water, or sewer services.

In the past, many in Congress, the Federal Communications Commission (FCC), and the Department of Justice have feared that if unregulated by both government and marketplace, the oligopoly would engage in economic practices that would be harmful both to consumers and to the industry as a whole. Lack of competition can lead to such problems as exorbitant cable subscription fees, television program production in the hands of a few large corporations, and the elimination of small business from the industry.

Government response to such economic problems has often been to pass complex new laws and regulations to counteract these trends. Unfortunately, government regulation of television—often an unbalanced political compromise between dominant corporate and less powerful forces (both corporate and consumer)—sometimes further complicates matters. Once enacted, rules are often difficult to administer fairly, target the wrong thing, or have unintended consequences.[45]

An increasingly pro-business atmosphere in Washington has also contributed to many of the changes. Although there have been some notable exceptions, the general trend has been for Congress and the FCC to loosen regulations that formerly restricted economic activities in the television industry. Often, these efforts have been in response to intense lobbying by powerful industry groups and sometimes even by consumers.[46] Although deregulation as a general trend is partly due to increased Republican power in Congress, it is also based on the notion, often articulated in the industry, that economic rules passed in the 1960s and 1970s to curb the power of the big three networks may no longer be needed. According to this theory, as cable has expanded and new channels have appeared, the threat of oligopoly control by the big three has lessened.[47]

For example, in the mid 1990s, the FCC did away with two important economic rules it had originally adopted some 25 years earlier to restrict the big three networks from exerting too much power over the television production industry.

The "financial interest and domestic syndication rules" (fin-syn) effectively barred the networks from owning or even investing in most of their own prime-time programs. The Prime Time Access Rule (PTAR) had the effect of restricting the number of prime-time hours of programming the big three networks could supply to local affiliates and so helped support independent program producers by ensuring a market for their programs outside network control.

By the mid-1990s, regulators felt that such rules gave unfair advantage to new competitors such as Fox, WB, and UPN, all of whom were exempt from their provisions.[48] The effect of this deregulation was to remove most of the restraints on big three network involvement in prime-time program production and syndication, providing an even stronger economic motivation for networks to merge with studios. For example, it is doubtful whether Disney would have found it economically advantageous to purchase ABC in 1996 had these rules not been rescinded.

Another important area of deregulation has been in the restrictions on ownership of television stations. Limits on the number of television stations a single person or corporation can own have been greatly eased.

Nontelevision interests have also been affected by a loosening of economic regulation. Deregulation means that telephone companies (the TELCOS)—once prohibited from offering cable TV services to customers—are now free to enter the television distribution marketplace. In addition, technical innovations such as fiber optics and digital compression now make it practical for a single cable to the home to offer a variety of communication services, including World Wide Web access, pay-per-view television, telephone, and who knows what else.

While deregulation will continue to have a major impact on the industry, Congress and the FCC have also retained many important economic regulations and even added some new ones. Cable systems, for example, must still abide by rules that require the carriage of local broadcast stations but prohibit the duplication of their programs. The Children's Television Act of 1990 requires that broadcasters limit commercial time on children's programs. Some new regulation has even been necessary to encourage the development of emerging television technologies. As mentioned earlier, it was only after intense lobbying by DBS trade groups, coupled with a series of ongoing antitrust investigations against a group of big cable owners, that Congress added a provision to the 1992 Cable Act that requires cable programmers to charge competitors equitable rates, thus making competitive DBS possible.[49] Likewise, the costly and complex rollout of high-definition digital television is only feasible with the FCC's imposition of national standards and rules for implementation.

Economics and the Issue of Public Access

Another important aspect of television deregulation is the issue of public access and coverage of controversial issues. Since the television industry is owned by a small number of private corporations, there is a distinct danger that programming, especially of news and public affairs, will avoid topics perceived as unpopular with the corporate world or as threatening relationships with important advertisers. Several of the major players in the industry, most notably Westinghouse (owner of CBS) and General Electric (owner of NBC), have major interests in other industries. Is it sensible to expect that these companies' television networks will aggressively pursue news stories that may run counter to their parent company's interests? For example, both Westinghouse and General Electric build nuclear power plants. Can we expect to see CBS and NBC assiduously cover the problems of nuclear waste disposal? It is true that the tradition of an independent television news operation is strong, and it has produced examples of journalists who courageously battle such pressures. Still, the fact remains that in a time of dwindling news budgets, there is little economic incentive for journalists or others in the television industry to challenge seriously parent company or advertiser interests.

Congress itself recognized the problem of concentration of media ownership and its effect on access years ago when it passed laws requiring broadcasters to provide access to candidates for public office on an equal basis.[50] But even these laws do not guarantee access to political candidates outside the mainstream who may have small budgets and fundamentally different ideas. The televised presidential debates, for example, are routinely limited only to participants from the major two parties. An exception was third-party candidate Ross Perot, who only gained access to the debates after spending millions on buying television time and attracting coverage accordingly. In addition, these laws define politics solely in terms of electoral events, giving short shrift to environmental and other social movements.

Beginning as early as 1949, the FCC also attempted to address the access issue with a series of rules that became known as the fairness doctrine. These required all broadcast licensees to provide "fair and balanced" coverage of "controversial issues of public importance." The fairness doctrine proved difficult to enforce and was strongly opposed by broadcasters, who argued that the rules actually reduced free debate because licensees feared legal complications resulting from their airing programs that might be perceived as one sided. Opponents argued that for commercial reasons, broadcasters offered bland coverage in any case and in doing so promoted the status quo. Whatever the case, an FCC made up largely of Ronald Reagan appointees eliminated most fairness doctrine rules in 1989.

Many broadcasters had also argued that the fairness doctrine had become obsolete, since the vast expansion of broadcasting and cable channels during the 1980s meant that there were far more voices to be heard. To a certain extent, this was true. Cable's expansion saw an increase in the availability of news and public affairs programs with the introduction of CNN and other all-news services, C-SPAN, and niche channels featuring documentaries. Yet at the same time, many of these new channels are owned or controlled by the same large corporations (see table 2.3) that also control many of the country's other major news outlets. The mergers of the 1990s saw even more consolidation. For example, the 1997 combination of Time Warner and Turner means the same company now owns both CNN and *Time* magazine—two of the nation's most influential news sources.

Public Television

An overwhelming majority of the hours we spend watching television is devoted to channels whose primary aim is to make a profit. But noncommercial public television attempts to offer an alternative economic and programming model. In most locales, public television supports itself with a combination of tax dollars, corporate underwriting, and voluntary viewer donations raised through regular fund-raising campaigns. The original idea behind the creation of public television was that a service was needed that would be free to program without the need to cater to advertisers. Since it wouldn't need to attract large audiences under the commercial constraints demanded by advertisers, public television would be able to offer alternatives—especially programs aimed at those segments of the population underserved by commercial TV, such as children, U.S. ethnic minorities, and the elderly. In addition, it was thought, a noncommercial service would be able to offer public affairs, educational, and cultural programming not seen as commercially viable for profit-oriented networks.

Yet many agree that public television has not fulfilled its original promise. In 1992, a task force sponsored by the Twentieth Century Fund reviewed the situation and recommended a fundamental structural change and significantly increased levels of federal funding.[51] At the same time, political conservatives agreed that public TV had problems, but they proposed the solution was to eliminate federal support altogether.

The seeds of today's problems date from public broadcasting's beginnings. In the 1960s, a private commission funded by the Carnegie Corporation proposed the new national system that was to become public broadcasting. The Carnegie Commission realized that if a national public system was to be successful, it would have to have two things: a reliable source of funding, and as much isolation from politics as possible. They therefore proposed a tax on the sale of TV sets to go directly into a trust fund that would finance the new system and reduce its direct dependence on an annual appropriation from Congress. Variants on this system support noncommercial broadcasting in Europe, most notably in Great Britain, where annual license fees on receivers support the BBC. To isolate public broadcasting further from political pressures, the Carnegie Commission also proposed that the system's directors not be political appointees. When Congress passed the Public Broadcasting Act of 1967, it rejected both recommendations, effectively defeating the goal of political insulation and resulting in a system that has been plagued by chronic political wrangling.

Although public television was supposed to encourage programs that were considered too controversial for the commercial networks, it has frequently drawn fire for doing just that. During the Vietnam War, conservatives charged PBS with "liberal bias" for airing controversial documentaries that questioned the propriety of U.S. policy. One result was that President Richard Nixon vetoed the 1972 Corporation for Public Broadcasting (CPB) funding bill.[52] The administration said that PBS had become too centralized and forced the system to place more program control in the hands of local stations. Several members of the CPB board resigned in protest only to be replaced with Nixon appointees. The move forced public broadcasters to seek increased financial support from nongovernmental sources, such as individual affluent subscribers and commercial underwriters.[53] Further cuts in federal funding came during the Reagan administration, and in 1995 congressional conservatives, many enraged by a PBS documentary on homosexuality, sponsored hearings that challenged PBS programming and proposed the elimination of federal funding.[54]

As a result of the steady decline in federal support since the 1970s, public broadcasting has developed an economic structure increasingly reliant on private and corporate funding, which has lead to particular kinds of programming inequities. For example, the need to raise funds through local donations leads to the criticism that elitist programs are aired to cater to the tastes of older, wealthier donors. Yet at the same time, other critics complain that public television stations in some markets air too many lowbrow, mass-appeal shows, supposedly the result of attempts by programmers to broaden the subscriber support base.

Structural funding problems affect public television producers at the national level in a different way. Since most federal dollars now go to local stations, producers obtain most of their financing from corporate underwriters. These corporate underwriters are not directly involved in program production, and they do not have the same influence on public TV generally that advertisers have on commercial programming. Nevertheless, public television producers must internalize the values and priorities of those who pay the bills in order to obtain financial support. These priorities include appealing to affluent viewers and avoiding anything outside the narrow center of political and cultural views as approved by AT&T, Exxon, GE, GM, IBM, Martin-Marietta, and other major corporations.

As William Hoynes has shown, the range of guests and commentary on the widely praised *MacNeil-Lehrer NewsHour* is no broader than on ABC's *Nightline*, to which it ostensibly offers a noncommercial alternative. Both are dominated by business and political elites, short on representatives of consumer and labor groups.[55]

Still other critics point to the decision of many public stations to expand their acknowledgment of corporate sponsorship, and indeed, changes in federal regulations regarding underwriting announcements have resulted in what sound very much like commercials. Critics wonder if public television is losing its noncommercial identity and, with it, its relative immunity from direct commercial pressures.

Despite its many shortcomings, over the years public television has frequently demonstrated what can be accomplished when TV is at least partially freed from the limitations and economic censorship of the market. Important and innovative programs such as *Sesame Street* and *The Civil War* have achieved widespread acclaim and support. But just as important, and despite political pressures from many sources, PBS has also managed to air controversial documentaries that would never be seen on the commercial networks. Examples include *Tongues Untied* (about being black and gay), *Dark Circle* (about nuclear contamination), and *Days of Rage* (a look at the Intifada, attacked by critics as pro-Palestinian).[56] As James Day has put it, "Public television has a life, a purpose, and a place in the profligate mix of U.S. media. What is needed is the vision to see it and the will to make it happen."[57]

Whatever its successes and failures of the past, public television today is under new economic pressures as it is swept along with the massive changes taking place in the commercial television industry. At the same time public TV has been hit with reductions in government spending, it is also facing not only the cost of conversion to HDTV but also increasing competition both for its viewers and for its programs. The economics of niche programming means that upscale cable channels such as the Arts and Entertainment Network (A&E), Bravo, the Discovery Channel, and the History Channel can offer narrowly targeted highbrow programming and attract an audience once thought to be the exclusive province of public television. There is also increased competition for the acquisition of the programs themselves. At one time, British and Australian television producers found public television to be their sole U.S. market. Today, several cable channels regularly feature foreign-made programs, and the number will inevitably grow. With the increasing diversity of programming available on cable, and especially the growth of subscription-based programming that is relatively free of advertiser pressures, public television faces a challenging future.

Conclusion

For years, the television industry in the United States was dominated by the big three broadcast networks and their affiliate stations. Virtually all viewing was of network programs, and virtually all television advertising dollars followed. The technological innovations that began in the 1970s led to the rise of new cable channels, DBS, and the economic upheaval we have today. Although the number of viewers—and therefore the level of advertising revenues available—have remained about the same, the industry has continued to develop new channels and programs. The development of the economic system of viewer subscription as a supplement to the traditional advertiser support is a major new factor in television economics. As convergence of both technologies and corporations continues, we can anticipate still more changes in the way programs are bought, sold, and distributed. Yet the underlying structure of the television industry remains the same: corporations in the television business will continue to shape the medium for their own profit, institutionally heedless of its consequences for the world in which we live.

FURTHER READING

Bittner, John. *Law and Regulation of Electronic Media.* 2d ed. Englewood Cliffs, N.J.: Prentice Hall, 1994.

Bullert, B. J. *Public Television: Politics and the Battle over Documentary Film.* New Brunswick, N.J.: Rutgers University Press, 1997.

Day, James. *The Vanishing Vision: The Inside Story of Public Television.* Berkeley: University of California, 1995.

"Fear Stalks the Small Screen." *Economist,* April 25, 1992, 81.

Gruley, Bryan, and Kyle Pope. "Television: So What Exactly Is Digital Television?" *Wall Street Journal,* April 3, 1997, B1.

Hoynes, William. *Public Television for Sale: Media, the Market, and the Public Sphere.* Boulder, Colo.: Westview, 1994.

International Television and Video Almanac. 1997.

Jarvik, Laurence Ariel. *PBS: Behind the Screen.* Rocklin, Calif.: Prima, 1997.

Kaye, Elizabeth. "The New Phone Sex." *Esquire,* May, 1994, 78–83.

McChesney, R. W., Ellen Meiksins Wood, and John Bellamy Foster, eds. *Capitalism and the Information Age: The Political Economy of the Global Communication Revolution.* New York: Monthly Review Press, 1998.

Miller, Mark Crispin. "Free the Media," *Nation,* June 3, 1996, 9 ff.

Powe, Lucas A., Jr. *American Broadcasting and the First Amendment.* Berkeley: University of California, 1987.

Quality Time?: The Report of the Twentieth Century Fund Task Force on Public Television. New York: Twentieth Century Fund Press, 1993.

Smith, F. Leslie, Milan Meeske, and John W. Wright II. *Electronic Media and Government*. White Plains, N.Y.: Longman, 1995.

"Video on the Internet: Webbed." *Economist,* January 20, 1996, 82–83.

"Who Is Watching America's TV Networks?" *Economist,* March 31, 1990, 63–64.

Williams, Raymond. *Television: Technology and Cultural Form.* New York: Schocken, 1975.

CHAPTER THREE

Advertisers and Their Audience

Advertising is one of the most fascinating aspects of American television. Our favorite shows are interrupted every few minutes by commercials that present clever and compelling slices of contemporary life and are frequently more entertaining than the programs they interrupt. In many ways, they also tell the critical observer more about American values.

The vast system that is the American television industry has evolved largely because advertisers believe that the billions of dollars they spend on producing and airing commercials have an impact on consumer behavior. Yet the thrust of these messages is that only by purchasing more consumer goods—many of them of questionable value or even harmful to either our health or the environment or both—can we achieve success and happiness. Despite the industry's creativity at discovering new revenue streams, it is likely that advertising-supported television will continue to dominate the industry for the foreseeable future, so viewers need to gird themselves with a critical perspective that will allow them to elicit television's pleasures without becoming a victim of its appetite.

Advertising is also big business. According to one estimate, spending on ads in the United States totaled about $161 billion in 1995, only about $36.2 billion (22.5 percent) of which was spent on television.[1] However, some critics believe that television ads have a disproportionate impact because of their prominence and public visibility. As table 3.1 shows, Procter & Gamble (P&G), the nation's biggest advertiser, spent nearly $2.8 billion on U.S. advertising in 1995, with $1.3 billion of that on television.[2]

Table 3.1 also shows the four other largest U.S. television advertisers and some of their major brands. It is worth noting that three of the top five television advertisers (P&G, Philip Morris, and PepsiCo) sell relatively low-cost fast-moving consumer goods. Only two advertisers on the list (General Motors and Chrysler Corporation) sell large-ticket items. One reason that fast-moving consumer goods are so heavily advertised is that they tend be purchased very frequently. Advertisers believe that they must constantly reinforce the merits of their particular brand just to maintain their market share of sales, and introducing a new product or brand requires an even greater advertising effort. For example, Procter & Gamble claims that for its popular brands such as Tide, Crest, and Pantene, its ads will reach 90 percent of the brand's target audience six or seven times each month.

The Development of American Advertising

Today's heavy emphasis on advertising by manufacturers of consumer goods is the result of an evolution that began in the second half of the 1800s when the United

TABLE 3.1. TOP FIVE ADVERTISERS, 1995

Advertiser	TV Ad Spending ($ millions)	Total Ad Spending ($ millions)	Popular Brand Names
Procter & Gamble Co.	1,291.0	2,777.1	Folgers, Crest, Tide, Cover Girl, Oil of Olay, Old Spice, Downy, Pantene, Nyquil, Pampers, Vicks, Pert, Scope, Head & Shoulders, Pringles, Cheer
General Motors Corp.	914.4	2,046.9	Automobiles: Chevrolet, Buick, Oldsmobile, Pontiac, Cadillac, Saturn, GM, Geo
Philip Morris Cos.	884.2	2,576.9	Beer: Miller, Colders. Tobacco: Marlboro, Merit, Virginia Slims, Benson & Hedges. Foods: Kraft, Post cereals, Nabisco, Maxwell House, Oscar Mayer, General Foods, Jell-O, Birds Eye, Good Seasons, Crystal Light, Breyers, Boboli, Minute Rice, DiGiorno, Louis Rich, Shake 'n Bake, Tombstone Pizza, Bull's Eye barbeque sauce, Budget Gourmet, Lenders, Claussen
PepsiCo	690.9	1,197.0	Soft Drinks: Pepsi, Diet Pepsi, Slice, Mountain Dew. Snacks: Frito-Lay brands (Fritos, Cheetos, Tostitos, Lay's chips). Restaurants: Pizza Hut, Taco Bell, Kentucky Fried Chicken
Chrysler Corporation	618.7	1,222.4	Automobiles: Chrysler, Dodge, Eagle, Jeep, Plymouth

SOURCE: Compiled from figures in *Advertising Age,* September 30, 1996. TV figures represent total 1995 U.S. ad spending on cable, syndicated, spot, and network television.

States underwent a massive social and economic transformation from a predominantly agricultural society to an industrial one. Americans who lived in rural areas flocked to the towns to work in new factories. Cities exploded with population. The new urban dwellers found city life far different from that in the countryside. For one thing, factory jobs paid wages that could be spent in the shops and stores that were now right at their doorstep. For another, many of the self-reliant ways of the countryside were no longer practical in crowded urban streets. Things that people used to do without or made themselves could now be more conveniently purchased in stores.

Take, for example, a product as simple as soap. In rural areas, people made their own soap in a hot, smelly, and time-consuming process, using the animal fats and wood ashes easily obtainable on the farm. City dwellers found it more practical to purchase soap from the corner store. As the demand for such manufactured goods increased, more businesses were created to profit from it. So the move to the cities gave impetus to a whole new class of what economists call "fast-moving consumer goods," items of relatively low cost that consumers purchase time and again and retailers sell quickly and in large volume. Today, supermarkets and discount stores thrive on the regular shopping trips American families make to buy their customary supply of these items.[3]

Another effect of urbanization was the rapid growth of the print media. New technology meant faster printing presses, but more important, the concentration of people in the cities meant that newspapers and magazines could be distributed quickly and easily to large numbers of readers. The nation's first advertising agency, N. W. Ayer, was founded in 1863, and shortly after that, a man named J. Walter Thompson (his name lives on in the modern ad agency) offered to design ads for clients.[4] Although advertising using newspapers, posters, and flyers had been around for many years, in the second half of the 19th century, it began to take on a new look. The Procter & Gamble Company, a soap maker based in Cincinnati, began setting aside a portion of its annual budget for newspaper ads and posters promoting a new product with the name "Ivory Soap." P&G and other companies of the era discovered that in order to sell fast-moving consumer goods repeatedly to the same customers, the product had to be memorable and easy to identify. Thus were born brand names, distinctive packaging, and advertising slogans. P&G enjoyed phenomenal success with its new product (still one of America's best-selling soap brands) and helped usher in a new age of advertising and marketing.

British author H. G. Wells, a contemporary observer of these developments, said that advertising was the art of teaching people to want things.[5] In other words, what P&G and other producers of fast-moving consumer goods had discovered was that these new urban Americans had to be taught to consume. It was not enough simply to tell people that a product was available; they had to be convinced that they needed it and would benefit from it. This realization ushered in a whole new approach to advertising—one that has left a profound mark on America and turned us into a society of consumers and a culture based on consumption of goods, many of which might never be purchased in a different sort of world.

The economic process of buying and selling goods was well established before the advent of advertising, so it is clear that advertising by itself does not cause people to buy things. We would all need food, shelter, and clothing whether advertising existed or not. However, as Michael Schudson points out, what a culture considers to be a basic need has more to do with the complexities of social relationships than it does with meeting one's biological requirements.[6] He explains, for example, how buying gifts for others is an essential part of establishing and maintaining social relationships.

The social aspects of buying things are so important to most people in modern America that many have described ours as a "consumer culture." Raymond Williams has explained infatuation with consumption by comparing the appeal of consumer items to the allure of magic charms in other cultures. While in some societies people chant incantations, wear charms, or burn incense to bring them happiness or success, many Americans buy products. For us, the magic is in what we believe the clothing, shampoo, beer, or cake mix will do for us above and beyond just satisfying our basic physical needs.[7]

For example, beer ads, which are almost always aimed at men, are frequently designed to encourage a feeling of fun-filled fantasy and often exploit young women in tight-fitting clothes to add the suggestion of easy sex. Through a constant repetition of these commercials (usually during televised sports events), drinking a particular brand of beer becomes magically connected with the pleasures men enjoy in having escapist fantasies—after all, alcohol helps to ease inhibitions and encourages such pleasures. The fantasies in the beer ads simply continue the fantasies of the male sports fans who vicariously participate in the games they watch.

A similar strategy is used in ads aimed at women, but the differences show institutional sexism at work. Commercials for food and over-the-counter medicines frequently associate the use of the sponsor's brand with motherly love and nurturing. Cake mixes and baking products are promoted as ways women can demonstrate both their technical competence as cooks and caregivers and their love for their families. Pillsbury states this explicitly in its decades-old slogan "Nothin' says luvin' like somethin' from the oven." Cold remedy ads frequently feature a wife/mother ministering to her husband and children by dispensing both tender loving care and the sponsor's product.[8] The use of the brand is subtly (and magically) linked with being a good mother and loving spouse.

Of course, it is one thing to discuss advertising's effects in the abstract and quite another to consider how it affects us personally. For example, just how effective is advertising in influencing your decision to buy a particular product? That, of course, depends on many complex factors outside the ad itself. Brand loyalty, for example, can be a powerful force. From Procter & Gamble's perspective, if your mother always used Tide detergent, you may never try any other brand, despite being inundated with hundreds of commercials for rival brands. But that doesn't mean well-established brands need not advertise. To the contrary, they spend millions of dollars on advertising each year just to make sure their customers remain loyal. On the other hand, you might be more receptive to an ad for a new product that promises some new benefit (real or imagined). A variation of this is the established brand that constantly advertises itself as "new" and "improved" in the theory that consumers are always willing to try something that promises new magic.

Many advertisers freely admit uncertainty about the effectiveness of their ads. A frequently quoted industry saying is, "I know I waste half my advertising money; the only problem is I don't know which half."[9] Yet under the right conditions, advertising, and especially television advertising, clearly sells products to some people who might have not otherwise bought them. If you doubt this, recall the example in chapter 2 of author Julia Child, who sold 10,000 copies of her new cookbook in 35 minutes on QVC. Home shopping channels are, after all, continuous advertisements.

The Structure of the Advertising Industry

Television advertising is only a small part of the much larger advertising and marketing industry that serves the producers of consumer products and services. Marketing researchers study consumer attitudes and buying patterns, designers work to create eye-catching packaging, and huge sales forces convince retailers to devote shelf space to their products. The stakes are high—millions of dollars in profits may be won or lost if a product gains or loses just a few percentage points in its market share or a few inches on a supermarket chain's shelf.

Advertising agencies help plan and coordinate advertising and marketing campaigns. This usually includes the overall development of a marketing and advertising strategy of which television advertising may be only one small part. An agency typically provides all sorts of services: planning an overall advertising strategy, writing and producing ads for radio, television, print, or direct mail. Once the ads are approved and ready, the agency oversees their placement in appropriate media (including television) and the day-to-day operation of the campaign.

Agencies are usually not paid directly for their services but receive "agency discounts" (effectively, a commission) from the advertising media in which they place the sponsor's ads. The larger the budget for advertising, the more the agency will make from the account. Therefore, landing or losing a single large account can make or break a small agency. Clients also expect their agencies to avoid conflict of interest by refusing the business of direct competitors. Just a few large agencies handle most of the national advertising in the United States.

The industry divides television advertising into five major types: network, spot, syndicated, cable, and local. Table 3.2 shows how the $36.2 billion spent on television advertising in 1995 was distributed among these five categories. Network ads are those that are placed on one of the major broadcast networks. Generally, network ads will be seen all over the country at the same time, so they have the advantage of reaching large numbers of viewers simultaneously. The cost of a 30-second network ad varies considerably with the size and type of audience the show is expected to deliver and other factors, but at the start of the prime-time fall 1997 season, it ranged from a low of about $55,000 for a spot on ABC's *Nothing Sacred* (a new series) to $575,000 on *Seinfeld* (a returning, top-rated show). A single, top-rated show such as *Seinfeld* can generate as much as $200 million in annual ad revenues.[10] On the average, prices for network prime-time ads have been steadily declining since the early 1980s as the size of the big three viewing audience has dwindled.[11]

Since advertisers spend so much money to air their commercials, they want to be certain the audience will pay attention to them. For this reason, great time and care are generally taken in the process of producing commercials at the national level. The average national commercial costs almost a quarter of a million dollars to produce.[12] The making of television commercials is estimated to be a $4.5 billion a year business, with about 60 percent of this done in and around Hollywood. Although there are many small companies that specialize in producing commercials, larger companies, such as Sony's Pavlov Productions, are also involved.[13]

Sometimes, however, the advertiser may want tighter control over ad placement, in which case spot advertising may be more appropriate. Spot advertising is the purchase of time by a national advertiser directly from individual stations, groups of stations, or local cable systems. Although more complicated than a network purchase, a spot purchase allows the advertiser to be geographically selective. Some advertisers, for example, may only sell a particular product or brand in certain areas of the country. By purchasing spot ads in selected markets, these advertisers can run commercials tailored to the locale. Other advertisers may run both network and spot ads. They use the network ads to reach large numbers of viewers and then supplement these with ads in areas of the country where they want to have more impact—perhaps where sales of a particular product are greatest. Usually, the only difference between a network and a spot ad is the way it is purchased. In fact, it is not unusual for the same commercial to air on a station as both a network and a spot ad.

TABLE 3.2. FIVE CATEGORIES OF TELEVISION ADVERTISING EXPENDITURE

Category	Advertising Expenditure ($ millions)	(%)
Network TV	11,600	32.0
Spot TV	9,119	25.1
Syndicated	2,016	5.6
Cable	2,670	7.4
Local	10,841	29.9
Total	36,246	100.0

SOURCE: *International Television and Video Almanac, 1997*, 18A.
NOTE: Figures are for 1995 in millions of dollars. Local figure includes both broadcast and cable outlets.

With syndicated advertising, commercials are purchased in non–network syndicated shows that are then distributed as a package to stations throughout the country. Advertisers frequently find that syndicated ads can reach the same number of viewers as network ads but at a lower cost.

The purchase of commercial time directly from national cable networks is the newest and fastest-growing area of television advertising. Similar to network advertising, national cable advertising has the added advantage of providing the sponsor with a much more demographically narrow audience. For example, an advertiser whose target audience is men can purchase ads on sports channels. More tightly targeted ad purchases can save the advertiser money by reducing the number of "waste" viewers who may see the ad but are unlikely to buy the product.

Finally, the term local advertising refers to ads purchased by local merchants on local broadcast stations or cable systems. Some national companies share the cost of local advertising with local dealers of their products in a strategy known as cooperative advertising (or, simply, "co-op").

Commercials are placed on American television in a structure that has been called a magazine format. That is, commercials from many different advertisers are scattered throughout television programs much like ads in a magazine are scattered among the pages of the articles. Today, a single advertiser will rarely be the sole sponsor of a program, but in the early days of television, sponsors almost always owned and produced the entire show. Their products' names were heard not only in the show's commercials but were also featured prominently in the design of the set, the titles and credits, and even the program's name. But as television advertising costs rose, so did the sponsor's risk. If a single-sponsor show flopped, the sole advertiser would bear the cost. With today's magazine format, the networks control the program and sell spots in it to many different advertisers. Of course, care must be taken to avoid placing competitors' ads too close together.

There are, of course, alternative ways of scheduling commercials. In some European countries, government regulations require all the television commercials for an evening to be shown one after the other before the prime-time shows begin. Most advertisers dislike this because they believe that ads are more effective when they are placed within programs.

The precise number of ad minutes that a television station or network will sell in any given hour varies greatly. With the exception of rules regarding children's commercials (see below), there are no specific governmental limits to the number of ads a broadcast or cable channel can carry. Indeed, in recent years we've seen the rise of the "program-length commercial" and, of course, home shopping channels.

Despite these exceptions, most advertisers know that few viewers will stay tuned for very long if they see nothing but ads. Scheduling too many ads too close together may cause viewers to change to competing channels, a danger made all the more likely with the proliferation of remote controls. On the other hand, having fewer ads reduces revenues. Traditionally, programmers have tried to balance commercial minutes by scheduling fewer commercials during an hour of prime time, when commercial prices and numbers of viewers are at their peak, and more ads during an hour of daytime or late-night shows.

Programmers are also careful how they place commercials within a program. The goal is to attract the audience and then hold on to them. Some television stations will show as much as 20 minutes of a movie before the first commercial break. As the movie progresses, commercials become more frequent on the assumption that the audience is intrigued by the story and won't change channels. For the same reason, on network prime-time shows, a short "hook," or attention-getting segment, is shown at the very beginning of the program to hold the audience through the first series of commercials. This means that television programs must be carefully scripted to meet the demands of commercial placement. A little-recognized part of the art of television is the creation of program formats and scripts that make commercial breaks seem like a natural part of the flow of television. In a strategy reminiscent of old movie serials, scriptwriters build action at a pace that peaks just in time for the commercial break, often leaving the characters in a cliff-hanging situation to ensure that viewers will stay tuned.

About two-thirds of all network television commercials are 30 seconds long and are grouped together in pods.[14] Each pod has a predetermined number of commercial slots, with the number of slots dependent on the time of day and other factors. Any of three other types of nonprogram material may also be found in a pod. One type is the promo, or promotional announcement. This is simply a brief announcement promoting an upcoming show. Although promos don't earn the network or station any revenues directly, they play a big part in attracting viewers to future programs and so have an important function in building and maintaining the audience and thereby enhance overall revenues. One recent strategy is to use a split screen to combine the credits for a closing show with a promo for an upcoming one. The aim, of course, is to hook viewers on the next show before the last one is over. A second type of nonprogram material is the ID, or identification of the station or network. Some IDs are required for broadcasting stations by government regulation, but they also play an important part in promotion, since they reinforce the name of the station or network for the viewers.

A third type of nonprogram material is the PSA, or public service announcement. This is an unpaid spot resembling a commercial but promoting a charitable cause. Stations and networks run PSAs for free or at low cost and so usually schedule them only when they cannot otherwise sell the time to advertisers. PSAs and promos also serve as convenient placeholders for a program's unsold commercial slots.

Commercial Placement in a Prime-Time Network Show

For broadcast and cable networks, the commercial slots during network feeds are divided between the network and the local outlet according to a prearranged contract. This means that in any given hour, a certain number of the commercials will be slots sold and inserted by the network (which gets all the revenue from those slots), and the remainder will be slots sold by the local station or cable company (which gets to keep local revenue). Some pods during an hour may contain network commercials exclusively, and others may contain both network and local ads. In most cases, the local commercials on broadcast networks are shown only in pods occurring at the top and bottom of the hour—times when the stations will also run IDs.

Although the number of commercial minutes does vary from time period to time period and channel to channel, let's take a look at one fairly typical hour of prime-time programming and see how the commercials were positioned. Table 3.3 indicates the placement of TV commercials we found in one hour of prime time on NBC. On this particular evening in 1997, an episode of *Frasier* was followed by an episode of *Caroline in the City*. By starting a stopwatch at the beginning of the first show, we were able to determine the length and location of each commercial. The times in the left column refer to the number of minutes and seconds after the hour's start. The hour contained a total of six pods—three in each show. During the hour, 28 commercials were shown for a total of 12 minutes of ad time, or 20 percent of the total hour. Twenty-three of these commercials were network ads, and five appeared to be spot ads aired by the local station (a strategically placed network promo helps cue local stations to insert their locally run commercials seamlessly).[15] Eleven promos were also shown, totaling 3 minutes and 25 seconds.

The episodes themselves consisted of about 22 minutes and 15 seconds of actual program material, including opening titles and closing credits, for a total of 44 minutes and 30 seconds for the hour, or about 74 percent of the total viewing time. The episodes were each divided into four segments separated by the commercial pods. The first segment consisted of the "hook" and opening credits and ran only 1 minute and 30 seconds for *Frasier* and 45 seconds for *Caroline*. Program segments two and three were the main story lines of the episode, with each segment running from eight minutes to 12 minutes and 20 seconds. Segment four in each show was the closing credits. Note that the closing credits of *Frasier* were separated from the opening hook of *Caroline* by only a 10-second promo—a strategy employed to minimize audience loss between shows.

Although there is variation among networks and shows, this structure is fairly typical for prime-time broadcast network programming. As we mentioned earlier, television programming that takes place out of prime time or on non-network stations will likely have an even higher percentage of commercials and other non-program material each hour.

TABLE 3.3. AD PLACEMENT IN PRIME TIME: A CASE STUDY OF *FRASIER* AND *CAROLINE IN THE CITY*

0:00:00	*Frasier* hook & opening credits [running time 1:30]
1:30:00	Commercial pod 1: Blockbuster Video [:30], Advil [:15], Fuji Film [:15], Fidelity Investments [:30], network promo/ID [:30]
3:30:00	*Frasier* Act 1 [running time 8:00]
11:30:00	Commercial pod 2: Diet Coke [:30], Easy Off [:15], Snackwells [:15], McDonald's [:15], promo/ID [:20]
	[Switch to local station]
	Cadillac [:30] (spot), Power Ade [:30] (spot), Mazda [:30] (spot), local promo [:05]
14:40:00	*Frasier* Act 2 [running time 12:20]
27:00:00	Commerical pod 3: J. C. Penney [:30], Olive Garden [:15], Downy Fabric Softener [:30], Centrum Vitamins [:15], Mazda [:30], promo [:20]
29:20:00	*Frasier* closing credits [:30]
29:50:00	Promo [:10]
30:00:00	*Caroline in the City* hook & opening credits [:45]
30:45:00	Commercial pod 1: Lite Beer [:30], "Nothing to Lose" [:15], Burger King [:30], Saturn [:30], promo [:20]
32:50:00	*Caroline* Act 1 [running time 10:00]
43:15:00	Commerical pod 2: Boston Market [:30], Blockbuster Video [:30], Mazda [:30], promo [:30]
	[Switch to local station]
	KIA [:30] (spot), local promo [:30], Mitsubishi [:30] (spot), local promo [:10]
46:30:00	*Caroline* Act 2 [running time 11:00]
57:30:00	Commercial pod 3: Neutragena [:30], Pantene [:30], Lexus [:30], promo [:20]
59:20:00	*Caroline* closing credits [:30]
59:50:00	Promo [:10]

Audience—The Commodity Advertisers Buy

Television advertisers place their commercials on television solely to reach (and, they hope, influence) people in the audience. As we discussed in chapter 2, when advertisers say they are buying "airtime," what they are really buying is the audience's time. Only if advertisers believe that viewers are watching their commercials are those commercials of any value. Once again, we can see how the viewers—you and I—are the commodity that the television industry sells to the advertisers.

When national advertisers buy commercial time, they (or, usually, their advertising agency) do so with much planning and care. By placing their commercials

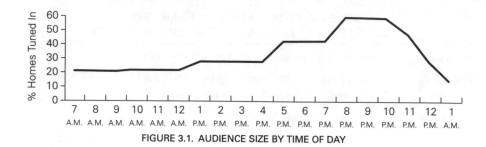

FIGURE 3.1. AUDIENCE SIZE BY TIME OF DAY

in the right programs, they can maximize their effectiveness—that is, they can reach the maximum number of potential buyers for the money they spend. Commercial placement boils down to two major considerations: the size of the audience the commercial will reach and, just as important, the composition of that audience.

How many people are watching a given program at a given time depends, of course, on how appealing the program is to the viewers, but other factors also come into play. For example, the time of day, day of the week, and even season of the year will affect not only how many viewers are available to watch TV but also their sex and age.

Figure 3.1 shows how the percentage of television viewers changes over a typical weekday.[16] The day begins with about 20 percent of U.S. television homes watching television. That level remains fairly constant during the morning and increases slightly during the early afternoon. A big increase takes place at about 4 P.M. as viewers begin returning home from work and school. By the beginning of prime time at 8 P.M., more than half of American households are watching TV. During "prime time," not only is the audience the largest of the day, but it is also the most diverse in terms of age and sex.

Another way that people in television discuss audience size is in terms of markets. Nielsen Media Research has divided the entire United States into 211 separate geographic regions.[17] Generally speaking, each region is centered on a particular metropolitan area reached by the same group of television stations. The population within each market is estimated and ranked according to size. Market size is illustrated in table 3.4.

The concept of market gives advertisers at least a rough idea of the potential audience for a particular television program or commercial in a given geographic area. For example, if national advertisers buy commercial time in the Boston market, they can predict that their ads have the potential of reaching 2.1 million different homes, or about 2.2 percent of the country (based on an estimated 96.9 million television households in the United States).

While market size is an important way for the industry to estimate the size of the audience for a particular ad, it also helps determine how much advertisers are charged for commercial time and how much television stations must pay when they buy programs. Market size is also used to simplify advertising purchases. For example, an advertiser might decide to buy spot ads in only the top 10 markets. As table 3.4 shows, about 29.9 percent of all television households are located in the top 10 markets. This means that a commercial aired only in those 10 markets could potentially reach about 29.9 percent of the U.S. population with televisions.

TABLE 3.4. TELEVISION MARKET RANKS

Rank	Designated Market Area (DMA)	TVHH* (millions)	% of U.S.
1	New York	6.7	6.9
2	Los Angeles	4.9	5.1
3	Chicago	3.1	3.2
4	Philadelphia	2.7	2.7
5	San Francisco	2.3	2.4
6	Boston	2.1	2.2
7	Washington, D.C.	1.9	2.0
8	Dallas–Ft. Worth	1.8	1.9
9	Detroit	1.7	1.8
10	Atlanta	1.6	1.7
	Total markets 1–10	29.0	29.9

SOURCE: Adapted from table in Nielsen estimates, January 1997.
*Television households.

Advertisers who wish primarily to target urban audiences find purchasing by market convenient. By buying time in only the top 25 markets, they can potentially reach 49 percent of the United States. If they expand their purchase to the top 50 markets, the percentage rises to 67. Since there are costs involved in contracting with and providing commercials to each station, some advertisers find it uneconomical to advertise in smaller markets. Then, too, small-market audiences tend to spend less money. The result is that smaller-market stations are on a much more precarious financial footing than their larger-market counterparts and must rely more heavily on income from local advertising and, consequently, that local advertisers' needs play a bigger part in determining what programs get seen in smaller markets.

Today, the industry is rethinking the concept of market as a way to predict potential audience size. Market boundaries, once determined by the range of a city's television stations, are now blurred because cable systems and DBS may greatly expand a station's coverage area. The Federal Communications Commission (FCC) has even established special rules restricting which channels a cable or DBS system may carry and others requiring carriage of all local stations. These rules are designed to protect the existing economic system of buying and selling programs that is based on the market concept, but as technology changes and deregulation progresses, we can expect to see such rules challenged. Despite the fact that cable has greatly extended the range of many stations and provided new competition for viewers, the basic principle remains; the more potential viewers in an area, the higher the price for commercials and the greater the potential revenues a station can earn.

For most advertisers, the size of the audience is not the only consideration. They are also interested in reaching their target audience. The target audience usually consists of those viewers who the advertiser feels are most likely to buy the product and is generally determined and monitored through extensive market research.

The most common way to describe a target audience is in terms of easily measurable demographic factors, such as sex and age, and, to a lesser extent, race. For example, marketing research will probably tell a manufacturer of laundry detergent that its product is bought most often by women who are between the ages of 18 and 49. This group might well become the target audience for the product, and television commercials would be designed and produced to appeal to that group. Furthermore, to maximize its advertising dollar, the company would place its commercials in programs that research has shown women 18–49 are most likely to be watching.

As we have seen, advertising-supported services must attract audiences that include substantial numbers of the type of consumer the advertiser wishes to reach. In the United States, this often means the young (18- to 49-year-olds) rather than the old, and the white majority rather than nonwhite minority. When the Fox network was created, it was faced with competing against the well-established big three networks and so adopted a strategy of programming to appeal to a younger demographic, and especially to young men. In this, it has been highly successful both in attracting a youth audience and in attracting important advertisers who saw Fox as an efficient way to reach this market. The newer networks, WB and UPN, have also aimed at a younger market, while at least one of the big three, CBS, has consciously programmed for an older market, hoping to attract advertiser interest in the aging baby boomers. Table 3.5 shows how the median age of viewers differs for each of the six broadcast networks.

Demographic targeting is often focused on the sex of the viewers as well. Because of inequitable domestic divisions of labor, women are still the major purchasers of fast-moving consumer goods. For that reason, audiences that have a large proportion of women are much in demand by advertisers that sell fast-moving consumer goods. This is made somewhat easier for them by the fact that men and women watch TV differently. First, women spend somewhat more time watching television than do men—an average of 4½ hours per day for women and about 30 minutes less for men.[18] Second, the ratio of men and women in the television audience varies greatly by the time of day and week. While nearly two-thirds of the adult audience watching TV on a typical weekday afternoon are women, that ratio falls to about 50–50 on weekend afternoons.

Because time of day and day of week are so crucial to proper ad placement, the industry divides time into standardized segments called "day parts." A day part is a time period during which the audience available to watch TV is expected to remain fairly constant in size and composition. A typical audience ratings report from the A. C. Nielsen Company (an industry leader) may divide data into more than 30 different day parts (many of them overlap) for the use of clients with different needs.[19] However, a few of these day parts are most commonly used and have been given names. The term "prime time" as it is used in the industry actually refers to the day part in the evening when television viewing is at its peak.[20] Advertisers associate each day part with a particular demographic mix of viewers, and by understanding these characteristics they can make good guesses about who will be in the audience at a particular time.

TABLE 3.5. MEDIAN AUDIENCE AGE OF
TV NETWORK VIEWERS

Network	Median Age of Viewer
WB	24.8
Fox	32.3
UPN	34.3
ABC	40.7
NBC	41.1
CBS	51.5

SOURCE: *Advertising Age*, May 12, 1997, S16.
NOTE: As of the 4th quarter, 1996, and 1st quarter, 1997.

Women as a Target Audience

Nowhere are the implications of demographic targeting in television advertising better demonstrated than in the industry's seemingly insatiable drive to reach women aged 18 to 49. In a society in which control is still largely in the hands of middle-aged white men, one important fact seems highly incongruous: women wield 75 percent of the purchasing power in America.

At one time, reaching large numbers of women was relatively easy for television advertisers. Thirty years ago, a few commercials placed in daytime game shows and soap operas would reach most women in the country, since the majority of them worked at home tending house and raising children. But in the past three decades, the number of women working away from home has doubled, and now fully 60 percent of them have outside jobs. The effects on television advertising and programming have been significant.

For one thing, daytime television viewing by women dropped after more of them exchanged the home workplace for one outside. For example, the soap opera *General Hospital* lost about half its audience between 1986 and 1996.[21] Advertisers who once relied heavily on daytime commercials had to find new ways of reaching what the television ratings companies call "working women," that is, women who work outside the home.[22]

The result has been increased advertiser demand for commercial time when working women are more likely to be in the audience—this means during early morning and evening hours. Two of the three broadcast network morning shows (ABC's *Good Morning America* and CBS's *This Morning*) were created largely in response to demand from advertisers trying to reach women before they leave for work. (NBC's *Today* has been on the air much longer, but it, too, underwent changes designed to attract more women viewers.)

The major impact of this increased demand to reach women, however, has been during prime-time evening programming. Few prime-time shows can survive unless they attract substantial numbers of women in the 18–49 demographic, since that is the target audience for many advertisers. If the shows attract men and older women too, so much the better, but most programs are designed to appeal to women 18–49. Shows with strong women characters such as *Designing Women, Murphy Brown,* and *Roseanne,* and, more recently, *Cybil, Caroline in the City,* and *Ellen,* were created explicitly to appeal to working women, often by giving voice (albeit a bland one) to women's concerns and objections to a male-dominated society. Made-for-TV movies frequently follow the formulas industry cynics have dubbed "disease of the week" (female hero or her loved one must deal with serious, often fatal illness) and "woman in peril" (female hero or her loved one is threatened or attacked and must recover or seek revenge). The industry specifically constructs both types in ways it thinks will appeal to female viewers. Of course, an even more successful strategy for producers (but difficult to achieve) is to create programs that will attract large numbers of both women and men viewers. One show that found a formula to accomplish this is *Home Improvement.*[23]

Although woman-oriented programming may seek to attract female viewers by portraying their concerns, few offer women feminist analysis of their problems. After all, the purpose of these shows is to sell women products that are manufactured and sold by companies still (for the most part) run by white males. It would not be in their interests for women to, say, refuse to purchase cosmetics, household cleaners, or convenience foods.

Even the once all-male bastion of television sports is being transformed to attract more women viewers. CBS's coverage of the 1994 Winter Olympics was, as one observer put it, "converted by CBS . . . into a form of light entertainment."[24] By emphasizing skating coverage (a favorite among women), interviews, and personality features, CBS attracted a 35 percent larger audience than the previous Winter Olympics. Although the networks generally expect to lose money but gain promotional value from the Olympics, CBS's strategy made the coverage profitable and cut deeply into the prime-time audiences of the other networks.[25] The coup shook up many traditional sports programmers and inaugurated a rush to bring more skating and gymnastics coverage to prime time.

Perhaps a better way to understand the implications of demographic targeting is to look at the ads themselves. For example, contrast the ads seen on daytime television, aimed at women at home, with those on weekend sports telecasts. Ads for disposable diapers are virtually never seen during a football game any more than commercials for beer are seen during soap operas. But a closer look at the commercials also reveals that advertisers manipulate the portrayals in their ads, regardless of product, exploiting whichever gender images or stereotypes they think will be most likely to please the audience targeted.

The commercials advertisers create are carefully crafted bundles of images, frequently designed to associate the product with feelings of pleasure stemming from deep-seated fantasies and anxieties. Indeed, many advertisers spend a good deal of money researching women's private thoughts. General Foods, for example, has employed psychologists to conduct focus groups of potential consumers, asking them questions such as, "If you were having a dream in which General Foods International Coffee played a part, what would it be?" Their answers were then used to help design television ads.[26] Advertisers seem quite willing to manipulate these fantasies and exploit our anxieties, especially those concerning our gender identities, to sell products. What's more, they seem to have no compunction about capitalizing on dehumanizing gender stereotypes to seek these ends.[27]

Three decades ago, Betty Friedan raised serious questions about the role of American women. Her book *The Feminine Mystique* became a best-seller and helped popularize the modern women's movement. Thirty years later, many of her observations remain convincing. She argued, for instance, that in America, "the really important role that women serve as housewives is to *buy more things for the house*"—and she held American businessmen largely responsible.

> It is their millions [of dollars] which blanket the land with persuasive images, flattering the American housewife, diverting her guilt and disguising her growing emptiness. They have done this so successfully, employing the techniques and concepts of modern social science, and transposing them into those deceptively simple, clever, outrageous ads and commercials, that an observer of the American scene today accepts as fact that the great majority of American women have no ambition other than to be housewives. If they are not responsible for sending women home, they are surely responsible for keeping them there.[28]

Just as it did in the 1960s, today's American business still has a vested interest in maintaining traditional gender stereotypes, for the production and sales of many American goods and services are still dependent on the exploitation of fears and anxieties connected to traditional gender identities. However, with a far larger percentage of American women working outside the home today, advertisers have had to co-opt a new working-women stereotype. Naomi Wolf in *The Beauty Myth* argues that as the women's movement took hold and women began entering the workplace in greater numbers, advertisers, especially those in the cosmetics and fashion industries, replaced the old images of women with a new mythology that women could only be accepted in this world of the "new woman" if they met rigid new standards of slimness, beauty, and fashion.

> How to make sure that busy, stimulated working women would keep consuming at the levels they had done when they had all day to do so and little else of interest to occupy them? A new ideology was necessary that would compel the same insecure consumerism; that ideology must be, unlike that of the Feminine Mystique, a briefcase-sized neurosis that the working woman could take with her to the office. To paraphrase Friedan, why is it never said that the really crucial function that women serve as aspiring beauties is *to buy more things for the body?* . . . *The beauty myth, in its modern form, arose to take the place of the Feminine Mystique, to save magazines and advertisers from the economic fallout of the women's revolution* [emphasis in the original].[29]

Although advertisers have adapted to women's changing roles in their own particular ways, many still retain archaic sexist notions. The belief that women are innately more irrational than men and therefore particularly susceptible to commercial appeals seems to be commonly held in the industry as evidenced by the many condescending TV ads aimed at women. That is not to say, however, that men are not also targeted for advertiser exploitation. Even though men buy fewer consumer goods than women, they remain an important target audience in a few specific product areas such as beer, financial services, and automotive products.

Advertising and Children

Children seem to be especially susceptible to the effects of television advertising. This rightly worries many of their parents. Cereals, snack foods, candy, soft drinks, and especially toys target the kid-vid audience. Saturday mornings have traditionally been considered "prime time" to reach children, but advertisers also concentrate on afternoon cartoon shows. Niche programming on cable networks such as Nickelodeon and The Cartoon Channel has also proven quite successful. As one industry analyst put it, "Many kids don't watch television anymore; they watch Nick."[30] In fact, by the 1997–1998 season, Nickelodeon was the overall children's programming ratings leader among all networks—broadcast and cable—and Nick's Saturday morning cartoon show *Rugrats* was the most-watched children's show, with a 5.4 rating. That is, an estimated 5.4 percent of all U.S. children (ages 2–11) tuned in to *Rugrats* on an average Saturday.[31] As you might surmise, television advertising aimed at children is a booming segment of the industry. In 1997, the industry sold $928 million in advertising during children's programming, up nearly 10 percent from the year before.[32]

Toy advertising has attracted special criticism in recent years, owing to the changing nature of the toy industry and its increased connections with the television and film industry. Toys are big business in the United States, with wholesale toy sales totaling $13.43 billion in 1995. Television toy advertising is also big—and growing. Much of the growth reflects the industry's need to reach consumers who increasingly buy toys at large mass-market merchandisers like K-Mart and Wal-Mart, where customers are expected to wait on themselves. When we wait on ourselves, merchandisers must rely on a sales pitch that has been previously internalized by advertising.[33]

Another factor, however, has been the growth of so-called licensed products—toys and other items associated with a movie or television character or even a sports star or team. Nearly half of U.S. toy sales are now of licensed products, and some of the big media conglomerates, most notably Disney and Time Warner, have entire divisions dedicated to the development, merchandising, and sales of licensed products based on movie tie-ins and cartoon characters.[34]

During the 1980s, toy advertisers and television producers developed several cartoon series either based on toys that were already popular or in conjunction with new toys that were being released. Some people considered this "toy-based programming" to be nothing less than program-length commercials aimed at children. The parents' group Action for Children's Television (ACT) and others convinced Congress of the need for reform, and in 1990 the Children's Television Act was passed, which required significant changes in the industry. The law limits commercials in children's programs to 12 minutes per hour during weekdays and 10½ minutes on weekends. In addition, new FCC regulations have eliminated some of the worst cases of toy-show tie-ins and require broadcasters to provide an average of at least three hours per week of programming specifically designed to educate and inform children. It is important to note that these restrictions apply only to those who hold braodcast licenses and not to cable networks. Although it is too early to know the ultimate effects of these changes, some industry observers are speculating that unless broadcasters can produce educational programs that are also entertaining, kiddy viewers may continue their migration from broadcast channels to cable.[35]

Programs: Attracting the Audience

Table 3.6 lists some of the major suppliers of the television programs we see and lists some of the shows with which they have been involved. As we saw in chapter 2, the major Hollywood studios have all become part of media conglomerates, so you'll note that with minor exceptions, the major suppliers of TV programs, home videos, movies, and CDs are the same major corporate players listed in table 2.3.

As we discussed in chapter 2, shows that are financially successful must be able to appeal to members of the target audience. At the same time, they must also be careful not to offend them. While some in the audience may applaud programs that deal with touchy issues such as extramarital sex, abortion, and homosexuality, other viewers may be offended. Producers and networks sometime walk a tightrope between the daring and the offensive, and which is which may depend on the intended audience. Keeping the audience happy also means that series writers must be careful not to have characters behave in ways that confuse or upset loyal fans. Some soap operas closely monitor viewer reaction and respond in their scripts by twisting plots in ways they think viewers want.

Buying and Selling Television Programs

A trade publication recently announced that during the 1998–1999 television season, NBC would pay $13 million for each weekly episode of the hit drama *ER*.[36] But exactly what is NBC buying? Although in industry jargon television programs are said to be "bought" by networks, in reality, this term is somewhat misleading. In actuality, it is not the television programs that are being bought and sold but rather the limited right to use the programs in particular ways for a specified time. Television programs fall into the legal category known as intellectual property and as such are protected under U.S. copyright law and international copyright agreements. Rather than selling all the rights to their work at once, owners of intellectual properties generally find it much more profitable to sell limited rights to use the work to many different people.

In the television industry, an elaborate system of buying and selling program rights has evolved. Since many programs can attract a sizable audience even after repeated showings, owners can realize profits from several different buyers over a period of many years. One need only tune in to any of a number of cable networks to see how long some TV shows can continue to generate profits. Several channels regularly run old TV shows, some of them dating from the early 1950s. Nickelodeon's "TV Land" channel consists of nothing but old reruns. A few programs, such as *Star Trek* and *I Love Lucy,* have attracted repeat audiences for many years both in the United States and abroad and have generated many times their original production costs for their owners.

One point here is important to understand. In the complex business world of the entertainment industry, the holder of the copyright is not necessarily the same person (or even the same corporation) who actually created the product. Only the most successful artists can demand profit participation as a condition of working on the show. Although standard industry contracts negotiated by unions and guilds offer some protection, the majority of people who work on television programs are fortunate if they work full-time and earn a living wage, and they do

TABLE 3.6. MAJOR U.S. TV PROGRAM SUPPLIERS

Parent Company: Supplier Names	Sample of Current and Past Programs Produced*
Time Warner: Warner Brothers TV, Castle Rock TV, HBO	*Suddenly Susan, Veronica's Closet, Built to Last, Jamie Foxx, Meego, The Drew Carey Show, Common Law, Living Single, Kirk, Life with Roger, Love Connection, Lois and Clark, Dark Justice, Jenny Jones, The Jane Whitney Show, Murphy Brown, Nick Freno, The Parent 'Hood, Step by Step, Family Matters, Friends, Full House, On Our Own, ER, Tiny Toons*
Disney: ABC Productions, ABC News, Walt Disney Studios, Touchstone TV	*Boy Meets World, Dangerous Minds, Life's Work, Home Improvement, Ellen, Hiller and Diller, Smart Guy, Soul Man, Teen Angel, Blossom, Empty Nest, You Wish, Home Boys in Outer Space, Brotherly Love, Unhappily Ever After, Live with Regis and Kathie Lee, Siskel and Ebert.* Partner with PBS in *Bill Nye the Science Guy.* ABC News productions including *Turning Point* and *20/20.* Foreign TV including *The Disney Club,* produced in 33 national versions, reaching 75 million viewers. Syndicated Disney afternoon block of programs, including *Shnookums* and *Meat Funny Cartoon Show,* and a Disney morning with *Ducktales.* TV versions of *The Little Mermaid* and *Aladdin*
Viacom: Paramount Network TV, Viacom Productions, Spelling TV	*Clueless, Sabrina, The Teenage Witch, George & Leo, Fired Up, Hitz, JAG, Jenny, Almost Perfect, Hard Copy, Melrose Place, Beverly Hills 90210, 7th Heaven, Martin, Diagnosis: Murder, Matlock, The Montel Williams Show, Frasier, The Sentinel, Sister, Sister, Wings, Entertainment Tonight, StarTrek* (and its spinoffs)

not get wealthy from their talents. Stars and writers who become millionaires are the exceptions. As in most American industries, most of the profits in television production are reaped by those few who provide the capital and assume the financial risk of production.

To understand better how programs are bought and sold, let's take the hit sitcom *Home Improvement* as an example. The series was created by Matt Williams, a Hollywood entrepreneur-producer who had previously helped create and produce *Roseanne.* Williams's company, Wind Dancer Productions, financed the production with the help of Buena Vista Television, a subsidiary of the Walt Disney Corporation. The series was originally created for broadcast on the ABC network, but the network itself did not own the show.[37] Instead, Williams and the other owners sold ABC the rights to the first network showing (including reruns) of *Home Improvement* episodes for a limited time. Once this period expired, the off-network episode rights were then sold to other buyers—in *Home Improvement*'s case, to individual television stations. The selling of such rights to individual stations is called syndication, and the show, having been already seen on a network, is then called an off-network series. Some hit shows such as *Home Improvement* will have their early episodes in off-network syndication while newer episodes are still being made for a network's first-run showing.

Since the price charged to syndicated program buyers for the rights to air

Parent Company: Supplier Names	Sample of Current and Past Programs Poduced*
News Corp: Twentieth Century Fox TV	*413 Hope St., Ally McBeal, Buffy, the Vampire Slayer, Dharma & Greg, Good News, King of the Hill, Nothing Sacred, The Practice, Relativity, Millennium, X-Files, The Simpsons, Sparks, The Visitor, America's Most Wanted, Chicago Hope, Picket Fences, A Current Affair, The Pretender*
Sony: Columbia Pictures TV, TriStar	*Between Brothers, Dawson's Creek, Gregory Hines, Head over Heels, Michael Hayes, Over the Top, Party of Five, Sleepwalkers, Tony Danza, Jeopardy!, Wheel of Fortune, Early Edition, Mad about You, Married with Children, The Nanny, Walker, Texas Ranger, Who's the Boss?, Seinfeld, The Ricki Lake Show, Love and Marriage, Ned and Stacy, Malcolm and Eddie*
Seagram: Universal TV	*Players, Timecop, The Tom Show, EZ Streets, New York Undercover, Sliders, Murder She Wrote, Coach, Northern Exposure, Law and Order, Something So Right, The Burning Zone, M.A.N.T.I.S.*
Westinghouse-CBS: CBS Entertainment, CBS News, CBS Sports	*Dave's World, Dr. Quinn, Medicine Woman, Touched by an Angel, Caroline in the City, Gregory Hines, Promised Land, Walker, Texas Ranger*, CBS News productions including *48 Hours* and *60 Minutes*
General Electric: NBC Productions, NBC Studios, NBC News, NBC Sports	*Homicide: Life on the Streets, Mr. Rhodes, The Pretender, Profiler, In the House, Players, Tony Danza, Union Square, Working*, NBC News productions including *Dateline NBC.*

SOURCES: Compiled from various sources including the 1997 *International Television and Video Almanac* and "Producer's Scorecard," *Electronic Media*, September 8, 1997, 20.
*List includes co-productions, and so some shows are listed twice. Not listed here but still an important factor are independent producers such as Steven Bochco (*Brooklyn South, Murder One, NYPD Blue*), Dreamworks SKG (*Spin City, High Incident, Ink*), Carsey-Werner (*Cosby, Cybill, 3rd Rock*), and Shukovsky-English (*Murphy Brown*) and others who alone or in partnership produce well-known programs.

the show is directly related to the program's anticipated ability to attract a desirable audience, a hit series such as *Home Improvement* can make millions in off-network sales. Industry observers estimate that Williams will personally make more than $100 million just from his share of the show's syndication rights.[38] As with the network rights, syndication rights are generally sold for a limited time, and so the program may be sold and resold to different buyers at different prices for years to come both in the United States and overseas.

The process of selling syndicated shows has been greatly altered by deregulation. The FCC's 1995 abolition of the Prime Time Access Rule now allows major market network affiliates to schedule off-network syndicated programs in the "access" period (the one-hour slot before prime time begins). This has been a boon to owners of popular network series such as *Friends*, since many more stations can now bid for the rights to run the show in syndication. Because of the rule change, *Friends* was sold into syndication at premium prices just halfway through its second network season, and it may set new records for income from a syndicated program.[39]

Of course, tremendously lucrative shows like *Friends* and *Home Improvement* are rare cases. Most television programs never make it past the preproduction stage, or fail to attract buyers, or flop once they get on the air. For every *Friends* or *Home Improvement,* there are dozens of flops, each representing a substantial loss of money for the program's financial backers and a loss of jobs for those who work on the shows.

However, not all television shows start out on networks—many are successfully syndicated directly to individual stations. This is called first-run or original syndication. First-run syndication is often chosen for shows with lower production budgets or with slim chances for extensive reruns. Most talk shows, such as *The Oprah Winfrey Show* and *Sally Jessy Raphael,* are first-run syndications, as are many game shows such as *Jeopardy!* and *Wheel of Fortune.*

The Special World of Television Sports Programming

The buying and selling of television sports programming constitutes a special category and merits special attention. In the United States, the sports and television industries have become unalterably intertwined. In chapter 2, we saw how Time Warner, Disney, and News Corporation all own professional sports franchises that provide an economical source of programming. Ted Turner, whose Turner Television is now part of Time Warner, began building his cable empire largely by televising games of the Atlanta Braves and Atlanta Hawks, which he owned.

In fact, the chief source of income for most professional and many collegiate sports teams is television rights, and there is a large market for their product. More than 20 national networks and dozens of regional ones carry significant amounts of sports programming.[40] Companies must bid for the rights to carry the most desirable games, and the resulting multimillion-dollar deals have turned American sports franchises into major players in the entertainment industry. Professional teams are economic monopolies in their cities and region and have been given special exemption from federal antitrust laws by Congress. When these monopolies band together into leagues, they represent some of the most economically powerful producers of entertainment programming in the country. Big-time college sports is also an important player, and top 10 football and basketball schools reap millions of dollars in revenues from their teams.

In exchange, however, sports must accommodate itself to television. Professional football games are started and stopped by a special sideline official who, taking his cue from the television crew, makes sure that the game is delayed long enough for the required number of commercials to be shown. Other major sports, such as baseball and basketball, also lend themselves to telecast because they have frequent breaks in the game for commercials. But the huge profits to be made from television have commercialized sports in ways far more serious than the addition of a few time-outs. Most of the labor disputes of professional sports teams and the corruption of "amateur" collegiate athletics are directly attributable to squabbling over how the massive income from television is to be distributed.

In recent years, network competition for television rights for professional football has become especially heated, and prices have skyrocketed. In 1994, CBS was outbid by Fox for television rights and suffered not only lost advertising revenues but also depressed ratings in its postfootball Sunday night programs. Worst of all, some CBS affiliates deserted CBS completely and joined Fox. In 1997, when CBS again had the opportunity to bid for football, it agreed to pay $500 million a year for the rights to air American Football Conference games. This was 150 percent of what NBC had previously been paying for those same rights. After the negotiations, one relieved CBS senior executive was quoted as saying, "With football, it's like we have our manhood back." Fox and ABC renewed their contracts for other game packages, but also at greatly increased prices. In total, the National Football League is to receive $17.6 billion for television rights during the 1998–2005 seasons. In exchange, the NFL agreed to allow broadcasters to increase the number of 30-second commercials per game by 3, to 59.[41]

Audience Measurement

If the viewers of television programs are the commodity that the industry sells to advertisers, how can a fair price for this commodity be established? Consider the problem. When advertisers buy time for commercials on a particular program, how can they really know who is tuned in? That is, how can they know what they're buying? Since the price they are willing to pay is based on the audience's size and composition, how can these things be measured on a day-to-day basis? The answer is they can't. No one can know exactly how many people watched a particular television program on a particular day. The best that anyone can do is to make educated guesses. This is where audience research comes in.

Television audience research has evolved as a way the industry tries to estimate and quantify something that it can never really measure precisely. In the business world, numbers often achieve a symbolic power all their own. If advertisers are going to spend billions of dollars each year to purchase television commercials, they want numerical "data" that tell them "precisely" what they've bought. Numbers—even numbers that are just estimates—seem to be precise, and many people in the industry (who really know better) fall into the habit of treating audience ratings estimates as if they are precise measurements. Unfortunately, this often means an overreliance on numbers that are simply educated guesses, and these guesses can range in their accuracy from fairly good to just plain wrong.

Most television ratings estimates today are based on data that are gathered in one of two ways: (1) using a box called a "people meter" that is permanently installed in a sample of volunteer homes around the country and intermittently asks who is watching the set, and (2) using diaries that are mailed to a sample of viewers who are then asked to report the programs they watch. Although both methods have shortcomings, under most conditions they probably do provide a good rough estimate of the number, sex, and age of those watching a particular program. In addition, ratings data, especially those from the meters, are gathered continuously during the season, so for a particular television series the repeated estimates become considerably more trustworthy.

Once data have been gathered on what viewers in the sample are watching, they are used to project viewing patterns for the nation as a whole. For example, if 18 percent of the metered homes watched *Friends* this week, the industry estimates that 18 percent of the homes with TVs in the United States also watched *Friends*. As long as the viewers in the sample of homes behave just like everyone else in the country, this makes sense.

However, some critics charge that the samples the industry uses systematically underrepresent the poor—especially minorities and the elderly. The industry has responded to these charges by conducting special studies on these groups and by making at least a token attempt to improve their representation in the samples. The fact is, however, that neither the audience research industry nor the advertisers care if the poor are undercounted. Advertisers want to reach those who have money to buy their products.

The 1998 cancellation of the relatively popular CBS program *Dr. Quinn, Medicine Woman* illustrates this point. Although the show generally won its Saturday night time slot and was ranked 72d out of 177 prime-time shows in overall ratings, it attracted mostly older viewers and so generated little revenue for the network. In explaining the cancellation, CBS president Leslie Moonves was quoted as saying, "Unfortunately, we get paid zero—not a nickel, but zero—for anybody over 55. Despite the show's very loyal and devoted audience, the amount of money we were getting per advertising spot was disastrous."[42]

This doesn't mean that everyone in the industry ignores minorities and the elderly. Many advertisers consider African American and Hispanic audiences with at least some disposable income to be important target groups, and they go to great lengths to be sure that ads reach them. Likewise, a few advertisers see older viewers as their primary target. Products such as laxatives and denture cleaners are generally purchased by older viewers, and companies that market these products develop specific advertising strategies to reach them. However, such advertisers often find it uneconomical to reach older consumers during prime time, choosing instead to buy ads at other times of the day or in newspapers or magazines.

Since ratings are just estimates based on samples, they have a built-in margin of error. This so-called sampling error comes from the fact that whenever information is gathered from a sample rather than from an entire population, some error may result simply from chance alone. Sampling error has nothing to do with the many other types of errors that can also creep into an audience estimate, such as undercounting of the poor or errors made in filling out diaries. Sampling error is simply a matter of chance and cannot be avoided. Audience researchers can even guess about how large the sampling error will be based on the size of the sample used. The smaller the sample size, the greater the sampling error is likely to be. Since it costs money to conduct audience research and the cost is directly related to the size of the sample, a trade-off occurs. To reduce the chance of sampling error, the industry must spend more money for a larger sample size. The accuracy of television ratings, then, becomes partly a matter of how much the industry is willing to spend on the research, or, to put it another way, the industry pays only for the accuracy it thinks it needs. The amount of sampling error that is permitted in a given set of television ratings is therefore far larger than that one would find in scientific research or even in most public opinion polling. Again, however, many people both inside and outside the industry forget this and treat television ratings as precise measures.

One way to avoid this trap is to mentally place a $\pm$ symbol after every ratings number you read. For example, if you're told that a particular TV show had a rating of "14.7," think of this as "14.7 $\pm$" or "14.7 percent plus or minus something." This helps to remind you that every ratings number is just an estimate and that it really represents a range of numbers (the same, of course, applies to political polls or any other kind of data drawn from a sample). How large the range might be depends on the sample size and how sure the industry wants to be. While statisticians actually calculate an estimate of this range, that really isn't necessary for most of us. We need only remember that no ratings number is precise. For example, if show "A" receives a rating of 14.7 and show "B" gets a rating of 14.8, did show "B" have more viewers than show "A"? Many in the industry would say it did, but if the sample size is typical of that generally used to calculate national ratings, these two estimates actually overlap when sampling error is considered. This means that it is quite possible that more people actually watched show "A" but that the show received a slightly lower rating through chance alone. That is, it just happened by chance that a slightly higher percentage of viewers in the sample watched show "B" than did so in the United States as a whole. Does this mean the ratings are worthless? Not at all. In this example, we can safely assume that both shows "A" and "B" had about the same number of viewers and that the number of viewers was roughly 14 to 15 percent of the television households in the United States.

The television and advertising industries produce and consume huge quantities of audience measurement information. Most large television stations and ad agencies have libraries filled with volumes of television ratings books and computers overflowing with audience research estimates. As you can imagine, the analysis of all this data can become quite complex, and we need not go into it here. However, there are a few basic concepts commonly used by advertisers that must be explained to understand why television programs and commercials are the way they are. First, let's look at some of the ways audience measurement information is presented.

Sometimes audience measurement estimates are simply presented as a number of viewers or television households (9 million homes watched *Friends* last night), but more frequently ratings are reported as a percentage. For example, *Friends* may be reported to have had a rating of 18.3 on a given evening. This simply means that the rating company estimates that 18.3 percent of all television households in the country (which means just about all households) watched the program, an estimate derived, as we discussed above, from a sample. A rating, then, may be defined as an estimate of the percentage of a population who watched a show.

You're probably familiar with national ratings reported in newspapers and trade publications that estimate viewing by all television households in the United States. If you happen to know the number of TV households in the United States, you can easily translate such a rating into an estimate of the number of households viewing. In 1997, the industry estimated there were about 98.6 million TV homes in the United States. This means that during that year, each national ratings point represented about 986,000 TV households. So when *Friends* was reported in one week of 1997 as getting an 18.3 rating, that represented about 18.3 times 986,000, or about 18.0 million homes. (You get the same answer by taking 18.3 percent of 98.6 million.) Ratings can also refer to smaller geographic areas. For example, a local news show might have a rating of 2.3. In the case of the local program, the rating simply refers to the percentage of all television households in the local market who watched.

Ratings are also reported for specific demographic groups. For example, a network show might be said to have received "a 15.6 rating for women 18–34." This would mean that about 15.6 percent of women in the age group 18 to 34 years of age watched the show. Demographic ratings are very important to many advertisers and have a major impact on how television shows are constructed; however, one point should be noted. Whenever a demographic group's rating is reported, it is based only on the members of the original sample who were in that group. Since there are far fewer women aged 18–34 in the sample than there are people of all types, the demographic rating will necessarily be based on a smaller sample size. This means that demographic ratings will have a larger potential sampling error—and should be therefore considered less accurate estimates than ratings drawn from the same sample that estimate viewership as a whole.

Another way the industry reports viewing estimates is as a share of the television audience. While a rating expresses the number of viewers or households watching as a percentage of the entire population, a share expresses the number of viewers or households watching as a percentage of those who were actually tuned in to TV at the time the measurement was made. As with the rating, the share estimate may be based on all households in the United States or on some other population, such as a particular demographic group. Since television viewing levels vary from day part to day part and by season, many people find the share a better way to compare programs within a particular time period.

Critics of all stripes regularly take potshots at the ratings system, and many of them are valid. As we noted above, the sampling system, while mathematically sound, does undercount poor people, and the methodologies used may not be as reliable as the ratings companies might like advertisers, television producers and distributors, and the general public to believe. Broadcasters regularly complain about what they perceive as the rating system's failings and point to examples of local stations that have had quite different ratings reported by competing companies. Then, too, affiliates of the big three networks have been frustrated to see their local ratings and revenues slide along with those of the networks. Others blame Nielsen's 1987 conversion to the harder-to-use people meter (a set-top box to monitor viewing in the sample of homes used for overnight ratings) as contributing to lower ratings.[43]

Ien Ang, in her book *Desperately Seeking the Audience,* argues that the ratings system itself is conceptually flawed. Ratings, she maintains, are statistical constructs that were developed to sell some sense of audience size to advertisers and broadcasters, but they cannot provide any explanation of viewer behavior. They were conceived as a way of bundling the abstract and amorphous mass of viewers into seemingly neat and attractive packages of audience-as-commodity that broadcasters could sell and advertisers could buy. For that reason, their results are presented far more systematically than the limited knowledge they gather might justify. What viewers do with television is far more diverse than any quantification can ever measure. Ratings, Ang argues, count only whether or not a set is watched at a given time: "they do not give any clue about the more specific question of what makes people watch the programmes, so that it is very difficult to use ratings to predict future success or failure"—or to make claims about audience taste or why people watch. Ratings can provide programmers with no real audience feedback of the what and why of viewers' likes and dislikes.[44]

Procter & Gamble: A Case Study
of America's Top Advertiser

To gain a better understanding of the scope and power of television advertising, let us take a closer look at the Procter & Gamble Company, the nation's largest advertiser.[45] (In chapter 6, we take a closer look at the commercials in one P&G-sponsored show, *Northern Exposure*.) As table 3.1 shows, the company spent $2.777 billion on U.S. advertising in 1995, with $1.219 billion of that on television. As we mentioned earlier, P&G was originally one of the country's leading soap makers, but over the years the company has diversified into food, paper goods, cosmetics, perfumes, and medicines. Today, it is one of the world's largest corporations and sells more than 300 different brands to nearly 5 billion consumers in over 140 countries.[46] The company claims that in North America and Western Europe, it sells $40 worth of its brands annually for every man, woman, and child.[47] Not only is P&G large and diversified, but it is also one of the country's most profitable corporations, with 1997 sales of more than $35 billion and net earnings of $3.4 billion.[48] Table 3.7 lists some of the company's better-known U.S. brands.[49] Most of the items P&G sells are of relatively low cost, but the company's volume is huge (such as the 400 million boxes of Tide detergent sold each year), and most analysts agree that the company's huge advertising budget contributes greatly to its continuing economic success.

More than half of P&G's income comes from sales outside North America, and in recent years the company has been aggressively expanding in the developing world.[50] P&G entered the mainland Chinese market for the first time in the late 1980s and within a few years was both that country's biggest TV advertiser and its most successful privately owned consumer-products company.[51]

P&G has been such a pervasive advertising force for so many years that some historians credit the company with the invention of modern American advertising.[52] P&G's first ad appeared around 1881—a successful campaign comparing Ivory soap with other soaps of the day. Soon, ads for Ivory and other P&G products became commonplace in newspapers and magazines and on billboards and trolley cars.

With the advent of radio, P&G began developing and producing programs specifically designed to serve as advertising vehicles. The most successful of these were its continuing daytime stories. These became known as "soap operas" because they all carried ads for cleaning products. "Ma Perkins," one early 15-minute soap, is reported to have mentioned the P&G detergent product name Oxydol 20 to 25 times during each episode, five days a week.[53] Another successful P&G radio soap opera was *The Guiding Light*, which, when television was developed, moved successfully to that medium and continues to this day.

The soap opera proved an ideal format for P&G ads. Since most of the company's products were purchased by women homemakers, daytime programs and their ads reached women while they were engaged in the washing and cleaning the products were supposed to make easy. By 1939, P&G was producing 21 radio programs and spending more of its ad budget in that medium than in newspapers and magazines combined.[54]

The advent of daytime television proved an even greater boon to P&G, and the company, through a subsidiary called P&G Productions, developed television

TABLE 3.7. PROCTER & GAMBLE'S BRANDS

Foods & Beverage	Health Care	Paper Products
Crisco	Chloraseptic	Always
Duncan Hines	Crest	Attends
Folgers	DayQuil	Banner
Hawaiian Punch	Fixodent	Bounty
Jif	Gleem	Charmin
Pringles	Metamucil	Luvs
Sunny Delight	Noxzema	Pampers
	Nyquil	Puffs
	Pepto-Bismol	Summit
	Scope	
	Sinex	
	Vicks	
	Vicks 44	

Laundry & Cleaning Products	Beauty Care
Biz	Camay
Bold	Clearasil
Bounce	Coast
Cascade	Cover Girl
Cheer	Giorgio
Comet	Head & Shoulders
Dash	Hugo Boss
Dawn	Ivory
Downy	Max Factor
Dreft	Oil of Olay
Era	Old Spice
Gain	Pantene
Ivory	Pert Plus
Joy	Prell
Mr. Clean	Secret
Oxydol	Safeguard
Spic & Span	Sure
Tide	Vidal Sasoon
	Zest

soap operas, with as many as 13 on the air at one time.[55] Some P&G soap operas, such as *Search for Tomorrow* and *Edge of Night,* left the air only after decades-long runs, and others, such as *As the World Turns* and *Another World,* are still running. However, with the advent of the women's movement in the late 1960s and the entry of many more women into the workplace, daytime viewership of soaps began declining, and P&G began seeking new ways to reach women viewers who were now out of the house during the day. At the same time, the company further diversified into products it thought "working women" were more likely to purchase, such as cosmetics and convenience foods. The company spent increasing amounts of its advertising budget in prime time, adding to an already growing demand for commercial time on programs that delivered large women audiences. To guarantee access to good prime-time advertising slots, P&G began investing in the production of prime-time television series (such as *Northern Exposure*) and by 1997 had signed agreements with both Viacom's Paramount and Sony's Columbia TriStar.[56]

The overwhelming pervasiveness of P&G ads means that their messages, both overt and subtle, have saturated our lives for decades. P&G commercials have left an indelible mark on all of us who watch television regularly—and especially on women who watch daytime television. In surveys conducted in 1985, 93 percent of the women shoppers responding could identify the P&G cartoon character "Mr. Clean," the bald genie featured in decades of ads for the product of the same name. Of that same group, only 56 percent could identify then Vice President George Bush.[57] Other P&G commercial characters from the past are also familiar to Americans: there was Josephine the plumber for Comet cleanser; Rosie the waitress who mopped up spills with Bounty towels; Mr. Whipple, the grocer who begged customers not to squeeze the Charmin toilet tissue; and Mrs. Olsen, the vaguely Swedish neighbor who assured viewers that Folger's coffee is "the richest kind" and helped to make that brand the nation's best-seller. P&G slogans have also become part of American popular culture. Generations of Americans have known that Ivory soap is "99 and 44/100% pure"—a slogan that dates from the 1800s. TV fans also know that "Choosy mothers choose Jif [peanut butter]" and that Folger's coffee is "the best part of wakin' up." The dollars P&G will spend on TV ads this year will buy a great many repetitions of its carefully crafted commercials.

P&G is well known in the industry for the conservative style of its commercials. For years, the company has relied heavily on what are known as "slice of life" commercials (because of their purported dullness, industry wits call them "slice of death"). The "slice of life" ad typically portrays white middle-class characters in a "real-life" setting. A problem arises, and one of the characters suggests the use of a P&G product to solve it. The product performs flawlessly, and the ad ends on an upbeat, happy note. Women who portray housewives in these commercials are carefully chosen to look "typical"—that is, they must appear neat and clean but not too pretty or glamorous, nor too ethnic or poor.[58]

One common technique used by P&G (and other advertisers as well) is known in the industry as a "guilt campaign." This involves airing commercials that imply that the viewer is not really a loving mother and homemaker unless she uses Downey to make her towels soft, Pampers to keep her baby dry, and Duncan Hines to bake cakes for her husband and children. Guilt ads frequently portray someone such as a husband, neighbor, or mother-in-law critically surveying a woman's cooking or cleaning. The message is clear: using P&G's products will give you love and respect and prevent others from thinking you a slob. More subtly, P&G ads continually reinforce the importance of homemaking and mothering skills to a woman's value and identity.

An especially interesting use of this technique is the portrayal of women in P&G ads as the family health care giver. Commercials for products such as Nyquil and Formula 44 often portray Mom as the family medical expert who is the only one capable of dispensing medicine to her suffering children or inept husband. The message: Dispensing medicine is good mothering and a token of love. Although Mom may be conditioned to think of herself as "only a housewife," she is told in these ads that she has medical skills on which the family relies. Some experts have suggested that the constant reinforcement of such messages can contribute to the overuse of nonprescription medicines or the use of illegal drugs.[59]

P&G has also been faced with increasing consumer awareness of the environmental impact of its products. Detergents and cleaners can pollute waterways, cosmetics and food products can be detrimental to health, and manufacturing and packaging produces wastes that must be disposed of. Motivated by government regulation but even more so by a fear of sales lost from increasingly concerned consumers, P&G has responded with environmental policies to address some of these concerns. For example, P&G has developed a Tide package that creates less waste and changed chemical formulas to reduce environmental damage. Logically, however, the most effective way to reduce environmental impact is to use fewer of these products in the first place, but, of course, none of the ads produced by P&G or other manufacturers suggest that option, since most companies' primary goal is not to reduce pollution but to increase profits. While P&G trumpets its attempts to reduce waste and pollution, the actual amount of product, packaging, and potential environmental impact continues to grow, along with the company's revenues. We'll discuss P&G's environmental impact more in chapter 6.

P&G also receives its share of the criticism that virtually all American advertising deserves relating to its portrayal of race and gender. Its cosmetics and suntan lotion commercials glorify a particular idea of feminine beauty, contributing to the cultural message that women should emphasize their physical appearance to attract men and that men should only value women who meet this somewhat arbitrary but still class- and sexuality-based standard. In addition, mainstream P&G ads focus on idealized white middle-class family life. Poor people, ethnic minorities, and single-parent families almost never appear in mainstream P&G ads. There are exceptions, but these are mainly found only when P&G targets minorities. Its ads in black-oriented magazines and commercials on Spanish-language television stations inevitably contain characters only from those minorities. Sadly, ads from P&G and most other advertisers reflect the racism and de facto segregation still present in American society.

FURTHER READING

"The Advertising Industry." A special supplement to *Economist,* June 9, 1990.
Ang, Ien. *Desperately Seeking the Audience.* New York: Routledge, 1991.
Barnouw, E. *The Sponsor.* New York: Oxford University Press, 1978.

Dominick, Joseph R., Barry L. Sherman, and Gary A. Copeland. *Broadcasting/Cable and Beyond: An Introduction to Modern Electronic Media.* 3d ed. New York: McGraw-Hill, 1996.

The Editors of *Advertising Age. Procter & Gamble: The House That Ivory Built.* Lincolnwood, Ill.: NTC Business Books, 1988.

Ewen, Stuart. *Captains of Consciousness.* New York: McGraw-Hill, 1976.

Friedan, Betty. *The Feminine Mystique.* New York: Dell, 1963.

Gross, Lynne Schafer. *Telecommunications: An Introduction to Electronic Media.* 6th ed. Guilford, Conn.: Brown & Benchmark, 1997.

Jhally, Sut. *The Codes of Advertising.* New York: St. Martin's Press, 1987.

Kervin, D. "Gender Ideology in Television Commercials." In *Television Criticism: Approaches and Applications,* edited by L. R. Vande Berg and L. A. Wenner, 235–253. New York: Longman, 1991.

Marchand, Roland. *Advertising the American Dream.* Berkeley: University of California Press, 1985.

Schudson, Michael. *Advertising, the Uneasy Persuasion: Its Dubious Impact on American Society.* New York: Basic Books, 1984.

Strate, Lance. "Beer Commercials: A Manual on Masculinity." In *Men, Masculinity, and the Media,* edited by Steve Craig, 78–92. Newbury Park, Calif.: Sage, 1992.

Swasy, Alecia. *Soap Opera: The Inside Story of Procter & Gamble.* New York: Times Books, 1993.

Williams, Raymond. *Problems in Materialism and Culture.* London: Verso, 1980.

Wenner, Lawrence A. "One Part Alcohol, One Part Sport, One Part Dirt, Stir Gently: Beer Commercials and Television Sports." In *Television Criticism: Approaches and Applications,* edited by L. R. Vande Berg and L. A. Wenner, 388–407. New York: Longman, 1991.

Wolf, Naomi. *The Beauty Myth.* New York: William Morrow, 1991.

For up-to-date information about Procter & Gamble, its products, and its environmental policies, see the company's Web site at www.pg.com.

CHAPTER FOUR

Signification, Discourse, and Ideology

In chapters 2 and 3 we analyzed the economic and institutional structure of U.S. television. Commercial television is not a passive, neutral provider of the programs we'd most like to see. Rather, it actively filters our priorities as viewers, as citizens, as beings on this planet, through those institutions that profit financially from television—networks, advertisers, production and cable companies. Thus viewers constitute a secondary audience, with these corporations as primary audience and constituency.

These corporations would like us to see the ratings system as an instrument of democracy, ensuring that programming responds directly to popular tastes and the will of the people. But as chapter 3 points out, if you're an affluent, younger adult, your ratings "vote" counts more than that of someone with less disposable income, since the advertisers will pay more to attract your attention. Even more important, the argument that commercial television gives us what we want ignores the choices made by television institutions *before* we choose what to watch. Since the makers of television are rewarded when more of us (especially affluent viewers) watch more television, promotions constantly try to sell us on what's on later in the day or evening, the next day, and later in the week. And programming, even on most cable channels like CNN and MTV, is almost always designed to please and entertain us in a bland and superficial way without asking us to think or confronting us with difficult or harsh realities. After decades of this kind of television, it has come to seem "natural" to most of us—the only kind of television we can imagine.

We often forget that television presents us with a fundamentally *partial* and *interested* view of the world. Virtually every year brings new channels, and the prospect of hundreds of choices can make it seem as though the medium were an entertainment and communication source of nearly inexhaustible abundance, providing for every desire and possibility, every interest and group. As it grows and takes more of our time, television then comes to mediate, even substitute for the larger world beyond the immediate space of our everyday domestic and work lives. As George Gerbner has said, television becomes not a medium but an environment.[1] It becomes a partial world unto itself, a diminished reality for us, a commercialized environment the easy pleasures of which obscure its alienation from our interests. Television is partial in two senses: it is self-interested, and it is radically incomplete. The problem is that this partiality isn't apparent most of the time; instead, television presents itself as our friend, a source of pleasure, entertainment, and useful information.

To make matters more complex, television deserves praise for its ability to break down social and geographic barriers, especially for those isolated by illness, old age, rural location, or social role, such as homemakers, usually women. Commercial television can bring a larger and often more educated and cosmopolitan view of the world, less racist and sexist, into people's homes. As an agent of modernization around the world, television can be genuinely liberating by demonstrating alternatives to traditional and repressive ways of life.

But even as it helps liberate people from patriarchal and other traditional social constraints, television too often equates freedom with consumption, happiness with commodities, and beauty with its own commercial values.[2] In substituting for other activities and ways of life, it obscures its own partiality. Much of the rest of this book explores this partiality and the concrete operations of the new, synthetic environment. This chapter begins the analysis of how the meanings and pleasures of television are made. Much as they'd like to control this process, the corporate makers of television cannot dictate it. All they can do is organize what we see and hear in as appealing and persuasive a way as possible. As viewers, on the other hand, we don't fully control the meanings and pleasures we produce, since we must use the materials, the programs and ads, provided us by the makers of television. In other words, the meanings and pleasures we get from television aren't produced by us alone, or by the producing institutions, but by a complex relationship of the two, within economic, social, and cultural frameworks.

This relationship seems on the surface to be one in which television simply provides us with programs we like to watch. On closer examination, though, it is a fundamentally political process, in which relative power and interests are defined and resources distributed, even when we're not aware of it. It is not political in the formal sense of voting and candidates and elections and issues. It is political in the sense that watching television involves us in an implicit contest with its makers over the meanings and pleasures, the possibilities of public and private life it represents. It's not an even contest, and we cannot begin to participate in it as equals unless we examine television more closely than it expects us to. Looking and listening more closely, and considering carefully the implications of what we find, will help us make explicit television's implicit assumptions—and our own.

For example, much television reflects back to us, the audience, our love and appreciation of nature—but in an abstracted, often hypocritical way. Programs and commercials are full of idyllic and picturesque images of the natural world, often presented like tourists' postcards or to sell products. But ironically, while television is glorifying nature, it's helping to alienate us from the object of its (and our) affection. Instead of watching the Discovery Channel (and it's one of the best things on television), we could actually be discovering for ourselves. Instead of learning to associate the beauty of nature with pollution-spewing cars or other products, we could be learning to be more at home in the natural world itself and thus more sensitive to the ways that natural world provides the integral basis for our social world. You don't have to be a "tree-hugger," or nostalgic for a world that never was, to reflect on the ways television substitutes for all kinds of other experience and helps destroy the very processes and experiences it praises.

We'll examine issues of reception, audiences, and identities, and how we can change from consumers to activists, in chapter 7. Here, and in chapters 5 and 6, we'll look closely at the actual images and sounds of television, within social and cultural contexts, for clues to the patterned relationship of makers and viewers. A long tradition of close analysis of literary, art, and film works will help us. So let's begin with the reason most of us keep returning to television, the source of meanings and pleasures: images and sounds.

Signification: Making Meaning Contextually

That is exactly what we see and hear from television—images and sounds. But if a friend asks you what happened on *Seinfeld* last night, you're not likely to say that you saw a couple of hundred shots of simulated domestic situations, brightly lit and edited in continuity, and heard synchronized voices of characters, music, and a laugh track, all interspersed with about 16 commercials and 11 promotional segments. Of course that is, more or less, what you saw and heard. You're more likely to tell your friend about the plot and the characters: Jerry did this, so-and-so said that. In other words, you transformed those images and sounds, that carefully edited sequence of shots and sounds, into a story, with characters, comedy, and beginning, middle, and end.

That transformation is called *signification,* the social process of making meaning. It's a process we ordinarily take for granted, because common sense usually tells us that the meanings are just *there, in* the images and sounds, programs and commercials themselves. But some reflection will show what a serious mistake this common sense can be. Think of the situation comedies of the fifties and early sixties like *Leave It to Beaver, Ozzie and Harriet, Father Knows Best,* and *The Donna Reed Show,* some still being rerun in the nineties. When these programs were first shown, nearly 60 percent of U.S. children grew up in families in which the father was the breadwinner and the mother a homemaker, and U.S. television largely ignored those of non-European descent.[3] Today, only a minority of U.S. families fit that model, women constitute almost half the paid workforce, and those of non-European descent are increasingly hard to ignore, on television and elsewhere. For most viewers today, these older programs are probably seen either as laughable illusions or as nostalgic returns to a simpler and more innocent time. But for no viewers can the meanings be the same as they were when these programs were first shown, 30 or 40 years ago. The programs, the images and sounds, are the same, but the meanings we make from them have changed. To start, black and white now means "decades old." So the meanings depend on historical context; as our society has changed, the meanings we create have changed.

Cultural context matters, too. Media researchers have shown that many television viewers in traditional societies "read" or understand characters and stories in imported U.S. programs according to their own cultural norms, of tight-knit extended families and generational obligation.[4] The viewers make a somewhat different story than most Americans do, in response to their distinct and shared frameworks of meaning. The immediate textual location can also radically change meanings. Daytime serials have ads for laundry soap, processed food, and other products targeted to women. Sports programs, in contrast, are full of beer, tire, and other ads aimed at men. How different, how startling the meanings would be if the ads in soaps and in sports programs were switched!

Meanings are context-bound. This insight and others are organized in *semiotics,* the study of signification and signs.[5] The basic unit of human culture and communication is the *sign,* composed of a *signifier* and a *signified.*[6] The signifier is the physical form as perceived by our senses—with television, moving electronic images and sounds. The signified is the meaning we create based on these perceptions. Since the meaning of a sign changes with all the other signs around it, with its larger context, and with the meaning systems of those who encounter it, there is no necessary relation between signifier and signified. The signified (meaning) is not *in* the signifier but in the relation between them as constructed by people interpreting and by other signifiers and signifieds that form context. Thus the relation between signifier and signified is *arbitrary* (unfixed, changeable by humans) but also *historical* (with variation limited and enabled by social forces).[7] As the examples above show, the meanings we choose tend to change over time and across cultures.

Television programs and ads, like all cultural products, are complex structures of signs. In a car commercial, the image of the car is a signifier, constantly building and shifting its signifieds or meanings. So is the environment through which the car moves, the words the announcer says and the way they are said (including the sex and accent of the announcer), the words that appear on the screen, and the music and other sound effects.

Many structures of signs, such as conversations and other actions, are fleeting and hard to analyze. But when we write something down or make a still or moving image or recorded sound, we construct a *text*. A text "has a physical existence of its own, independent of its sender or receiver."[8] It is a structure of signs, a coherent network of signifiers and meanings made in collaboration with viewers or readers. Films, songs and symphonies, photographs and magazine covers, novels and short stories, newspaper and magazine ads and stories, radio and television programs and commercials are all texts. Structured cultural artifacts, texts become important elements in and symptoms of larger social patterns and structures. If we know how to "read" them insightfully, they can give us useful information about our society and its history as well as about their more obvious subjects and meanings.

Unlike older media such as novels, paintings, and films, television's texts hurtle at us virtually one on top of the next, with no time and space between them. Like driving down the freeway with billboards, other cars and the landscape whizzing by, or strolling through a mall past shops and people within a synthetic environment, the programs, commercials, and promotions of television form a continuous *flow* rather than discretely experienced texts.[9]

What do we gain by calling a TV program, commercial, or any other human artifact a text, composed of signs? First, we draw attention to the active, structured, and cultural way in which meaning is produced. Although meaning seems to be in the object (the signifier) itself, it's actually produced in the rule-governed relation between producers and us, the receivers. Those rules are called *conventions* and *codes*, and they organize our human communication into a complex but relatively orderly process.[10] Texts are the material products of that process, the mediations between producers and receivers of meaning.

But there's another, more important, more general process that we attend to when we begin to think of television and communication in terms of signification, signs, and texts. As human beings, we *make* the society and culture we live in; they do not drop out of the sky or exist only as the result of natural processes. Collectively we make our own world from and within the natural one. Unfortunately, so often the products of our work and dreams are mysterious to us. We have made them, but they appear to have taken on a life of their own. Like Frankenstein's monster, they turn on us: because we don't understand them, large institutions like government and corporations are mystifying. Even our own everyday processes of communication are mysteries. We know how to use the tools of language, how to understand television and film and even some computer languages. But we're operating from "inside" these systems; we don't fully understand their rules or implications. This means that we're alienated from the products of our own culture and society, that they often rule us instead of the other way around. Institutions, including television, seem so big and complex today that we despair of comprehending them. But we must. A fish may not be aware of the water in which it swims. But we humans must be aware of and democratically control our institutional environment or it will alienate and destroy the natural one and us as well.

Television is not a deity that determines our actions, although it may seem that way sometimes. It has been made by humans, and it can be changed by humans. In fact, it is being changed every day, by the millions of decisions producers and owners and viewers and critics of television are making. The problem is that this institution is almost too familiar; it needs to be defamiliarized. Most of us have our favorite shows, our habitual times for watching. We take it for granted because it's always there, seemingly so obvious, always pouring out its messages. We have to use the (at first) strange language and concepts of signs, texts, conventions, and codes to deliberately make television strange. Television's sheer ubiquity makes it seem difficult to analyze, but that same ubiquity makes the analysis imperative.

Conventions and Codes

How do we put the jumble of signs and texts together to make sense and meaning from television? Conventions and codes are the unstated and often unconscious agreements, the cultural practices that enable us to connect immediately signifiers and signifieds into signs by quickly apprehending the whole rapidly shifting context of signification. Although these conventions and codes are tacit, usually invisible to their users, they are learned. But we don't go to school to learn the codes and conventions of television (or film, video games, and other visual media) as we do for written and spoken language. We learn them through practice, through watching television and other experiences, and thus we might not be aware that we have learned. We may be able to read, write, and speak English, but few of us can explain the codes and conventions of the language; we are users of language, not linguists or semioticians. How much more invisible, then, are the codes and conventions of the signifying systems of television that seem not even to be signifying, in which the meanings just seem to be there? Those signifying systems, called realisms, which seem to reproduce transparently the look and sound of a preexisting reality, will be analyzed in chapter 5. Chapters 4 through 7 will explore many of the ways television signifies and the politics of that process.

In a car commercial, it's a seemingly simple process to recognize the picture of the car on the screen, since it's an iconic sign—it resembles a real car. The literal, *denotative* meaning of the car is pretty simple, too: we recognize it easily as a vehicle with wheels in which people ride. But that's like saying MTV is about music. A car commercial develops a whole range of *connotative* meanings as well, meanings that derive from, reproduce, and inflect widely shared social values through cultural codes and conventions.[11] Although these meanings are not the same for everyone, they usually follow familiar and predictable paths.

Most of us have probably seen enough car (and truck, motorcycle, and sport utility vehicle) ads that with some reflection we can identify the conventions that structure this type of text. The vehicle gleams with reflected light as it moves through the landscape, the center of attention. Camera, editing, and sound construct it as silently powerful, beautiful, and swift. Variations on this formula targeted to the family market stress the safety of children, the impossibly spacious and quiet interior, or other features. The car is often implicitly gendered, associated with the stereotypical traits many in our culture still ascribe to women or men. It may be pretty to look at, "a flashy possession, boy-toy, or wife."[12] Alternatively, it can be tough, solid, and hard like its presumed masculine owner. In both these versions, the ad's conventions help shore up threatened traditional gender identities and values. The conventions are changing, though, since about half of all cars are now bought by women. Increasingly in recent years, car ads stress high-tech and computer imagery in both design and performance. Above all, the automobile as represented gives us *freedom*, provides *command* and *control* over our environment, whether that environment is a natural landscape, city or suburbs, or other people. Whether gliding smoothly through beautiful scenery, bouncing or flying through rough mountainous terrain, or eliciting the admiration of passersby and riders alike, the car and its environment usually move in a coordinated dance that celebrates this freedom, this command over space and time.

This summary of codes and conventions of car ads demonstrates how we make meaning from and with television. In pointing to general patterns that structure our experience of particular texts, semiotics brings hidden assumptions to the surface for examination and questioning. If you recognize your experience of car ads in the description of these codes and conventions above, you've begun to demystify television. But both the cultural codes and conventions and their analysis are rooted in social values. In trying to sell cars, for example, commercials appeal not just to the values of freedom and command and control of the world, values most of us would probably endorse in the abstract. They usually also assume, as part of those values, something more that would make many of us uneasy: domination of the environment, alienation and separation from it. That vehicle moving through the landscape is not part of it. As a triumph of modern engineering and manufacturing, cars represent one end point of the Enlightenment tradition of scientific and technical progress, of the domination and control of nature. As a triumph of sophisticated computer imaging and special effects, "nature"-oriented car ads represent the culture industry's homage to what it helps to destroy. Thus nature is doubly alienated, as people increasingly isolated from the natural environment watch pictures of cars sold through their association with a simulation of that environment.

Advertising and Conventions of the Commercial

In the 19th century, if someone wanted to sell you some food, they might announce it in the local market or put an ad in the newspaper, mentioning perhaps price, size, and freshness—by today's standards, a relatively casual approach. Today, though, advertising, like food production, is a major industry. And as we saw in chapter 3, advertising today cannot depend on rational appeals to stimulate demands for the products that will bring higher profits to television's sponsors. Instead, advertisers and marketers conceptualize the problem of selling in a different way. They seldom tell us that we should buy their products because they are less expensive than comparable products, are well made or durable, or, in the case of food, are healthful and tasty and nontoxic. They begin by finding out, through marketing surveys and interviews and focus groups, what are our strongest values, deepest fears, and most fervent hopes. Then they try to associate their clients' products (including political candidates) with these intensely held values and emotions.[13]

This is the central convention of most national television advertising: the association of products with widely held values and solutions to common problems. Automobiles may pollute the air and waste precious fossil fuels, but in ads they are often seen in beautiful natural landscapes, pure and unspoiled. After-school snacks may be full of chemicals and processed sugar, but in commercials they are often a way for working moms to alleviate their guilt at not being able to be at home when their children return from school. Pizzas may be full of deadly fat and grease, but on television not only are they impossibly beautiful, they also bring families, friends, and business associates together.

Now cars are convenient and necessary in a society organized around consumption and individual mobility, kids enjoy their after-school snacks, and pizzas have some nutritional value. But the point is the deliberately irrational nature of the claims of modern advertising. Enormous technical rationality (money, artistic talent, organizational and logistical resources) is expended to fundamentally irrational ends.

A Commercial for Cascade

In order to look more closely at the conventions of television, let's examine a typical commercial. This one is for Cascade dishwashing detergent, from Procter & Gamble, part of a series that appeared often in the late 1990s. Chart 4.1, similar to a storyboard used in the production of television and film, schematizes the visual and sound phenomenon in writing and still images.

As we indicated earlier, a central strategy of national television advertising is to associate the product with strongly held values or solutions to important everyday problems of the audience, even if these solutions are blatantly implausible. Here the point of the story of the young couple seems to be that Cascade can solve a potential conflict between the two over "sharing household chores." But before we analyze this commercial closely, we need to understand its larger social and historical sources and context. Like viewing itself, close analysis of any cultural artifact never proceeds in a social vacuum, and we need to make explicit both our own assumptions of value and the reasons why so many ads and programs address problems of domestic labor.

Women's Double Shift

Until recently most Americans were part of families in which men were the primary or exclusive wage earners. And with a few relatively short downturns, men's real wages (adjusted for inflation) increased steadily for more than a century. But in the early 1970s, owing to a restructuring of the global market economy and corporations moving U.S. factories overseas, men's wages in the United States began to decline. In addition, from the fifties to the seventies the divorce rate increased to around 50 percent as a result of legal reforms as well as complex changes in family and work patterns, including new choices for both women and men. In the last four decades women have entered the paid workforce in unprecedented numbers and now constitute almost half of all paid workers in the United States, though usually still earning significantly less than their male counterparts.[14] Some middle- and upper-middle-class married women work to maintain their family's standard of living in the face of declining wages. Many other women, especially single mothers, work to prevent or slow the descent into poverty that for women so often accompanies divorce. Even more than programs, television commercials tend to ignore this unfashionable second group and, as in the Cascade ad, focus on conventionally attractive young wives.

But as women increasingly work outside the home, their domestic duties have not declined. To women's traditionally unpaid domestic labor—cooking, cleaning, child care—has been added a second, paid shift. Increasingly, women have two full-time jobs. Thus in dominant heterosexual relationships of marriage, a major issue and structural conflict is "sharing household chores." Many women rightly feel that domestic work should be shared more equally when both husband and wife work full-time, but many men haven't yet adjusted to the new situation regarding what was until recently "women's work." In programs like *Home Improvement* these issues tend to be represented obliquely in the context of boyish, immature husbands and responsible, mature wives. In ads they are often addressed more directly, if more improbably. Snack foods as symbols of love for your latchkey kids and fast-food restaurants when you're too exhausted to cook are common commercial solutions for harried working moms. As the decline in men's real wages and women's longer hours have become long-term trends and increasingly impacted marriages, as both cause and effect of conflict in people's lives, program and ad producers have taken note. Marketing surveys and focus groups have revealed the anxieties and stresses of women juggling job, domestic work, and family responsibilities. As more women experienced these problems in the eighties and nineties, more commercials during programs targeted at women presented products as solutions. As so often before, in a market society a public, social problem was redefined by advertisers as a matter of private consumption, buying a substitute for public discourse and political action.

We can see these larger social problems and issues worked out, addressed, and deflected in the form and style of particular texts. While signification, codes, and conventions are abstract concepts that help us understand general patterns and systems, we experience the meanings and feelings of television concretely, through the experience of particular images and sounds. Those who make programs and commercials responding to the gender inequities described above trade in those images and sounds. We can fully articulate our own interests—as humans and citizens of the planet, not as they define us, as consumers—only by understanding the material specificity of television as closely as its makers do. We need to be able to analyze technique, to connect means to ends. Dozens of talented people spend weeks and months and hundreds of thousands of dollars making a commercial that lasts 30 seconds. Then we watch it, often casually, usually more than once, amid hundreds of other ads and programs. Most ads are

CHART 4.1. CASCADE COMMERCIAL

Shot or Sequence	Approx. Total Duration in Sec.	Image	Sound: Voice & Music
1 Medium Long Shot 	4	Wife sitting on couch, smiling and nervous, addresses us.	Wife: I think men and women should share household chores, don't you?
2–4 Medium Long Shots 	3	Husband in kitchen juggles large piles of dirty dishes, almost dropping them. Three short shots, jump cuts convey nervous, edgy feeling.	Loud, brassy music. Wife continues over: I cook, and my husband Bill does the dishes.
5 Medium Shot 	2	Similar to shot 1, but closer and shorter	Music stops. Wife: He's terrific at it.
6–8 Medium Long Shots 	3	Similar to 2–4. Husband eats leftover food off plates, glancing to see if his wife is looking.	Music continues and builds. Wife: He always scrapes the plates and he never . . .
9 Medium Close-up 	2	Closer, shorter shot of wife, panning up to face.	Full musical stop before climax. Wife (continuing): . . . ever overloads.

Shot or Sequence	Approx. Total Duration in Sec.	Image	Sound: Voice & Music
10–14 Medium Long Shots	5	Continuation of 2–4, 6–8. Four quick shots of husband overloading dishwasher in fast movement, then longer close-up of pouring Cascade box.	Big musical climax. Male voice-over: No matter who does the dishes, Cascade does the dirty work.
15–16 Close-up	6	Split-screen close-up of glass plate to compare Cascade with other detergent. Quick dissolve to result: Right, Cascade side is clear, left side spotted. Hand removes plate.	Music under voice slows, softer, to high pulsing voices. Voice-over (continuing): Dishes washed without sheeting action are left looking dirty, but Cascade with sheeting action gets them so clean they're virtually spotless.
17 Medium Close-up	2	Holding glass plate, husband addresses us, points to plate; wife comes up behind, hugs him.	Husband: Perfect. Wife: Mmmmmmm, just like you, my love.
18 Close-up	3	Box and bottle of Cascade on counter. Title on right: So Clean, It's Virtually Spotless	Fast, brassy music again, with a ping at the end.

designed to bypass our rational and critical abilities, appealing to the more vulnerable realm of feeling and association and building up that dimension in us at the expense of logic and rationality. We need to slow things down, examine television's signs and texts and conventions more closely and carefully, in order to reflect on the medium's implications for us and others.

Television Genres

Television can be an overwhelming experience—dozens of channels, thousands of individual texts in immediate sequence and juxtaposition. How do we sort it out? Some of television's conventions help us differentiate *genres,* or types. A genre is a matrix of conventions shared by makers and viewers, an implicit agreement that helps us categorize different kinds of programs and commercials and thus simplify meaning making.[15] Programs entertain us, commercials persuade us to buy, and promotions preview what's on next hour, day, or week. Situation comedies are brightly lit, loosely episodic, half-hour comedy programs often built around the personas and one-liners of stand-up comics like Roseanne Arnold, Bill Cosby, Tim Allen, or Jerry Seinfeld. Dramatic shows, usually an hour long and more carefully lit, characteristically center around police (*NYPD Blue*), lawyers (*L.A. Law*), doctors (*ER*), or investigators (*Murder She Wrote* or *The X-Files*). News, sports, daytime soaps, cartoons, music videos, and other genres have their own conventional features that make them quickly recognizable. Each of these types of programming attracts a distinctive demographic mix of viewers, usually with one segment predominating—children for cartoons, men for sports, older adults for news and public affairs, and women for soaps. But there's a great deal of intermixing of genres and their conventions: cartoon plus sitcom equals *The Simpsons,* for example, while the "dramedy" combines drama and comedy and the "warmedy" is a warm comedy.

In some ways, the Cascade ad is like a situation comedy. The earnest wife and her wacky husband are stereotypes out of a sitcom, where the diversity of the U.S. population and the television audience is figuratively funneled into the narrow commercial conventions of formulaic entertainment.

Direct and Indirect Address

Yet one of the ways this commercial differs from a situation comedy is that in it, characters and an announcer address us directly. Perhaps the most basic convention operating here, one that makes the others possible, is the distinction between direct and indirect address. In direct address, a narrator or character speaks to us, the audience, on the soundtrack. Sometimes this voice is synchronized with the image of the person speaking, with her or his eyes looking as if directly at us. When the person is not shown, it's called voice-over narration because the voice over the images is explaining them.

Indirect address, in contrast, creates a world in which, although the camera seems always to be in the right place at the right time, the characters don't seem to know it's there, since they never look at it—toward us. It's a relatively self-enclosed world, like that of the realist theater (from which it derives), with its invisible "fourth wall" for the audience. This world of the story action, often called the *diegesis* ("recounted story" in Greek), is a basic convention of narrative fiction television and film, including situation comedies, dramas, and other programs and commercials.[16] Video and computer games also often try to create this diegetic world. It "includes events that are presumed to have occurred and actions and spaces not shown onscreen," according to David Bordwell and Kristin Thompson.[17] It excludes *nondiegetic* elements like credits and background music. Here we see the wife in what appears to be the living room and the husband in the kitchen. Though we cannot see it, we probably assume that the two spaces are contiguous both out of common sense and because he glances nervously offscreen in shot six, checking to make sure she doesn't catch him licking off the plates.

This commercial combines direct and indirect address. The little story of the young couple begins with her addressing us and ends with him addressing us, yet they also exist within the diegesis. Thus the ad combines the indirect address of situation comedy with the direct address of those commercials in which people speak, with a disarming ingenuousness, as if personally to us, the individual viewer. And the advertiser also addresses us directly, not as the advertiser but in that pleasant, impersonal, authoritative male broadcasting Voice of God, as well as in the final written titles, "So Clean It's Virtually Spotless."

Conventions encode social relations of power, and many commercials aimed at women today follow the same pattern as this one. The woman speaks first, but the Voice of the Product has the last word. Often she presents a problem that is solved by the product and explained by the male voice. This commercial presents a variation on that pattern. The young wife voices a mildly feminist principle ("I think men and women should share household chores, don't you?"), but the immediate problem is one she apparently doesn't see. Her husband, who nearly drops large piles of dishes and licks off the plates instead of scraping them, overloads the dishwasher at precisely the moment she claims that he doesn't. She doesn't seem to realize what we are taught and Bill understands implicitly: Cascade's magic prevents a possible conflict between the couple. It not only solves dishwashing problems; it solves potential marital problems as well. Men are from Mars and women from Venus, and only the product can keep them together. Man and wife are happy at the end, he in his boyishly unhousebroken masculinity, she in her apparent ignorance. Only we and the Product know the truth.

Narrative Form

This commercial has a beginning, middle, and end. Though we might find it, like many ads, silly and annoying, if it were to end anywhere before the last shot and sound, we would likely be frustrated and unhappy. Why? Because it is not a random collection of shots or events; it has *form*.[18] It presents a set of formal conventions that cue certain expectations in most viewers. These formal conventions constitute "the overall system of relations that we can perceive among the elements" in the whole text.[19] They unify the text, give it coherence. Perhaps the most common type of form in television is *narrative*, telling a story in images and sounds. Bordwell and Thompson define narrative as "a chain of events in cause-effect relationship occurring in time and space. . . . Typically, a narrative begins with one situation; a series of changes occurs according to a pattern of cause and effect; finally, a new situation arises that brings about the end of the narrative."[20] As viewers we construct the events represented into patterns of causality, time, and space, following the expectations generated by formal conventions. Characters are usually the agents of this narrative causality, and conflicts within and among characters and between characters and their environments produce the changes in situation from beginning to closure.

The Cascade commercial is primarily formed as a narrative, although the narrative is clearly subordinated to persuasive or rhetorical ends. It becomes a demonstration of the need for the product, which comes to the fore in shots 14 through 18 as resolution of the narrative conflict. Let's consider form first and then examine the text even more closely for its style.

Digression: What's at Stake—Subjectivity and Discourse

Before we proceed, however, we need to reflect a bit on the implications of this analysis. Chart 4.1 reduces the ad to a storyboard, translates something that happens through time into a spatial diagram. In other words, it partially reifies the experience, turning a process into a thing. Of course this is necessary in order to "slow down" a process that ordinarily happens too fast for us to analyze. But while taking apart and putting back together this reified object, we should not forget that this "thing" is also a diagram of human activity.[21] It's an artifact of the work of its makers and of the conventions that enable them to communicate, however imperfectly, with its viewers. But for our purposes it can be a chart of the activity of viewers. How do we make sense from these images and sounds? What gives us pleasure and displeasure? How does this work on a microtextual, second-by-second level? Television creates a kind of preferred pathway via cues, pointers, timing, sequence, omission, design, and other devices, along a more or less directed line of viewer activity in following its stories, performances, spectacles, and commercial propaganda. As viewers we may follow this pathway or deviate from it to various degrees. In this process, much is at stake for each of us as citizens and as humans.

Americans watch a lot of television. Watching television now ranks third, after working and sleeping, in sheer quantity of time spent on it. As in many advanced industrial countries, people come home after long hours of often stressful work and use television to unwind, forget, and escape. Much of television's function in many of our lives derives from its ability to distract us from or compensate us for bad jobs, bad relationships, and other unpleasant realities. That distraction has its rewards—not least its ability to help us cope, to get us through the night or week—but there's no use pretending that it doesn't change us, from early childhood to old age. In the face of declining real wages, most of us in the United States are working longer hours in order to shore up our living standards, but it would seem that fewer of us then have the time and energy for active leisure and for family and community building.[22] As Juliet Schor has pointed out, "the globe's only other rich, industrialized country with longer [working] hours than the United States—namely, Japan—is also the only nation to watch more television."[23]

It's not just the quality of our leisure time that's at stake. It's the quality of our selves and subjectivities. Social institutions like families, communities, schools, towns, churches, and corporations have existences beyond the scale of individual lives. They create the conditions for individual lives and subjectivities. Television is one of those major institutions.

But television is more than corporations and technology, images and sounds. Its *ways* of seeing, hearing, and understanding are also institutions. Those institutionalized, systemic social processes of making sense are *discourses*.[24] Like discourses, we are social to the core. Institutions construct us, and discourses are institutions that, among other things, represent and construct our subjectivities.

They are able to do so—to both limit and enable our control over our own destinies—because they represent and signify not only things, concepts, meanings, and feelings. They also represent and signify the positions and processes from which those representations and signs may be decoded, become legible.

Sense making helps constitute us as sense makers. Texts articulate, or join together, discourses and subjectivities. When we are growing up, parents and other figures of authority (including television) define and position us in the ways they address us (and control our behavior). Even as adults, our subjectivities are in process, changeable. In maturing, we have learned, more or less, to act as well as be acted on. But discourses and other institutions still position us, address and construct us as individuals and social beings.[25] It is only from the positions made possible by institutions that we can change and improve those same institutions.

Since texts are the location for the circulation of various discourses, we may trace the concrete operations of discursive positioning by asking, for example, Who does this Cascade commercial think we are? What are the human and subjective traits it appeals to? What does it assume about us as viewers? In our analysis we'll focus on two discourses that this ad shares with many other commercials and programs on television. In pitching Cascade dishwashing detergent, the ad deploys popular discourses on gender (femininity and masculinity) and on consumption (commodities solve domestic and other problems). And because discourses like these help organize and form texts (and our social subjectivities) in concrete ways, we'll analyze them in relation to the specific techniques of form and style.

Analysis of Narrative Form

In this ad the narrative conflict is not between husband and wife; the product shows how to avoid such a problem. The conflict is between her claims and what we see. It begins simply, with her talking to us. Since the target audience is probably adult women, the wife's initial statement about men sharing household chores is designed to address an all-too-familiar problem shared by many women viewers. The first half of the commercial intercuts (three times) shots of the wife with shots of the husband. Her voice continues over images of him, and loud, jazzy music is also added over these shots to contrast the two characters and help construct the incongruity of Bill in the kitchen. She addresses us quietly and earnestly from the living room, while a few feet away, in the kitchen, chaos is breaking loose.

We should understand the wife's voice here, both synchronized with her image and continuing over images of her husband, as a bid for power. Within the narrative form of the ad, it represents an attempt to tell the story, to control the narration. It's a story of marital cooperation and equality, of wifely pride in his skill in cleaning the dishes. But for many women (and some men) in the audience, it's also implicitly a bid for power and equality as well, insofar as they recognize their own aspirations and their own domestic situations in the televised image and voice. The ad begins with the most direct appeal possible, as if instead of mass communication this were interpersonal dialogue, seemingly unmediated, one woman speaking honestly and candidly to others. In this rhetorical hook, the commercial uses women's consciousness of the need to share domestic work not only in their own lives but as a matter of public discussion—part of the popular discourse on gender, masculinity, and marriage in talk shows, magazines, newspapers and other mass media, and public and private conversation. Like many real women, the one on-screen wants her husband to be a "new man," more sensitive than the traditional model, more partner and companion than boss, willing to share unpaid domestic work because they share paid work. However commercials and programs may deflect, distort, and trivialize the problems they seem to solve, those problems are usually important to the target audience. Market research ensures that producers know what the target audience cares about. The solutions may be imaginary, but the problems are quite real—at least to those being sold.

The woman bids for power here by trying to make her voice that of the story, by becoming the narrator. We can analyze narration, the storytelling process, along a continuum from restricted to unrestricted or omniscient.[26] When we know only what a character in the story knows, narration is restricted. But when we know more than any of the characters, the narration is omniscient. In shot 1 we are restricted to the woman's narration. But in shot 2 the image track changes to a shot of Bill while she continues to narrate. In news, documentary, and most television and film stories with voice-over narrators, the images would illustrate the words of the narrator. The power to explain images is an important one in dominant television and film, and it is usually reserved for conventionally authoritative voices and images, mostly male.[27] Here it is as if the female character were attempting to extend her narrational authority by expanding the range of the story information she presents. If her voice-over narration becomes omniscient, then "she" is no longer just a character within the diegesis but an unrestricted guide to the diegesis and the story itself, the very embodiment of narrational agency and power.

Instead of illustrating her words, though, the images of her husband begin immediately to undercut them. In shots 2–4, while she says that he does the dishes, we see him comically juggling large piles of dirty dishes, almost dropping them. In shots 6–8, while she says that he scrapes the plates, we see him licking off the plates, glancing to see if she's coming into the kitchen. And in shots 10–13, just after she claims that he never ever overloads the dishwasher, we see him do so.

Thus the first half of the commercial (about 15 seconds) quickly establishes a contrast between her voice-over narration and another narration, in images of Bill. In her story of marital harmony, he's a "new man" with terrific kitchen skills. The images show us a comic bull in a china shop, a barely domesticated guy one step from kitchen disaster. Thus the contradiction between her words and his images forms a larger narration from the juxtaposition of two parts. The omniscient narration is not hers, and it denies her narrational authority. She is revealed as naive.

In about 15 seconds, the ad has established the initial narrative conflict and then sharpened and focused it through two changes. The contradiction between her words and his images heightens, from juggling dishes to surreptitiously licking plates to overloading the dishwasher. Within the story, what's increasingly at stake is the possibility of conflict between husband and wife if she discovers what's really going on in the kitchen when she's not there. As Bill moves the dishes, then prepares them for washing, then (over)loads the dishwasher, narrative suspense increases.[28] A deadline is at hand. Will she find out? What will happen next? With such narrative organization all the images and sounds constructing the diegesis function to generate, delay, and complicate, then answer such questions. This form is designed to move the narration forward toward climax and resolution at a carefully calibrated pace, much like the rising and falling action of traditional dramatic form. At this point, readers of literature turn the pages faster, moviegoers focus more on the screen and less on their popcorn, and television viewers are probably less distracted by other events.

As this mininarrative speeds toward its climax, the wife is firmly pushed back into the diegesis as a character, lacking the power to narrate. The gender implications of these formal and technical patterns should be clear, especially when the wife's voice is replaced by the male announcer's, as Institutional Voice of the Corporation. "No matter who does the dishes, Cascade does the dirty work." Translation: Even if your husband isn't quite as terrific in the kitchen as you'd like him to be—even if it's you who does them—our product will make sure your dishes are clean. Cascade cleans up your relationship as well as your dishes. At the moment of crisis, of maximum danger to the couple's relationship, the product arrives. No cavalry ever rode to the rescue more dramatically, and no hero ever saved a damsel in distress more conventionally.

At this point the narrative is temporarily suspended in shots 15 and 16, which are nondiegetic inserts, outside the narrative world of the ad. They represent a pseudoscientific demonstration of the product's effectiveness by comparison with a generic competitor, a demonstration long conventionalized in television and other advertising. A glass dinner plate, divided in half by a line down the middle of the screen, goes through a simulated dishwasher cycle in a few seconds. The left side has spots; the right, Cascade side appears clean and clear. This shot/ sequence, the longest in the whole ad, aims to hold attention on the action of the product at the moment of peak narrative and dramatic suspense. All the cumulative action of the characters, plus the social resonance of the problem of women's double shift, is refracted onto the scientific magic of a dishwashing detergent.

Repeated in thousands of texts every day, in myriad forms and styles, such arguments become integral contributions to a discourse of consumerism. Define your problems, even those most intimate ones of your identity and subjectivity, in ways that can be solved by commodities. Other issues are peripheral or incomprehensible. You can buy happiness. When a meaning of an ad is stated so baldly, it sounds stupid, since such signifieds are ordinarily only briefly glimpsed in the rush of signifiers. But this is true of most ads and many programs. What, then, does it say about the social uses of this ubiquitous medium that a moment's critical reflection on so many of its meanings reveals a pattern of overwhelming brainlessness and mendacity? From such recognition grows the cynicism so widespread today.

In what he calls publicity, John Berger has analyzed advertising and commercial culture as a coherent and systematic discourse.

Publicity is not merely an assembly of competing messages: it is a language in itself which is always being used to make the same general proposal.

Within publicity, choices are offered between this cream and that cream, that car and this car, but publicity as a system only makes a single proposal.

It proposes to each of us that we transform ourselves, or our lives, by buying something more.

This more, it proposes, will make us in some way richer—even though we will be poorer by having spent our money.

Publicity persuades us of such a transformation by showing us people who have apparently been transformed and are, as a result, enviable. The state of being envied is what constitutes glamour. And publicity is the process of manufacturing glamour.[29]

As a discourse, advertising and commercial culture are reductive and impoverished, making diverse cultural meadows into monocultures. *In the Cascade ad, a major social problem and a pervasive source of women's anger, usually suppressed, becomes another way to sell soap.*

At the end of the dishwashing demonstration in shot 16, the ad returns to the narrative. The last two shots bring closure to the problem presented in the opening. Bill is perfect because the plate is perfect. His wife is happy in her idealism. The product appears last, making clear that Cascade, not the couple's relationship, is the ultimate moral of the story. Like the godlike hero of mythology descending to intervene in human affairs, this hero appears in a different kind of space than human characters do. Not just another household object, it appears, packaged, in bright close-up to save the day. Alternatively, it appears in "scientific" demonstrations to work its magic invisibly. In his brief identification with the plate and the product (Perfect!), Bill takes on some of this commodity magic. The circle is closed, the story complete, ordinary humans ennobled (him) or humored (her) by Cascade.

Analysis of Style

In our close examination of the narrative form of this commercial, we have watched it in slow motion, as it were, analyzing its sequence and organization through time and space, from beginning to end. Together with our analysis of the real-world gender relations that form part of the social and historical context for the text, which help make it understandable, this close attention to form has enabled us to interpret some possible social and intersubjective meanings of the ad. But before we turn to larger issues of discursive positioning and ideology, we need to pay even closer attention to the images and sounds of this 30-second text. The patterns and choices we find there will add new dimensions to our understanding of the social meanings of the ad through the techniques of their construction.

When we say that a person (or a group or a car) has style, what do we mean? Usually it indicates that the person has made choices in dress, gesture, friends, and other individual characteristics that are distinctive, recognizable, and often pleasurable. *Style* in television, film, literature, art, and music is similar. It is the repeated and salient use of particular technical choices characteristic of a single work or group of works.[30] Your friend with style works with such materials as clothing, hair and jewelry, bodily movement, and all those choices of place and association we call lifestyle. Those who make television (or video or film) work with such materials as editing, sound, lighting, setting, costume, acting, color, framing, and camera movement. In both cases, the concept of style draws attention to the concrete use of the materials or medium at hand. Style focuses on the cultural significance of the repeated and patterned technical choices made by people as social agents.

In the Cascade ad, style supports the narrative form analyzed above in two ways, by constructing the contrast between the wife and husband, and by demonstrating the development of this contrast and conflict toward crisis and resolution. The wife is calm, confident, and direct in the first half of the ad, whereas the husband is nervous and furtive. Some of these impressions and meanings come from the most obvious elements, the acting and dialogue. Yet other elements and techniques also affect our understanding in ways we are less likely to be conscious of. Since we tend to focus on characters and people when we're watching TV, all those technical choices that *construct* the characters, and condition our response to the whole text, are harder to notice. Thus the contrast between her calm confidence and his nervous unease is the difference not between two real people but between two opposing sets of stylistic techniques that produce the *effect*, the representation of real human traits and conflicts.[31] Graphically, shots of the wife are static, with little movement in the frame, and one very smooth tilt up to her face in shot 9. Shots of the husband in the kitchen, in contrast, are full of his movement. More important, editing compounds this contrast of stasis versus movement. Her shots are single takes, where his are short sequences of three to five shots, each about a second long, joined by jump cuts ("an elliptical cut that appears to be an interruption of a single shot").[32] Thus the nervous, jumpy effect around him comes as much from the editing as it does from any actions of the character.

These and other contrasts concretize the dynamic changes in the narrative as well. The temporal and rhythmic relations between shots are often controlled by shot length, and her shots become shorter (from four seconds to two), whereas his sequences of shots become longer (from three seconds to five). The effect of his discourse dominating hers comes in part from this "invisible" editing device.[33] It also comes from the loud, jazzy music during his lengthening shots in contrast to the lack of any sound but her voice during her shorter and shorter ones. And, of course, she moves from direct to indirect address, while he shifts from indirect to direct at the end. If the power to address us directly is significant, this pattern would reinforce the others in representing the ascendance of masculine over feminine and the symbolic reassertion of patriarchal control.

This reassertion of traditional gender hierarchy is inseparable from the reformation of the couple at the end. The product brings the couple into the same frame in the next-to-last shot, as color and music suggest such a reconciliation. The wife wears a bright orange blouse, the husband a light blue shirt. Since marketers know that bright orange (or green, blue, yellow, or red) attracts attention on the supermarket shelf, it is a popular color for soap or other packaging, and indeed the Cascade box has bright orange letters on a dark green box. And since marketers also know that light blue connotes cleanliness to its target audiences, Cascade and most other powdered soaps are colored light blue. It is not so much that the wife's bright orange attracts attention and the husband's light blue symbolizes cleanliness. More likely, the general and probably preconscious association of each character with a color, coupled with the unification of those colors in the product, reinforces the magical power of Cascade. The traits of the characters, including the colors of their clothing, are chosen more for their contribution to this commercial rhetoric than for any realism or plausibility.

Music plays a similar role. We've noted that loud, jazzy music associated with Bill's kitchen high jinks contrasts with silence during shots of the wife. During the last shot, the loud music returns for only a second or so, but this time with a soft "ping!" at its end. The soft "ping!" suggests both the softness of the wife's femininity and the sound of clean glassware after the ministrations of Cascade. The modification of "his" music by hers and/or the product's further supports the ad's suggestion that perhaps you can have your husband and shared household chores, too.

Thus style and form combine to organize the discursive elements and techniques into a coherent text. But this coherence is not socially neutral. Insofar as it represents those interests who made it, and what they may want from its receivers, the text implies and constructs a model viewer. By cueing us how to "read" them, television texts, through massive repetition of patterns similar to those just analyzed, help construct and reconstruct us as human subjects. They don't control us, but they do help establish the conditions and limits for human action and social change.

Subject/Discursive Positioning

Thus while we as human subjects produce discourse, discourses, along with other institutions such as families, schools, churches, and nations, reciprocally produce and reproduce us as human subjects. The Cascade ad, like the thousands of other texts that we encounter each day, is not a fixed unit but is inflected and activated in its concrete encounter with different viewers as readers. Likewise, "our subjectivity is a contradictory mix of confirming and contending 'identities,'" made and remade by social discourses and practices.[34]

As indicated earlier, a useful way of thinking about the text-reader relation, as mediated by discourses, is the concept of discursive or subject positioning. Like a sales representative who treats us as buyers in the hope that we will become buyers, the Cascade ad tries rhetorically to place or position us as prospective consumers of Cascade in order that we may become so. Through mode of address, form, style, and other discursive techniques and strategies, it hails or interpellates us as having those traits it wants us to have, drawing from market research into our values and cares. When institutionalized in many thousands of commercials as well as in shopping and buying as pleasurable and self-confirming social activities, this positioning or hailing helps construct an identity and role for us as consumers.[35] We don't necessarily always accept or fit into this identity—there are others, some alternative, even oppositional, and the process is always fluid and shifting—but the viewer as consumer is clearly a central and defining position for television viewers.

Who does this ad think we are? We might usefully think of subject positioning as multiple and sequential, with the text taking us through a set of preferred readings or positions, with some limited options at various points. This can operate through processes of identification, for example. Following is one analysis of this positioning through address and identification.

Demographically, the commercial's makers aim primarily at adult women, secondarily at adult men. As previously indicated, the ad begins with the desire of many women in the audience for their husbands to "share household chores." So it articulates this as a principle directly back to that audience, in the form of an identification figure speaking in direct address. Within a few seconds, the process of positioning through sympathetic identification moves quickly through three levels of engagement with the character. First we almost instantaneously *recognize* her as a human figure, a character similar to a real person. Next, many of us are *aligned* with her, placed in relation. The initially restrictive narration spatially promotes attachment to her as she bids for narrational authority. And her disarming directness provides the simulation of access to her subjectivity. For many women and other viewers this may proceed to *allegiance,* the positive moral and ideological evaluation of the character, constituted by sympathy, understanding, and full identification.[36] Insofar as "she" speaks for some of the hopes and aspirations of such viewers, their subjectivities are at least partly implicated in the ad's discourses: they are successfully positioned, even (or especially) if they are not conscious of the process.

This distinction between alignment and allegiance, however, points to the possibility of a very different interpretation of the whole commercial, one we have so far neglected. What if, instead of being ignorant and naive about what's happening in the kitchen, she knows exactly what's going on there? What if her apparently innocent idealism is ironic and she is winking at the target audience: I wish that my husband, and yours, was really "terrific" and "never overloaded" the dishwasher, but who believes it? Like most men, of course, as we women know, he's incompetent in the kitchen and perhaps elsewhere. (Examples: Tim Allen's character on *Home Improvement,* Al the husband on *Married with Children,* Homer on *The Simpsons,* and numerous other men on sitcoms and commercials.) We can hope or pretend, and laugh about it, but meanwhile we need Cascade to make him, and the relationship, seem perfect.

In this second interpretation, the female character holds narrational authority through the force of sarcasm, and the images of Bill in the kitchen illustrate rather than undercut her now satirical narration. She becomes the voice of the text rather than the butt of its joke. She pretends not to know what's going on in the kitchen because, as a woman, it's one of her many jobs to manage the relationship. Although there is no hint of sarcasm in her voice, her earnest ingenuousness can be read as over the top. If the target audience is to identify with her, their allegiance may depend on seeing her as knowing and worldly rather than naive and ignorant.

Thus the ad develops a positioning strategy typical of recent U.S. commercial television. Like the obsequious salesperson, it flatters and compensates viewers as knowing, sophisticated, and ironic *in both of the interpretations.* In the first interpretation we are invited to feel superior to both of the characters. We know, and the product knows, but she doesn't. We may share the character's values, but we wouldn't defend or articulate them as she does, thus risking ridicule, because that wouldn't be cool and pseudoworldly. In the second interpretation we get to feel superior to the husband, venting our hostility at incompetent men through the wife's satirical irony. The interpretations diverge at one level and then reconverge at another.

In both interpretations, whether we see the wife as knowing or not, the ad flatters *us* as knowing. Aren't you wised-up and smart, it says, knowing about the ways of men. Cascade knows it too. You're a princess for putting up with him, and for getting Cascade to make it all work. Women viewers are hailed as experienced and worldly, their knowledge about relationships and commodities confirmed as valuable and useful. This knowledge *is* valuable and useful, but if the second interpretation seems more enlightened and feminist than the first, both are vitiated by the ad's obsequious insincerity. Mark Crispin Miller calls this superior stance "The Hipness Unto Death": to protect itself from ridicule, advertising and much of the rest of television and commercial culture adopts an ironic stance, an I-can't-be-fooled-because-I've-seen-it-all-and-don't-believe-any-of-it attitude.[37] And advertising positions us to adopt this stance through an unearned ego massage.

These two preferred readings, the ways the text "wants" to be read, are more than a simple positioning. Sympathetic identification, ironic distance, indifference, boredom, and other positions and responses can occur sequentially, simultaneously, and in multiple combinations through repeated, often inattentive viewings. Throughout, though, the narrative and rhetorical problem-solution structure serves to flatter the subject of commercial propaganda.

For male viewers, perhaps a secondary audience, an equally stereotyped though perhaps simpler positioning is offered. Cascade will make you look good! For men who care about cleaning the kitchen, or even unconsciously about pleasing their spouses, the ad provides a place, an entry point for persuasion. For those who share more feminist analyses of gender in the kitchen, the ad allows them to feel superior as well.

Are We Influenced?

At this point, you might well be saying to yourself, nobody watches television that way. You're partly right, although the makers of television have spent much time and money and talent on this short text. They have designed and analyzed it in more detail than we have, though with opposing aims.

But are we really influenced by such techniques? We watch and listen so casually, even distractedly, especially to commercials, which we often try to avoid. The answer to this question is multiple. Certainly ads seldom produce an immediate need for the product (though there are those pizza and other food and beer commercials). Few of them try. In general, advertisers want only to associate their product with positive values. They know that more advertising doesn't necessarily produce more sales. So why do they spend billions a year on it? A short answer is that they're afraid not to. In the competitive markets for convenience foods, household products, and other consumer items hawked on television, advertisers need constantly to promote new products and continually flog consumer desire lest it lag. The best way to do this is to avoid the critical faculties and appeal directly to emotions and associations. So the Cascade ad needs only to associate the product with the solution to a domestic problem familiar to its audience. It makes little or no difference that when we state the association baldly—Cascade prevents domestic problems over shared work—it sounds ridiculous. In fact, viewers are more likely to remember and discuss clever ads than to ridicule bad ones off the air, and even bad ones are often remembered (making them "good" by advertisers' criteria). Far from protecting us from them, our distraction may allow their message to penetrate through repetition and habituation, the familiarity that stimulates involuntary response. For most advertisers, all the elaborate and professional techniques of persuasion aim at the moment when we are pushing our cart down the supermarket aisle (or similar point of purchase). If we remember anything of their message—perhaps it's only the color of the box—then we may pick out the Cascade from the clutter of other products. That's enough. But to find and affect that moment of decision, to make it a matter of emotional association rather than rational analysis, advertisers are willing and able to bring to bear the most grotesquely outsized apparatus of claims, strategies, howlers, feints, and general eye candy imaginable. Beyond the waste of material goods promoted by commercialism, advertising wastes talent by the truckload and contributes to making all claims equally trivial by making all possible claims.

Since many commercials and whole marketing campaigns fail to persuade people to buy, what difference do they make? Perhaps the most important effect is quite unconnected to the purchase of the particular product advertised. It stems from the association, endlessly repeated, between the commodity and aspirations, hopes, dreams, and solutions to real human problems. The larger problem of advertising lies in its aggregate, unintended influence, in its increasing domination of the public realm. It lies in the narrow and conformist discourse of consumer culture constituted by hundreds of thousands of ads telling us over and over again that we can buy happiness.[38] Programs send similar messages, with their relatively affluent characters whose problems are solvable in 22 or 43 minutes. While most of us would like to believe that we're not influenced by commercials (though others may be), advertising is like the air we breathe and the water we drink. But it's a new and synthetic cultural environment, not a natural one. With our acquiescence, powerful corporate and political interests, not biological evolution or divine intervention, have shaped this environment that increasingly shapes us. Even the Internet, that sprawling, decentralized generator of new forms of public, genuinely popular culture, is increasingly commercialized. Through sheer ubiquity and colonization of values, ads influence us although—and even because—we're not aware of it. Miller puts it this way:

> Hectic, ironic, and seemingly unintended, the ads do not stand out—and so TV has all but boxed us in. Whereas, out on the walls and billboards, the ads were once overt and recognizable, TV has resubmerged them, by overwhelming the mind that would perceive them, making it only half-aware— as every adman knows: "People don't watch television like they're taking notes for an exam," says Lou Centlivre, Executive Creative Director at Foote Cone Belding. "They're half-conscious most of the time when they're watching television." "People don't really attend to TV commercials. It's more of a subconscious or subliminal effect," observes Fred Baker, a Senior Vice-President at McCann-Ericksen.[39]

Commercial television, the showroom for ads, increasingly dominates public space in airports, schools, waiting rooms, and other places people congregate. It helps make homes into centers of consumption, places where families learn to inflate their needs and define themselves in marketing categories. It is becoming nearly compulsory, or at least unavoidable.

Isn't It Intentional?

A second question now occurs. Our analysis and interpretation of the Cascade ad makes certain claims about the meanings of its signifiers. But where do these meanings come from, and how do we know if we're making a mistake in interpretation? For many people, it seems commonsensical to ask whether these meanings were intended by its producers. How can we ascribe meaning to something if it wasn't in the minds of its makers?

This is an important question whose answers go beyond the purview of television. First, the way we use language ordinarily seems to be quite instrumental. We think we're trying to translate our ideas and intentions directly and efficiently into words and are seldom aware of how the medium of language (the structured organization of words as signs into sentences and discourse) helps determine what we can and cannot say or write. We don't begin with intended meanings (signifieds) and find signifiers to match them. Rather, we begin with a vocabulary of signs and the codes and conventions to combine them. Our intended meanings don't exist outside a medium, language, or signifying system.

This is more complicated when we write about a nonlinguistic medium—television or film, painting, dance, sculpture, even the special use of words in poetry. When we ask those who work in these media to interpret their artifacts for us, we often get vague or unsatisfactory answers. One reason is that, to the extent the works are nonlinguistic, they are seldom easily translatable into language. If the artist or producer had wanted to make something whose meaning was easily paraphrasable, she or he would logically have chosen to work with words.

More important, we can never say exactly what we mean, in the sense of producing an utterance whose meanings are limited to our conscious intentions. Once produced, the text has a life of its own. People will use it for their own purposes. (This doesn't mean that all interpretations are equally valid, though, only that interpretations are arguments with evidence primarily about texts and their conditions, not about makers.) Television and filmmakers, artists, and others contradict themselves, change their minds, and sometimes lie when they discuss their intentions. This doesn't mean we shouldn't attend to their statements, only that we shouldn't take them as final authorities. Intentions can be multiple, unconscious, contradictory, and confused. Like other texts, statements about intentions need interpretation because their meanings and intentions are not *in* them but in the social interaction between them and their human makers and receivers.[40]

This is especially true for cultural products like television shows and ads, made by organizations rather than individuals and designed to appeal to many different groups of people who otherwise have little in common. In the 1970s, Norman Lear's *All in the Family* was a major hit. Carroll O'Connor played Archie Bunker, a working-class white man prejudiced against women, homosexuals, ethnic minorities, and others unlike him. Lear, a liberal, intended the show partly as a plea for tolerance through the satirical depiction of Archie as bigot. But audience studies showed that for a large number of viewers, the satire was invisible. They identified with Archie, agreed with him, and thought he was the hero of the program. They openly shared his bigotry.[41] The meanings and effects of Lear's program had outrun his intentions. The place of his text within social contexts was different than he expected, producing different meanings, at least for many viewers. Like Lear, we cannot control the meanings we produce, and we cannot arbitrate meanings simply by appeals to makers' intentions. Meanings are not the property of authors. Between intended and resultant meanings lies an inescapable gap.

Thus the meanings we interpret here are social or symptomatic. They emerge from an analysis of the place of television texts within society and history and include speculations about the meanings for different audiences.

Intention and Determination

There is another, more dangerous error that we may fall into when dealing with large, powerful, and impersonal institutions like television networks and media conglomerates. An easy way out when thinking about the complex but specific meanings of television programs, commercials, and other particular cultural products is to appeal to the intentions of writers, producers, directors, and others involved in their making. Another easy way out when thinking about the larger meanings and effects of television and other major institutions is to ascribe these effects to the direct intention and control of those at the top of the corporation—conspiracy theory. Both of these notions give too much power to a few individuals and fundamentally misunderstand how people function in organizations and institutions.

The value and worth of the individual has been a historical strength in U.S. society, based in traditions of civil and personal liberties and encoded in the Bill of Rights of the Constitution. Similarly, the concept of the "marketplace of ideas," so important to our liberties, can describe a place where ideas freely compete in the search for truth. But it can also describe a place, like commercial television, where ideas are bought and sold as commodities.[42] In a large-scale, complex society like this one, most of us spend most of our time positioned within various institutional roles and practices, which make us as subjects and frame the choices within which we act. This is not to deny our individual agency and freedom, only to understand their limitations and dimensions in order to show how television and other major institutions can only be changed through collective action. Institutions don't just dominate and oppress us; they also enable, even empower us if we know how to negotiate them. The larger and more bureaucratic these institutions, the more authority and responsibility are diffused throughout the organization, not usually lodged in any one or a small number of persons. The exhortation to consume and the stereotyping of women and men need no centralized direction by the mythic string-pulling bosses of conspiracy theory. Such discourses and practices are institutional imperatives, largely though incompletely internalized by virtually everyone with any power, as described by Miller:

> Within the culture of TV, however, there is no such easily legible intention, for the marketing imperative does not now originate within the midst of some purposeful elite, but resides in the very consciousness and day-to-day behavior of the media's general work force. Contrary to the dark guesswork of the vulgar Marxist, the TV newsman, for example, usually needs no guiding phone call from his higher-ups in order to decide the bias of his story, but will guide himself, as if on automatic, toward whatever formula might "play," i.e., fit TV's format, goose up the ratings, maintain (or boost) his salary. Similarly, the ad maker need not consult, wizardlike, the secret findings of some motivational researcher (although there are plenty of such findings), but need only look into his/her racing heart in order to discover a scenario that

might startle and attract fifty million other hurrying consumers—all ironists, as s/he is. . . . More disquieting even than the old nightmare of conspiracy is the likelihood that no conspiracy is needed.[43]

Here the institutional structure of television finds or trains the individuals who will perform the functions necessary to its success. Determination and causation are more often cumulative, dispersed, structural, and "leaky" than centralized, efficient, or individual. In the real world, things happen in more complex and less linear ways than they do in television and film narratives. The collective, long-term practices of individuals—in making commercial television increasingly central to our lives, in marginalizing alternatives, in consuming—become structured into powerful television institutions, which then reciprocally limit and determine the lives of those who helped create them.[44] In the case of television, it's not so much that it's monolithic and all-powerful but that meaningful change will probably have to come from outside its major institutions, which are structurally dedicated largely to an economy and culture of waste. Other meanings and effects are present but not preferred.

Ideology

The concept of ideology brings together several of the concerns of this chapter. *Ideology* is the discourses, representations, and other cultural forms and practices of signification that naturalize and legitimize social relations of domination—patriarchy, racism, homophobia, class inequality, ecological destruction.[45] Ideologies are so bound up with discourses, as in the ideologies of gender and consumption in the Cascade ad, that we might usefully speak of *ideological discourses*. The concept of ideology emphasizes that discourses, conventions, and representations are never socially neutral or innocent but rather partial, interested, and political. Ideological discourses operate, paradoxically, by disappearing, since they are unexamined assumptions and practices. They fill the space between signifier and signified, enabling them to seem inherently connected. Once we can "see" them as ideological, as interested, they begin to lose their power over us, although their ubiquity as everyday practices makes them difficult to avoid and even more difficult to change.

The process by which ideological discourses become invisible is *naturalization*, representing the social and historical as natural.[46] When a discourse that represents the interests of one group is so widely accepted that it seems to be universal, unquestionable, and inevitable, it's been naturalized as ideology. In the Cascade commercial, the notion that men can't (or won't) learn how to wash dishes (without the magic product) is naturalized. In positioning and addressing us, the ad assumes it as given. But of course many men are learning to do these domestic jobs. The ad tries to represent its product as necessary to an already ongoing change in gender relations. We can only see this once we denaturalize and defamiliarize the ad's ideology.

More difficult to denaturalize are the formal and stylistic aspects of ideological discourses, their concrete technical ways of seeing and hearing. In the Cascade ad, the way the woman's discourse is contradicted, and the man's (and the product represented by a man's voice) brought forward, can be found throughout television and much contemporary culture. It's not so much that this is false (although we find it wrong) but that people think it's true: whole, complete, objective. It's not so much that these ideological lenses are distorted but that we take them as our own eyes.

Ideology also points to the reciprocal relation of human agency and social structure in television institutions. It is both practices and forms, both the activities of makers and viewers and the long-term reified results of that activity, the structures, that, in alienation, turn on us and seem to operate independently of our will. Television can only continue to function as it does through the collective, tacit agreement of its viewers. And there are signs that Americans are increasingly dissatisfied with television and consumer culture. Forty-nine percent say they watch too much TV, and 82 percent believe that "most of us buy and consume far more than we need."[47] Taking control of our relation to TV begins with understanding how our practices are sedimented in its forms and structures. Television is always changing; the question is, who controls that change?

FURTHER READING

Allen, Robert C., ed. *Channels of Discourse, Reassembled: Television and Contemporary Criticism.* 2d ed. Chapel Hill: University of North Carolina Press, 1992.

Andersen, Robin. *Consumer Culture and TV Programming.* Boulder, Colo.: Westview, 1995.

Anderson, Alison. *Media, Culture, and the Environment.* New Brunswick, N.J.: Rutgers University Press, 1997.

Bordwell, David, and Kristin Thompson. *Film Art: An Introduction.* 5th ed. New York: McGraw-Hill, 1997.

Dines, Gail, and Jean M. Humez, eds. *Gender, Race, and Class in Media: A Text-Reader.* Thousand Oaks, Calif.: Sage, 1995.

Merchant, Carolyn, ed. *Ecology.* Atlantic Highlands, N.J.: Humanities Press, 1994.

Miller, Mark Crispin. *Boxed In: The Culture of TV.* Evanston, Ill.: Northwestern University Press, 1988.

Mosco, Vincent. *The Political Economy of Communication: Re-thinking and Renewal.* London: Sage, 1996.

O'Sullivan, Tim, et al. *Key Concepts in Communication and Cultural Studies.* 2d ed. New York: Routledge, 1994.

Williamson, Judith. *Decoding Advertisements: Ideology and Meaning in Advertising.* New York: Marion Boyars, 1984.

CHAPTER FIVE

Television Realisms

In the previous chapter we developed a series of concepts to help us analyze and criticize television. Form and style combine, through the actions of makers and viewers, to form ideological and other discourses. This chapter examines some of the most important ideological discourses of contemporary television—realisms. Not everything on television seems realist, and at the end of the chapter we will return to the larger flow of ads, promotions, and program segments within which realist and nonrealist texts appear.

Because it combines and confuses several overlapping meanings, realism is a notoriously vague and sloppy term in contemporary usage. It can indicate a hard-headed refusal of idealism and the impractical; it can be a synonym for plausibility or verisimilitude; more precisely, it is "the use of representational devices (signs, conventions, narrative strategies and so on) to depict or portray a physical, social or moral universe which is held to exist objectively beyond its representation by such means, and which is thus the arbiter of the truth of the representation."[1] It is the second of these meanings that we ordinarily intend when discussing television or other media and artworks. If we don't like something on TV, we may say that it isn't realistic or plausible, as if our standard of judgment were whether something could happen in real life. But how do we have independent knowledge of the "real life" of the characters on any of the *Star Trek* series? How many of us who find *ER* or *NYPD Blue* "realistic" have experience in an emergency room or a big-city police department? In fact, most of us get most of our information about such "real" situations not from real life but from television, movies, and books. In other words, our judgments of plausibility are based on comparing a program or ad not against direct experience of an objectively existing world but against already conventionalized and mediated knowledge. There is no such direct experience; whether through media or not, all our experience of the world is mediated through discourse and signification. "We won't find a circus scene set in ancient Rome 'realistic' if we spot a gladiator wearing a wristwatch—but we tend not to be upset by the fact that he's speaking English. Thus realism of this kind is above all conventional—we learn to recognize a fictive world as 'real' by means of certain devices."[2] *Realism is not real.* It is a signified produced by signifiers, an *effect* of a set of technical choices made by producers to enhance the credibility and authenticity of their product. It is an ideological discourse. All images are equally real.

The distinctive characteristic of realism is that it tries to efface itself as a discourse. In other words it wants to become invisible, for its choices to disappear. Realism can only succeed in seeming real and natural if it seems to be a transparent window onto a preexisting world, a neutral record, in image or sound, of reality. *Realism is a central strategy in the naturalization of ideological discourses.*

Notice that we are not claiming that nothing is real, but only that our changing sense of the real is socially and culturally constructed—partly through television realisms—just as we ourselves are constructed. Of course the material world we live in does exist, but the meanings we make and the discourses we use are multiple, shifting, and form an often illusory but effective sense of the real. If realism is not real, then we need to examine and demystify the conventions and discourses that signify it.

Television Realism One:
Narrative Fiction in Indirect Address

Appropriating and modifying older traditions of realism from literature, popular theater, photography, journalism, and film, television has developed at least two major kinds of realism. The first is an adaptation of the narrative realism developed in Hollywood movies: narrative fiction in indirect address. What are the conventions of this discourse? Here we can use the concepts developed in chapter 4 in our analysis. Most generally, indirect address means that the text addresses us indirectly: no narrator, seen or heard, speaks to or looks at the camera as if at us. In many music videos, documentaries, and other types of programs and ads, no one acknowledges us, the audience, or our intermediary, the camera (and microphone and sound recorder). In documentaries without narrators, the world of the film is presented as the real world, uncontrolled and unscripted by the filmmakers. In music videos, though, we understand by implicit convention that we are seeing a performance staged for the camera and controlled by the director. Occasionally performers will look at us, breaking the illusion of a self-enclosed world oblivious to our presence as well-placed observers.[3]

This illusion, of looking and listening in as privileged, unseen, even voyeuristic observers, has been highly developed in the most pervasive mode of indirect address, narrative fiction. When we tell one another stories, it's obvious who's telling. But television stories, like film stories, are *shown*. They seem to have no tellers, no narrative source. Things just happen. The narrative can seem less mediated, more immediate and real than one related in words.

In this first, deceptively simple sense television narratives seem realistic. Of course on some level we always know that fictional narratives are staged and directed. We've provisionally suspended our disbelief and everyday skepticism in order to allow them to be fictions. But after almost a century of constructing stories in images and sounds, the film and television industries have developed a formidable variety of formal and stylistic conventions, a by now familiar syntax that creates a diegetic world. This syntax makes their *narration*—the process of showing stories—more pleasurable because seemingly more realistic. "Realism seems to demand of us that before we can be entertained by a comedy or police drama, we must first concede that the *mode* in which the fictional story is presented is *not* constructed, but is merely the natural representation of the way things are: a *story* may be fictional, but the way it is related tells it like it is."[4] Thus *how* television presents narratives to us, in its usually invisible form and style, produces the pleasurable effect of realism. We typically identify with characters in the story by following and sympathizing with their actions and emotions. But before we can do this, and in order to do it, we must make a prior, closer, and less conscious identification with the narration itself, with the way it is represented.[5] Identification is "the process by which the individual merges at least some of another's identity with his or her own."[6] So identification with realist narration involves a temporary merger of at least some of the viewer's identity with the position offered by the text.

As viewers, we identify with the invisible guide that organizes narrative events through space and time into a coherent story with a beginning, middle, and end. Enormous quantities of money, talent, and technical expertise are deployed in order to create a narration within the seemingly self-enclosed diegetic world of indirect address. This narration gives and withholds story information, usually showing us more than the characters know but not everything we want to know until the end. Although everyone in this diegetic world is pretending that we're not there, everything is organized and staged and edited for us. It has no reason for existing except for our pleasure and consumption. Realism seems a strange term for such a phenomenon!

Characters are arranged, photographed, and edited so we can see their significant gestures and expressions. Techniques of camera, lighting, editing, and sound are designed to present the story and characters while effacing the audience's awareness of technique. If they succeed, as they almost always do, realism is the result. *Thus realism is not the illusion that we are seeing the real world but the illusion that the way the fictional narrative is presented is not a way at all. The realist effect is the illusion that there is only the world of the fiction, not a system of representation.* Naturalization of this system makes realism an ideological discourse. In order to become more critical viewers—and more conscious citizens of the planet—we need to demystify and denaturalize the discourse of realism, which usually promotes television as consumption. The larger goal is not to create more acquisitive, consuming individuals but to understand concretely our social interdependence.

Narrative Fiction: Conventions of Form

Narrative realism (or the classical Hollywood mode) usually appears to be driven by goal-oriented characters.[7] They want something, and their desires and motivations are usually personal and individualistic—to raise a family, find romance, catch the criminals, solve the mystery, or find themselves. Largely absent are the public, social, and collective dimensions of real people's lives, their part in larger historical changes and conflicts of gender, class, ethnicity, and sexuality.[8]

This is, once again, a strange kind of realism. Most of us spend most of our time as part of institutions—families, schools, religious groups, governments, and businesses, among others. In real life our desires and goals are seldom as personal and individualist as those of television characters.

The relentless focus on individual psychology and private emotional life at the expense of the social and the public in television stories ratifies the pseudo-individualism of commercial culture. Thus television's commercial ideology begins with its very form, its unstated presumption that human nature is mostly individual. Defining characters in programs in terms of their personal psychological wants and needs provides an appropriate environment, a showroom for the commercials, which also focus on seemingly individual wants and needs in order to hyperdevelop them. This is seldom a conscious intent of television producers, writers, and technicians but rather an unexamined assumption, something taken for granted like stereotypes. While "realistic" programs about fictional characters seem to extol individualism, for the first time in human history scores of millions of real people are consuming the same cultural products. The "realism" of television is mostly a representation of the private, especially domestic, sphere of consumption, presented most often in that sparkling and brightly lit televisual style of the product showroom. While programs and ads superficially promote individualism, the idea that everyone is unique and special is undercut by commercials' conformist message that we can best demonstrate that unique individuality by buying those wonderful things that millions of others are buying.

In the conventionalized realism of television's narrative fiction, stories and characters are radically simplified, made formulaic so they can be consumed. Realist narrative as a viewing experience models consumer behavior: use it up and forget about it, or become a fan and fetishize it.

Most television narratives are either series or serials. In a series the setting and characters are generally the same across episodes, while each episode presents a different story. A serial carries its story threads through multiple episodes, sometimes weaving some of them together.[9] Soap operas are extended serials, in which particular stories and character relationships can continue intermittently for years, even decades. Although prime-time network programming usually favors series, more serial narratives have appeared there recently, perhaps in an attempt to use narrative continuity across episodes to hold on to audiences who might otherwise choose newer cable channels.

Other important formal conventions of narrative realism include its linearity and economy. We speak of a narrative *line,* a series of questions and answers, problems and solutions. One leads to the next, then the next, to form a larger narrative for the whole program or ad. Even situation comedies like *Seinfeld,* which are mostly one-liners and little comic situations strung on a minimal plot line, usually have a small problem the solution to which will take 22 minutes and pull us gently through the sequence of events toward a conclusion. The economy of this form lies in its smooth production of only those narrative questions that will be answered, only those problems that will be solved. Too many unanswered questions might jam up the smooth narrative apparatus, complicate the consumption of television as commodity. Once again, though, such flattering economy is hardly realistic or natural in the sense of "like real life." Seldom in the real world do events unfold explaining themselves for us, making their meaning transparent to our understanding. Almost never does life answer all our questions, place us in the privileged center of narrational comprehension. And yet we often judge television stories formed on these principles of linearity and economy against a narrow standard of realism as plausibility.[10]

Even the exceptions to this pattern can be seen as evidence for it, since, like other aspects of television, narrative is rigorously functional and instrumental in relation to its targeted audience(s). An example would be the fashion for what became known as "quirkiness" in prime-time network programming from the mid-eighties to the mid-nineties in such programs as *Hill Street Blues, L.A. Law, St. Elsewhere, Northern Exposure,* and *Picket Fences.* Losing educated, affluent viewers so prized by advertisers to emerging cable networks in the eighties, the big three broadcast networks looked for ways to hold these valued viewers with "quality television." One solution was quirkiness: not just quirky characters, but quirky, elaborate plots, digressions, and gratuitous literary references, to roughen and complicate the texture of those smooth commercial formulas and stereotypes. Thus quirkiness is one version of realism as plausibility, the realism of idiosyncratic characters and of moderate doses of narrative contingency and chaos. Valued viewers, many educated to appreciate more complex plots and idiosyncratic characters than the networks were providing, were apparently attracted by the new programs. But like every successful innovation on commercial television, quirk was turned into a commodity, a formula and mannerism, and declined in the mid-nineties as audiences seemed to tire of it. The lesson? Quality television often differentiates its characters and stories from more formulaic and commodified shows by making a new and exclusionary quality—realism as quirkiness, for example—into a formulaic commodity.

Narrative Fiction: Conventions of Style

As we noted in chapter 4, the concept of style draws attention to the materials or medium at hand. An individual commercial or program may develop a distinctive style. The Cascade ad analyzed in chapter 4, for example, uses nondiegetic music, editing, color, and other stylistic choices from among the materials of the medium to sell soap and gender roles. Some music videos use style in quite novel and imaginative ways. But the most common style is the least distinctive, the style that is most naturalized and thus ideological, because it doesn't seem to be a style, a way of seeing and hearing, at all. Formulated between about 1907 and 1917 by directors, editors, and writers in Hollywood and later in other film industries, and central to the narrative realism or classical narrative form analyzed in the previous section, the *continuity style* is designed to produce the realist, diegetic space and time within which the narrative takes place.[11] And it does so more or less invisibly, self-effacingly, so that the narrative seems to tell itself, instead of existing only as the product of human choice. The continuity style is a collective industrial style used with variations in virtually all U.S. narrative television and film, and with modifications in many other countries' television and film industries as well. It is so efficient as an industrial practice that, for dominant narrative realist television and film, it is cross-cultural and globally ubiquitous.[12] Our analysis of this style in television is indebted to its analysis in *Film Art: An Introduction,* by David Bordwell and Kristin Thompson.

Narrative and the Continuity Style

Moving images and sounds on television are iconic signs—they look and sound like similar things in the world. But they are presented in shots that have breaks (cuts or edits) between them. As gaps in the smooth flow of narrative information and viewer attention, these breaks are a potential problem.[13] The primary purpose of the narrative continuity style is to generate the illusion of a smooth, unbroken continuity across cuts by focusing our attention on story and characters and away from style. We may look at shots and listen to a sound track, but in our minds we seem to be privileged witnesses in a real-seeming world whose coherence can be assumed. The continuity style helps translate perceptions efficiently into stable, realist, consumerist understandings of character and story. It serves both clarity and commercialism.

On the big screen in a darkened theater, the realist illusions of the continuity style, the linearity and economy of narrative realist form, and indirect address often produce a strong effect of voyeurism, the visual pleasure, sometimes sexualized, of looking from a hidden, privileged vantage point at someone unaware of the look. On the smaller television screen, in a (usually) domestic space with frequent interruptions both from commercials and from other things happening, the voyeuristic effect is often weaker. In the movie theater, realism usually makes for a fascinated spectator, and expensive home theaters attempt to re-create the conditions for such voyeuristic pleasure. On television, realist continuity is often subsumed within a larger flow of apparently heterogeneous televisual imagery. The general effect is more often one of distraction.[14]

Much television, however, tells stories in continuity style. In order to analyze more closely the workings of the continuity style, we'll use the example of the first part of the opening scene from an episode of the popular situation comedy *Home Improvement*.[15] Whereas most 43-minute dramatic programs are shot like theatrical and television movies, with one film camera, 22-minute situation comedies, like soap operas, game shows, and talk shows, are usually shot on videotape with multiple cameras on a brightly and evenly lit stage, often before a live audience. The bright, even lighting, single setting, and multiple cameras make taping much faster and thus cheaper, since the program can be shot in sequence like a play, with few interruptions for crew to move cameras or lights. There are a few differences between single- and multiple-camera styles, but the conventions of continuity style are generally followed in both.

The continuity style is designed to anticipate and cue viewers' responses, to construct the story from the viewpoint of a pleasurably omnipresent camera. The illusion of smooth continuity from one shot to the next, and from one narrative action to the next, is produced by a combination of techniques and narrational strategies. The narratives are usually divided into scenes, "segments that take place in one time and space."[16] Commercial television groups these scenes into units to keep us watching through the commercial breaks and even into the next program. As viewers we are invited to ask a series of questions, the answers to which will lead us to new questions and so on. The process draws us in through each scene and from one scene to the next, into and through the commercials. The questions need not be conscious, but they guide our sense of the show. In the beginning of this opening scene from *Home Improvement*, we are invited to ask some or all of the following questions, depending on our familiarity with the show: What is Tim doing? (Working on his car.) Who is this new guy? (Joe, a new neighbor.) What's he like? (Loud and obnoxious.) How will Tim react to him? (Pleasant but evasive.)

The Continuity Style One: The 180° System

In order to generate this line of questions and answers in an easily consumable way, the dominant television and film industries have developed a practice of shooting and editing that ensures an apparently stable, predictable, and easily understood diegesis. The organizing principle of this practice is the 180° system. According to this system, in any narrative scene a center line or axis of action can be drawn between its central characters.

CHART 5.1. OPENING, *HOME IMPROVEMENT*

Shot or Sequence	Approx. Total Duration in Sec.	Image	Sound: Voice & Music
1a Long Shot 	8*	Dark garage, antique car gleams in foreground left. Camera rises to frame Tim as he enters through door in rear, switches on light, and raises garage door off right. Credits appear throughout this shot.	Low, soft jazz.
1b continues 	10	As camera moves right to keep him in left center frame, Tim crosses left to car, begins to work with head under dash.	Music continues.
1c continues 	3	After camera stops and reframes, Joe Morton runs in from offscreen just right of camera.	Music continues.
1d continues 	4	Stopping beside car, Joe looks at Tim working. Startled, Tim hits head on dash.	Music stops. Joe (loudly): Hey, tool man! Tim (softly): Owww! (Audience laughter.)
1e continues 	8	Tim stands to greet Joe; they shake hands.	Joe: I watch you on TV all the time! I love you! Tim: Hey, I love you, too: Who are you? Joe (shaking Tim's hand with exaggerated enthusiasm): Joe Morton, your new neighbor! I just moved into the house across the alley! Tim (extracting his hand from Joe's grip): Hey, all right, I saw the moving van. Did I see a 50-inch square TV?

Shot or Sequence	Approx. Total Duration In Sec.	Image	Sound: Voice & Music
2 Medium Long Shot 	3	Cut-in to closer shot past Tim in profile to Joe, frontal.	Joe: Do you know what's great on the big screen? *Tool Time*!
3 Medium Long Shot 	2	Reverse angle: Tim frontal, Joe in profile.	Tim: Yeah, well. So, welcome to the neighborhood, Joe. What line of work are you in?
4 Medium Long Shot 	7	Same as shot 2.	Joe: I'm in meat! You know how they call you the tool man? (Hits Tim, then himself on chest with rolled newspaper) I'm the meat man! (Turning to show back of his jacket) Morton Meat! You heard of us? Eight locations, best meat in the Midwest (pulls pen out, hands it to Tim), want a pen? (Audience laughter.)
5 Medium Long Shot 	11	Same as shot 3. Tim looks at pen.	Tim: There's a cow on there. (Audience laughter.) Joe: Yeah! Turn it upside down, see what she does! (Tim turns pen upside down; it makes mooing sound.) (Laughter.) Joe: That's great!
6 Long Shot 	6	Joe slaps Tim on the back. Cut matches on action of slap. Camera tracks left and back to reframe as Joe walks behind, then to left of car.	Joe: Hey, this hot rod's a beaut! What year? Tim: It's a '33. Joe: Oh really? It looks more like a '34 body on a '33 chassis to me. Tim: No, it's a '33.

*Shot 1 is 33 seconds in duration; numbers for segments 1a to 1e indicate time elapsed during that segment.

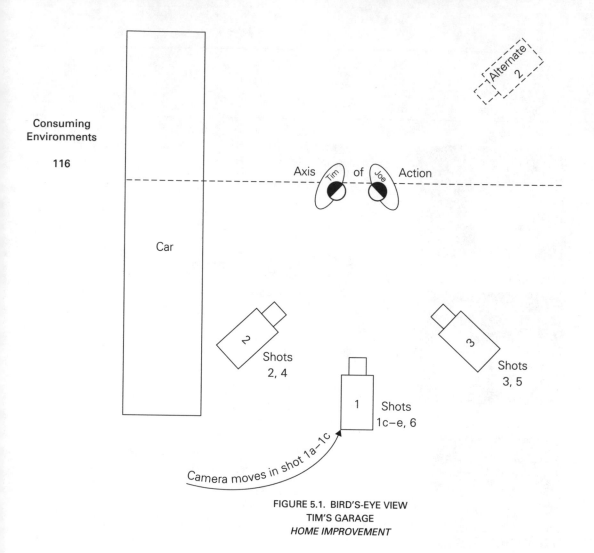

FIGURE 5.1. BIRD'S-EYE VIEW
TIM'S GARAGE
HOME IMPROVEMENT

Figure 5.1, an overhead view of the *Home Improvement* scene, shows the center line passing through Tim and Joe. According to convention, the camera should, in general, stay on one side of the axis of action or half circle (180°) formed by the line. The stated purpose of this practice or rule is to prevent viewer confusion by ensuring that there will always be some common space from shot to shot and that screen direction—"the right-left relationships in a scene"—will remain consistent.[17] For the same reasons, cameras at football and basketball games and other sporting events generally stay on one side of a line from one goal to another. This presumably keeps viewers spatially oriented, including those who are inattentive.

To understand what might be confusing about crossing the 180° line, imagine camera position 2 on the other side of the line, approximately in the position of Alternate 2 on the chart. In that case, shots 2 and 4 (see chart 5.1), shot from alternate camera 2 position, would show Tim on the right looking left and Joe on the left looking right.[18] Note, though, that in shots 3 and 5, intercut with 2 and 4, Tim is on the left looking right and Joe is on the right looking left. Thus in cutting back and forth across the line from shot 2 to 3, then 4 and 5, Tim and Joe could seem suddenly to switch places, and some inattentive spectators might get confused. And if Tim and Joe were moving through the space as in a chase, they might appear inexplicably to change directions, back and forth. By keeping screen direction consistent throughout this part of the scene (the line will shift when Joe moves in shot 6), it is argued, the 180° system avoids potential spatial confusion. In a larger ideological sense, though, the 180° system helps restrict potentially complex, multicentered scenes with many characters to spaces organized around two characters, usually stars. Thus it is both centralizing and reductive. In addition, by keeping the characters in roughly the same left-right relation to one another from shot to shot, the system, like other parts of the continuity style, focuses attention on the characters and deflects it from the shot changes in editing and other techniques.

Is the 180° system necessary? Are viewers so easily confused? Directors, writers, and editors sometimes ignore the rules of screen direction to little or no discernible negative effect, especially on such shows as *Homicide* and *ER*. In the scene between Tim and Joe, the characters don't look very much alike, and there are plenty of performance, lighting, and other cues to differentiate them. So the convention may have more to do with maintaining the realist effect through hiding cuts than with preventing confusion. It may be one more underestimation of the audience's intelligence.

The Continuity Style Two: Analytic Editing

The 180° system provides a kind of foundation for the other elements of the continuity style, a basis for making narrative space appear to be stable, predictable, and easily readable. Beyond maintaining screen direction, the continuity style provides conventions for editing and shot choice. In order to reinforce viewers' sense that they are oriented in a "realistic" though fictional space and time, the first shot in a narrative scene is usually a long shot of the whole space—an *establishing shot* (chart 5.1, shots 1a–1e). Once the larger space has been established, it will be *analyzed* with medium shots and close-ups into smaller component spaces to generate and regulate the flow of narrative information (shots 2–5). Finally, the scene or scene segment usually ends with a *reestablishing* long shot (shot 6), reorienting viewers in space before moving to another part of the scene or to the next scene, repeating the pattern. (In a variation on this pattern, one or more close-up or medium shots will precede the establishing shot.) In the conventional symmetry of establishing, analyzing, and reestablishing space, the shot sequence of analytic editing constitutes a reassuringly predictable stylistic foundation for the less predictable movement of narration.

This predictability, though, is for viewers almost entirely implicit or preconscious. The surface experience of watching a narrative on television or film is of the camera and editing *following* a preexisting story and characters. When we are watching *Home Improvement,* it seems as though Tim and Joe are acting naturally, and camera and cutting just seem to know in advance what they are going to do. In fact, the invisible narrators (producers, writers, director, and technicians) construct story and style together. Choices of camera position, movement, and editing, like those of character position and action, lighting, setting, and sound, actually help *constitute* the characters and story that seem so self-evident to viewers. With our participation, these techniques construct the realist illusion that characters and story precede and exist independently of their representation on television. On some level, of course, most of us know that the actors are not making up their lines as they go along and that almost everything that happens in a fictional television story is controlled and rehearsed. But do we realize that the continuity style actively anticipates, cues, and manages our responses rather than leaving things up to us? Why do we so often talk about the characters as if they were real people?

To understand this active organization of viewers' responses, we must analyze stylistic techniques as closely as television writers, directors, and editors do. But our purpose is different from theirs. They succeed by managing our responses; we, on the other hand, want to understand and control this power, hidden in television's *way* of telling stories. In the opening of the *Home Improvement* episode, the camera quickly establishes the first relationship of the scene, between Tim and his antique car, with a long shot across the car to Tim entering the garage in the background. The smoothly rising camera and careful lighting frame the figure neatly and clearly, anticipating our desire to identify the character. As Tim moves left to the car, the camera moves right to keep him in the left center of the shot. When the camera stops moving (shot 1c), the shot is still slightly unbalanced along the left-right axis by the empty space on the right side, implicitly waiting for Joe's appearance in the right center of the frame (shots 1d and 1e) to restore the rough left-right symmetry conventional in realist shots. The nondiegetic music conveniently stops just before the first line of dialogue (shot 1d). The first cut-in closer on the characters, shot 2, is motivated by Joe's response to Tim's question: "Did I see a 50-inch square TV?" "Do you know what's great on the big screen? *Tool Time!*" As the conversation develops, viewers presumably want closer shots of facial expressions and gestures. Style and narration help us want closer shots, then instantly supply what we "demand." Shots 2, 3, 4, and 5 cut back and forth on dialogue lines, always framing the speaker frontally, the listener in profile. (If one of these characters were a conventionally attractive woman, she would more often be framed and lit in partial profile to draw attention to and sexually objectify her body.) It is as if the omniscient camera as narrator knew in advance where to be, when to start and stop. Could supply influence demand here? Did we learn to enjoy the seemingly effortless omniscience and easy consumability of the continuity style because its makers stimulated demand by supplying it, by positioning us as wanting it? By teaching us its codes—and not to notice them?

The Continuity Style Three:
Shot/Reverse Shot and Eyeline Match

Shots 2, 3, 4, and 5 are variations on a familiar convention of continuity editing called *shot/reverse shot*. According to this convention, typically used for conversation scenes, a shot of one character looking left alternates with a shot of another character looking right. Notice how, in shots 2–5, the framings are medium long shots with both characters appearing in both shots rather than each character in a separate shot, or over the shoulder of the other character. This "two-shot" (two characters in a shot) framing is characteristic of situation comedies, which are usually shot by two or three cameras. Since there are at least two cameras shooting this conversation at the same time, they may be staying relatively far from the characters in order to avoid showing the other camera in the shot.

FIGURE 5.2

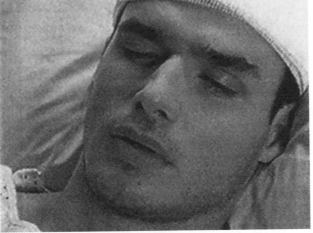

FIGURE 5.3

Another reason may be generic. As their name suggests, situation comedies find comedy in situations, in the interpersonal byplay of one-liners and character reactions. To give each character a separate shot in such scenes would be to isolate them when the focus is on their often simultaneous interaction. Thus the generic code of sitcoms favors long and medium-long shots of two or more characters. In contrast, melodramas like *General Hospital* and *Melrose Place* focus their narratives much more on the (imaginary) subjectivities of individual characters. So the genre emphasizes close-ups of faces to signify those subjectivities. Although shots 2 through 5 in our *Home Improvement* example function much like a shot/reverse shot sequence, they do not constitute such a pattern because both characters appear in both shots. An example of shot/reverse shot editing appears in two shots from an episode of *Melrose Place,* figures 5.2 and 5.3.[19] Here the close relationship of the characters Amanda and Jack is partly constructed by the choice of close-up shots for this scene. Equally important, though, we can see how the shot/reverse shot pattern within the 180° system functions to stabilize the imaginary space even when the two characters are not shown in the same shot. Since there is little or no space common to both these shots, there is, according to the assumptions of the continuity style, more possibility that inattentive viewers might be spatially confused than in the *Home Improvement* scene, where both characters are present in both shots.

The shots from *Melrose Place* stabilize the space by following the conventions of shot/reverse shot editing. Thus in terms of the way the characters are presented to the camera and so to us, the close shots of Amanda and Jack on *Melrose Place* are closer versions of the shots of Tim and Joe on *Home Improvement*. In both scenes, the center of attention in each shot is one character, presented more or less frontally to us and facing obliquely off frame to the left or right. The reverse shot shows the other character in a similar fashion though obliquely facing the other direction. The major difference is that in the *Home Improvement* scene the camera is farther away and so includes the second character in the shot as well. (In addition, Amanda looks down at Jack on the hospital bed, and he faces up.) The shot/reverse shot pattern often includes the second character from behind, over the shoulder, or in profile. As you can see from the overhead diagram of Tim's garage, Tim and Joe don't face each other directly but turn slightly toward the camera(s). This "cheating," borrowed from realist theater and film, presents them frontally to the camera while maintaining plausibility.

Since characters are in separate shots in the shot/reverse shot pattern, a complementary technique often helps to hold the spaces together. In the *eyeline match*, a character looks at something offscreen in the first shot, and the second shot shows what the character is looking at.[20] It might be an object, or a second character who is not looking back, as in the *Melrose Place* scene, in which Amanda seems to look at Jack but he has his eyes closed. If Jack opens his eyes, it will appear as if the two were looking at each other. With one character looking obliquely off right, the other obliquely left, the illusion that their gazes are meeting is quite strong.[21] The combination of one or two eyeline matches with the shot/reverse shot can powerfully link two characters in two separate shots along the imaginary eyeline. Note that close-up shots of each character alone in the frame don't have to be shot in sequence, or even at the same time or place. The syntax of the continuity system ensures that we the audience will put the pieces together according to convention, actively constructing the illusion for ourselves. The continuity style self-effacingly supports narrative form in promoting our absorption in story and character.

The Continuity Style Four: Match on Action

The eyeline match links two shots through the look of a character. The *match on action* links two shots even more tightly through the continuation of a movement across an edit or cut. The movement begins in one shot and is completed in another with no perceivable gap or overlap in the action, so we will follow the movement and not notice the cut.[22] In the *Home Improvement* scene, the cut from shot 5 to shot 6 is a match on action. The action is Joe's movement of slapping Tim on the back and stepping away to the back and left. It begins at the end of shot 5, just a second or two after the image shown in chart 5.1, shot 5, and continues through the cut as Joe crosses left behind Tim at the beginning of shot 6, just a second or two before the image shown in chart 5.1, shot 6. Joe's movement perceptually hides the discontinuity of the cut, as do dialogue lines and other sounds carried across the cut. The cut to the long shot also reestablishes the space and omnisciently anticipates Joe's movement to the left. Like the other parts of the continuity system, the match on action naturalizes the discourse of narrative realism. It helps promote the sense that the two-dimensional screen is a window onto a three-dimensional world, imaginary but real-seeming, pleasurable in the ways it draws us through its space and time. In fictional realism we seem to be within a coherent and self-enclosed diegetic world entirely designed for our viewing pleasure though never acknowledging our existence.

Television Realism Two: Nonfiction in Direct Address

Narrative fiction creates a diegesis, an imaginary space and time that usually seems realistic or plausible. But we almost always know that fictional stories are "made up," that their reality is figurative. The codes and conventions of narrative fiction cue us to suspend disbelief at apparent divergences from everyday reality.

In contrast, nonfiction television (and film and other media) usually claims implicitly to present literal, unmediated reality. Like fiction, nonfiction looks and sounds like what it refers to, the real world. Like fiction, nonfiction is coded to seem uncoded.[23] But nonfiction seems *more* immediate, more transparent, more real.

In the previous section we analyzed the conventions of narrative fictional realism: controlled lighting, balanced visual compositions, linear and economical story forms, and the continuity style, including analytic editing, shot/reverse shot, eyeline match, and match on action. Although fictional realism in indirect address seems to be unmediated, all these elements tacitly signify *control* over what is happening in front of the camera. Nonfiction genres like talk and stand-up comedy shows, infomercials, "reality TV," and other programs with hosts (*Good Morning America, America's Funniest Home Videos*) use some of these and similar techniques of control. Even news and documentary, in their images of anchors, correspondents, and interviewees, present a nonfiction discourse clearly preorganized and controlled like narrative fiction, for easy understanding.

However, central to news and documentary, exemplary nonfiction genres, is another set of codes and conventions. They include a shaky image produced by a handheld camera, an image that does not always capture its object in pleasing, balanced compositions; haphazard lighting and often monochromatic color; discontinuous, jumpy editing; and sound that includes extraneous noise, sometimes interfering with our ability to make immediate sense of what we hear.[24] These conventions of news and documentary nonfiction realism have very different meanings from those of narrative fictional realism. They signify that what we see and hear has not been controlled or staged but discovered. Thus it must be more literally real, more credible than fictional realism. *Its very lack of commercial polish and apparent control signifies raw authenticity.*

Seeing is believing: the problems with this widespread assumption are threefold. First, it ignores the selection, control, and mediation exercised by *all* video makers and filmmakers in the processes of preproduction, shooting, and editing, control that makers cannot choose to relinquish. Second, and perhaps more important, because these conventions automatically carry the authority of documentary truth, they can be copied to lend this authority to any argument, regardless of its merits. By using these conventions a video maker or filmmaker can make fiction look and sound like nonfiction, can appear to discover reality while staging it. Reenactment of earlier events on such tabloid shows as *Hard Copy* and "reality television" like *America's Most Wanted* has crossed this line in the nineties. In a more complex case, Oliver Stone's 1991 film *JFK* mixed fiction, documentary, and simulated or staged documentary to argue that President John Kennedy was killed and his assassination covered up in 1963 through a conspiracy that included his successor, President Lyndon Johnson. Stone was attacked not only for his conspiracy theories but for combining documentary film from 1963 with pseudodocumentary film staged for *JFK* so that most viewers couldn't tell the difference. His fictional images, charged some critics, by copying the documentary conventions in the 1963 film, sought from the audience an unwarranted and unethical presumption of documentary authenticity and truth to shore up his claims. Stone was deliberately confusing evidence and speculation, fact and fiction, through sophisticated technological fakery, it was alleged.[25] The lesson here is not so much whether Oliver Stone was right or wrong, though that is important. Rather, it is the unreliability of the conventions of documentary authenticity as guarantors of reality and literal truth. These conventions were always subject to manipulation; as technical means for simulating them improve, we will have to find ways of judging evidence and truth claims that are more thoughtful, analytic, and complex.

This brings us to the third and most radical reason for rejecting the presumption of reality in nonfiction conventions — radical because it questions not just the reality claims of particular documentary techniques but even deeper assumptions about the relation between images and their sources as well. Film and still photographs make indexical signs, images caused by light from the world as well as by the actions of their human makers. This is assumed to be particularly true of documentary and news, reflections of nonfiction reality. But the technical practice of image and sound recording is changing rapidly. New technologies of digital sampling increasingly replace the analog technologies of photography and sound recording and even videotape. This enables big-budget movies like *Jurassic Park, Twister,* and *Titanic* to meld convincing and "realistic" images of dinosaurs, tornadoes, and a ship at sea with those of human actors. It also makes possible the televisual simulation of moving images "peeling" off to reveal other moving images underneath, and other similar "eye candy" seen often in graphics-driven promotions, ads, and sports or magazine programs.[26] Bill Nichols describes this momentous technological change from representation or reproduction to simulation: "The image becomes a series of bits, a pattern of yes/no choices registered within a computer's memory. . . . There is no original negative image as there is in photography against which all prints can be compared for accuracy and authenticity. There may not even be an external referent. Computer graphics can generate highly realist renderings of real-life subjects from software algorithms rather than external referents. The implications of all this are only beginning to be grasped."[27] As more and more image and sound recording becomes digital, it is easier and more common to change these recordings in myriad ways, even to generate realistic new images and sounds by computer. The aura of truth of realistic images and sounds must erode.[28] We have to learn in new and more conscious ways that seeing and hearing are not believing.

While this brave new world of reality simulation struggles to be born, reminding us again that surface appearances can be unstable and untrustworthy, we cannot forget what is at stake. Ultimately, escaping is not an option. This planet, this social and political and natural world, is the only one we have. And nonfiction realism on television, especially news and documentary, implicitly claims to represent directly to us this world and this planet in all their diversity. It is a principal way we know the world beyond the space of our own lives—serious business if we want a voice in our own world and our common fate.

Nonfiction television shows us important things we need to know about the real world and gives us seemingly incontrovertible evidence: Rodney King being beaten by Los Angeles police, or the space shuttle *Challenger* exploding during launch, or extraordinary sports performances. Such images and sounds continue to compel belief. This has really happened; it's not made up. An old and very strong ideology tells us this is real. A press conference, an interview, and images from a nature documentary silently declare themselves as unmediated actuality.

Yet it is precisely the power of these images to mimic the real world that seems to demand an intervening narrator, a voice to explain them. Unlike those fictions carefully organized to show us meaningful stories seemingly without tellers, nonfiction images of the real world can be radically incomplete, fragmentary, without context, and meaningless. The solution is the narrator, anchor, host, or voice-over, who explains and organizes the images (and sounds) as evidence in an argument, addressing us directly.

Thus while television and film fiction usually lacks a narrator addressing us, nonfiction usually maintains direct address. This convention began with documentary film in the 1930s, when sound-recording equipment became widely available but largely limited to the studio. Until the early sixties, most documentary and news film was silent, with commentary and narration added later. Light, quiet cameras with synchronous sound recorders and improved microphones have created new options, but most news and documentaries are still dominated by the voice of the narrator or correspondent addressing us, telling us what the images mean.

Nonfiction television includes a number of genres—news, documentary, sports, talk shows, stand-up comedy, "reality television," infomercials, home shopping—using variations on the conventional host or narrator in direct address. Narrators are arguably the voices of television's framing or metadiscourse discussed at the end of this chapter, the announcers who connect programs, commercials, and promos with a flow of phrases. These include "it's on later," "stay tuned," "tomorrow morning, don't miss . . . ," "and then," and "right after these messages." Commercials honor this voice by imitation, trading on its credibility by using it to recommend products. And, of course, nearly lost in the flow and clutter are the network and station identifications, often crowded almost to invisibility by the voices of commodities.

Television News: A Hierarchical Discourse

Adapted from radio, print journalism, and documentary film, network news was one of television's first nonfiction genres, and it has developed the convention of the narrator/anchor into the cornerstone of a whole hierarchical discourse of authority and mediation. Other nonfiction genres play variations on this system. Because network news conventions continue to be the models for those in documentary, public affairs, local news, and other, lighter nonfiction programming, and because television makes claims about the real world most explicitly through these news conventions, we will focus our analysis of nonfiction realism on network news—ABC, CBS, NBC, CNN, CNBC, and MSNBC. As in our analysis of fictional narrative realism, we will concentrate on the long-term formal and deep structural features of network news rather than specific patterns of content. Although the content or meanings we make from television news are of the highest importance, far too little attention is paid to the ways in which that content is framed, even constituted by the forms of address of this powerful discourse. Whatever else network news may tell us, its very way of presenting itself—and of hailing or positioning us—reinforces its hierarchy of authority and its deliberate confusion of the gravity of the news with the constructed personalities of its anchors and correspondents.[29]

The Anchor: Hierarchical Authority and Simulated Eye Contact

In television news, images and sounds of the world out there must be explained and contextualized. On this quite defensible imperative, however, is raised an entire hierarchy of authority. Nonfiction images and sounds are not just mediated but framed, enclosed within this hierarchy. At the top of this hierarchy is the anchor, who legitimates the news institution itself. The image and sound of the anchor dominate and frame the whole program, as in figure 5.4 from the *ABC World News Tonight with Peter Jennings* for September 4, 1997.

Why are anchors so dominant in U.S. news programs? In most other countries, the news is presented by readers, relatively anonymous presenters. In the United States news readers are deliberately tied to the news they read and have become anchors and news stars with fans, high salaries, and public personas. Not accidentally, many news viewers think of watching Peter Jennings, Tom Brokaw, or Dan Rather instead of ABC, NBC, or CBS. Both acknowledging and promoting their centrality as the commodity that sells the news, anchors' names are even part of the titles of their news programs. CNN, CNBC, and MSNBC are developing their own news stars. Anchors and other prominent television journalists are selected, groomed, and retained largely on their ability to seem to project themselves out of the set into our homes, to appear to speak to us person to person, authoritatively but almost individually. Television industry people sometimes call this rare and lucrative quality "breaking through the glass," indicating an illusion of three-dimensional reality and human presence similar to that produced by fictional stories and stars.

Are U.S. viewers genetically programmed to prefer news anchors as journalistic stars to news readers? Not likely. The major difference is institutional, in strong traditions in other countries of broadcasting as public service (or the voice of the state) versus the dominance in U.S. television of commercial priorities. Most U.S. news programs work hard to *personalize* the news, systematically confusing the presenter with what is presented. The news is not necessarily the most profitable operation for a network, but its unique role, seriousness, and centrality in national public affairs give it a special prestige and status. Personalization associates this seriousness and prestige of the news with those who read it, so that viewers wanting to stay informed will think of Peter Jennings or some other trusted network figure. In the early 20th century the film industry learned

FIGURE 5.4

how to develop stars as reliable identification figures to promote consistent, habitual movie attendance and reliable profits. Similarly, commercial television news operations must, for private profit, attach their constructed journalistic stars to viewers' interest in the public world of news. The commercial imperative tends gradually to annex the public world of news to the publicity world of celebrities and spectacular commodities.

Personalization and construction of anchors as media stars happen in several ways. In order to "break through the glass" and establish a pseudopersonal rapport with viewers, anchors—and to a lesser extent other television journalists—must be serious but not staid, attractive but not too glamorous. Their star images must be clear but manipulable. If Dan Rather seems too tough and hard edged, get him a sweater to soften the look.

Anchor connotes weight, solidity, holding in place against changing currents. The news anchor mediates and frames virtually everything in the program—all reports by correspondents and implicitly the commercials as well. Introducing each report and usually returning afterward, even if only for a few seconds before a commercial break, the anchor is the symbolic center of a global news system, apparent gatekeeper for scores of distant correspondents. (Actually, of course, the gatekeepers are unseen news producers.) With a news center full of computer and video monitors often arrayed behind, seemingly bringing in instantaneous reports from around the nation and the world, the figure of the anchor condenses the key news values of responsibility, seriousness, and objectivity so crucial to the credibility of the impersonal news institution.

Perhaps most important for the commercial process of personalizing the news, this face is looking at us. Not at us personally, though we are perhaps encouraged to imagine it so. *The central convention of news, documentary, and indeed most nonfiction television, direct address signifies institutional authority. Only the anchor, and correspondents introduced by and relayed through the anchor, are allowed to address us directly.* They represent the news institution. All others are told not to look at the camera, or they appear in indirect address, as if the camera were invisible. The power of direct address is jealously guarded by television news institutions, for it is key to their symbolic hierarchy of authority.

The convention of direct address through simulated eye contact by television anchors has a history, and its technological tool is the teleprompter. When television news began in the 1950s, anchors read both from mechanical teleprompters near the camera and from news copy held in their hands. They looked down from the camera to these papers from time to time. Since the seventies, though, these papers held in the hands have become largely residual, and anchors (and politicians) now look steadily out at us while reading their copy. This apparent optical impossibility has been made possible by a more advanced teleprompter, in which a screen displaying the text to be read fits directly over the camera lens without blocking it. This simple but significant technological change makes it possible for anchors and others to appear to be telling us things that come from them rather than from something they are reading. The device concretely fuses reader and read, making the words an expression of the anchor rather than of an impersonal news institution. By this intimate association the authority of the news tacitly augments the authority of the anchor. Reciprocally, then, the news comes to seem significant not only for itself but because Dan Rather or Tom Brokaw has told us about it. Not surprisingly, many of us identify with the anchor in a manner similar to the way we identify with fictional characters, or the way some viewers develop "parasocial" or pseudopersonal relationships with home shopping hosts as discussed in chapter 2. Ideologically, anchors become more like authoritative personal friends or neighbors telling us what we want to know rather than what they really are, representatives of powerful commercial institutions with a partial view of the world.

Correspondents: Extensions of the Anchor

Like anchors, correspondents are representatives of the news institution. As such they have the authority to address us directly. But correspondents generally appear only through the relay of the anchor, who introduces and often concludes their reports, sometimes links several reports together thematically, and generally mediates all news material. The discursive relay from anchor to correspondent, and then at the end of the report from correspondent back to anchor, frames each report as second level of authority in the representational hierarchy of network news. The signifier of this relay at the beginning of the report is the replacement of the anchor's voice and image ("With a report from . . . , here's ABC correspondent . . .") with that of the correspondent, who usually opens the report by speaking to us, explaining the images, and often appears as well in synchronous sound. The symmetry of closure signifies the report's end, the correspondent's voice-over ("This is . . . , ABC News, in . . ."), and usually image as well, followed by that of the anchor. Thus the correspondent's voice and image partially frame the often uncontrolled images and sounds of the news-generating world. They do so in order to facilitate the more complete framing and management of those uncontrolled images and sounds by the controlled world of the anchor.

Ordinarily, the anchor acknowledges this relationship only through a slight turning of the gaze to the side, away from simulated eye contact with us, while passing discursive authority to the correspondent. The anchor's gaze returns symmetrically from the side to us once again immediately upon returning after the report. In actuality, the anchor is probably most often turning toward a video monitor to watch the correspondent's report. Yet this practical function is almost

FIGURE 5.5

never revealed. Instead, the anchor's small movement just before and after the report, contextualized within the smooth flow of coordinated items, becomes another signifier of the news institution's (and the network's) command and control of time and space.

Extensions of and assistants to the anchor, correspondents also derive some of their authority and legitimacy from their location. Behind them as they speak, and in images they narrate, the White House, battlefield, crowd, or other location provides evidence and credibility. They know partly because they are there, as in figure 5.5, a typical shot of ABC News correspondent Linda Patillo in Jerusalem.[30] But we should be skeptical, remembering that in this age of near instantaneous communication, in most cases the anchor could be telling us the same things the correspondent does. Someone is not *necessarily* better informed because he or she is on the scene. And again, seeing should not be believing. Miles Harvey recounts that "during the January 26, 1994 broadcast of *World News Tonight with Peter Jennings*, reporter Cokie Roberts appeared on camera for what Jennings described as a live report from Capitol Hill. But Roberts was not on Capitol Hill. Apparently unbeknownst even to Jennings, she was standing in a studio in front of an electronic backdrop of the U.S. Capitol. To give the fake report just that little extra touch of reality, Roberts had put on an overcoat."[31] Only later was the ruse discovered and the ABC correspondent and producer reprimanded. Cokie Roberts's career has not suffered discernibly from this small postmodern mistake. And why should it? No one noticed at the time, since we couldn't tell the difference between a picture and a picture of a picture.

Interviewees and the Rest of Us

Correspondents and sometimes anchors interview people as part of their reports, and interviewees form the third level of authority in the news. These interviewees are usually experts or institutional spokespersons or chosen to typify a particular situation. As such, what they say illustrates a larger argument made by the network representative, including the argument that there are two sides to the issue being covered. Since they do not represent the news institution, they are told not to look at the camera.

FIGURE 5.6

FIGURE 5.7

In figures 5.6 and 5.7 from *60 Minutes,* CBS correspondent Steve Kroft interviews molecular biologist John Gofman about the dangers to humans and the environment of putting 72 pounds of plutonium, theoretically enough to cause cancer in everyone on earth, in the Cassini space probe to Saturn atop a rocket that fails once in every 20 times it is launched.[32] Note the similarity in the editing of this nonfiction sequence to the editing of the fictional *Melrose Place* in figures 5.2 and 5.3. Both use shot/reverse shot and eyeline matching to construct a spatial and temporal relationship between people or characters in separate shots. Here neither the expert nor the network representative addresses us directly, which is normal for an interview.

As we noted earlier, though, correspondents frame their reports internally, in direct address, as anchors frame them externally. Their voices are usually heard first, or right after an illustrative lead-in, and they sum up the meaning of their report at the end. Having the last word is an important convention of news mediators. Just as networks generally do not use any film or tape they have not shot, and clearly mark it when they do, they do not allow the subjects of news stories to

FIGURE 5.8

frame their own stories.[33] This is particularly true of those of us at the bottom of the hierarchy of authority in television news. We are not allowed to control the camera, the microphone, or the editing deck. Neither journalists nor interviewees, we appear on the news only when we become unknowing visual evidence for the arguments of others, high-ranking sources or network or station representatives. Almost always their voices literally replace our own, their explanations managing our images.

Figure 5.8, part of the same *60 Minutes* report on the dangers of nuclear power in the space program, illustrates the marginalization of ordinary people on the news. *60 Minutes*, like most commercial media, frames this issue as a disagreement between expert scientists like Gofman and NASA's own experts. But they forget that the issue was brought to public attention, including that of *60 Minutes*, largely through the efforts not of experts but of many ordinary citizens. Rather than kooks and weirdos, these folks constitute a public conscience, telling us that NASA is nuclearizing and militarizing space, sending plutonium, the most toxic substance known to humans, as our gift to the universe for centuries to come.

Whereas the experts are almost always white male professionals, the active, informed citizens more often reflect the diversity of America itself, with more women and people of color.[34] These citizens of the planet include 87-year-old Peg McIntire (on the right in fig. 5.8), at a demonstration at Cape Canaveral in Florida; others in the Florida Coalition for Peace and Justice; and people around the world. To paraphrase Margaret Mead, never doubt that a small group of committed citizens can change the world; indeed, it is the only thing that ever has. Why do too many people today mistakenly believe that one ordinary person can't make a difference? One reason lies in the message tacitly built into the very form of even a good news program like *60 Minutes:* your voice doesn't count, because this is an argument among experts. Peg McIntire was not quoted or even identified in the *60 Minutes* report and probably would never have been shown demonstrating on CBS if there had not been an expert like Gofman to legitimate her protest. As Bill Nichols puts it, "Those who neither address us nor address those who address us (through interviews) are the truly dispossessed. . . . Not all sights are equal in the eye of the camera, or of television news."[35]

Declining Attention to News:
A Crisis in Democratic Discourse

Justifiably suspicious of the unearned authority of seemingly unmediated images and sounds, television news erects its own hierarchy of authority to mediate and explain them. But this mediating hierarchy serves less the public interest of informing viewers and more the private network interest of personalizing, managing, and profiting from the news.

In the process, the concerns and experience of most ordinary people, relegated to the bottom of this hierarchy, are not addressed in the current form of television news. The formal hierarchy in television news' address to and positioning of its viewers undoubtedly contributes to a more widely reported dissatisfaction with its content. Network news is steadily losing viewers just as newspapers are losing readers. Americans increasingly find the news media generally, and television journalists specifically, to be arrogant, sensationalistic, and cynical.[36] In a terrible downward spiral that degrades both the news and the publics it is supposed to inform, television news responds to flat or declining revenues by becoming more commercial, focusing on celebrities and eye-catching graphics, thus driving away at least some viewers and breeding cynicism and ignorance among those who remain.

The form of television news contributes to this crisis. Form is the symptom of unstated assumptions, the trace of everyday ideological practices. Instead of promoting citizen involvement in public affairs, the hierarchy of commodified stars, experts, and mediators shuts us out, and we become bystanders and consumers in a democracy without citizens.[37] Instead of contextualizing experience and information, television news decontextualizes, providing too many short, disconnected segments, factoids, and sound bites. We need help connecting our personal experience and private lives with the larger public and political world, and television news in too many cases obscures that relation.

A prominent example is national politics. Television journalists are our unelected representatives, supposedly asking the questions we need answered in order to be informed citizens. The mediating hierarchy analyzed above serves democratic purposes only if it continually justifies the authority delegated to it by the public and the audience. But because of commercial pressures and the growing insularity of celebrity journalism, television news, even more than the media generally, has decided that news "consumers" want presidential and other newsworthy political campaigns covered as if they were horse races or political games. While out in the country ignorance of the issues, confusion, anger, and alienation from the political process grow to dangerous levels, television and other journalists keep insisting they're giving us what we want.

However, James Fallows shows that "when ordinary citizens have a chance to pose questions to political leaders, they rarely ask about the game of politics. They mainly want to know how the reality of politics will affect them—through taxes, programs, scholarship funds, wars."[38] Is it possible that the "demand" to cover politics as a game, like the "demand" for journalists to become celebrities and journalism personalized, derives more than a little from supply? Multinational corporations like Westinghouse, General Electric, and Disney now own the broadcast and cable networks, as detailed in chapter 2. They increase pressures to make news divisions profitable, have been known to censor stories of corporate wrongdoing such as tobacco company cover-ups and defective equipment in GE nuclear plants, and use the news and the rest of the network to sell their products and represent their interests.[39] Are the most powerful corporations on the planet, which routinely manipulate the policies of national governments, merely passive and democratic reflectors, servants of the desires of the news or any other audience? Or is it primarily their needs being met by the supply of news and infotainment, our demand that must adjust to their supply—or go elsewhere?

C-SPAN, public television (sometimes), some cable access, and many newspapers, magazines, and on-line sources and forums provide public and non- or less commercial alternatives. But commercialized journalism must constantly work to marginalize or co-opt these, must try to rechannel the frustration, alienation, and anger generated in part by its own conventions into new but equally commercial conventions. Robin Andersen points out that "the new cheap formats of tabloid television, the news magazines, and 'reality' dramatization formats featuring 'real' people, together with talk shows," have in the last decade or so been in part a response to viewers' need for new televisual forms for public involvement and expression of experience.[40] They have in common an elimination or radical modification of the role of the anchor, narrator, or host, usually to give at least the impression that real life or more popular concerns are being addressed. These new genres mutate and rise and fall quickly in popularity, and they are often more exploitative and commercialized than traditional television news, but they also speak to unmet needs for popular participation, frank discussion of public issues, and taking stands on those issues.

The media frenzy in late 1997 prompted by the death of Princess Diana Spencer well illustrates this dynamic and contradictory process. The media both articulated and exploited the popular outpouring of grief at Diana's death. Issues emerged of responsibility for the car accident that killed her, of her role as spokesperson for charities and other campaigns on a world stage, of the proper role, even the legitimacy of British royalty. These issues crossed and blended the public and private realms in complex ways. Other, deeper problems were largely unaddressed, such as the commercial forces driving the international celebrity system that created the mythology of Diana's life and death.

Such media spectacles, in addition to their more obvious private or emotional dimensions, in many ways represent desperate attempts by millions of people to have conversations about public problems and issues—to form public spheres, one of the conditions of democracy—in a private, commercial system designed to turn those problems and issues into commodities. As George Gerbner puts it, we've got stories to tell in a media system designed by and for "a handful of global conglomerates with something to sell."[41]

The conventions of television news as nonfiction realism in direct address are precisely that—conventions, tacit agreements between makers and viewers. Perhaps many viewers are unhappy with this tacit agreement and wish to renegotiate it. Perhaps it doesn't seem so real or so useful anymore. More ominously, some people are losing interest in public and political life generally. Certainly the authoritative—and authoritarian—voice of conventional wisdom in direct address helps limit public discussion to the narrow constraints of elite interests. We need a wider range of participants in our public and political life, and the hierarchical structure of the conventional realism of television news is part of the problem.

Beyond Realisms: Freeways, Malls, Television, and the Net

This chapter has analyzed two kinds of realism that together account for much of what we see and hear on television. However, these realisms, and nonrealist programming like music videos and animation, are embedded within and framed by a larger discourse that is far from realist. This larger television discourse consists of a flow of apparently heterogeneous fragments, a montage or collage of program segments, commercials, and promotions, some realist, some not. The experience of watching television only intermittently resembles the experience of looking at realist images as if they were windows on the world. Even less often is it like reading realist stories or novels, which tell unified and plausible stories about worlds much like our own. And when realist movies are shown on television, recut, reframed, and segmented by commercials, they become part of television's discourse. That is, they become like everything else, fragments in the discursive flow, part of some new and very different metadiscourse constructed through the combined choices of programmers, advertisers, and you with a remote control. We will explore this flow more in the next chapter. Here we will trace some characteristics of this flow that fragments and reframes television discourse in decidedly nonrealist directions.

The vastly increased speed of modern transportation and communication, the rise of consumption as a way of life, and other major historical developments have made television increasingly central to everyday life in contemporary market societies. As Margaret Morse has suggested, "Freeways, malls, and television are the locus of an attenuated *fiction effect,* that is, a partial loss of touch with the here and now, dubbed here as *distraction.* This semifiction effect is akin to but not identical with split belief—knowing a representation is not real, but nevertheless momentarily closing off the here and now and sinking into another world—promoted within the apparatuses of the theater, the cinema, and the novel."[42] If innovative fiction depends on a clear but often complex relation between two well-defined worlds, real and imaginary, the experience of freeways, malls, and television often exists in some nonspace in between, displaced or separated from one's surroundings.[43] Driving on a freeway, shopping in a mall, and watching television can create a similar kind of "zombie effect," "vegging out" by losing the sense of place and time, being somehow *elsewhere,* semialert but distracted.[44] The freeway driver hurtles past an often abstracted landscape, floating disengaged from the real places behind the glass windows of the car. The mall shopper strolls through a synthetic consumer environment, past glass shop windows displaying fantasy dramas of acquisition. The television viewer remains stationary but can seem to move through space and time before worlds summoned to the glass screen by remote control. As chapter 1 shows, these forms of "mobile privatization" are historically linked. In all three, "a 'bubble' of subjective here and now strolls or speeds about in the midst of elsewhere," with everyday experience commercialized by billboards, store windows, and TV ads.[45] "The freeway is what makes it possible to drive coast to coast and never see anything"; the mall is a "TV you can walk around in."[46]

The Internet suggests new analogies with this contemporary triumvirate of the not-quite-real. We speak of channel surfing and surfing the Net, as if riding the board from wave to wave resembled riding the remote from channel to channel or the mouse from Web site to Web site. Microsoft's Windows programs, many video games, and other software are designed to give the computer screen a third dimension through the illusion of depth. This brings cyberspace closer to diegetic space, a Window onto a semireal world with color, movement, sound—and ads. As multinational corporations organize the partial convergence of microcomputers and television, they commercialize the Net with proliferating ads, ever in search of the fugitive attention of those with the most disposable income.[47]

Beyond Realisms: Televisuality, Reflexivity, and Intertextuality

As television was developing its own distinctive forms in the fifties and sixties, it moved more slowly than it does now, and commercials were more likely to be little realist narratives, 30-second versions of the programs with the product as hero. But as commercial pressures increased, ads became faster and denser, promotions more frequent and more strident, and even programs picked up the pace. This produced "clutter," ads, promotions, and programs elbowing one another in competition for viewers' increasingly jaded attention, which made it necessary to "break through the clutter" with even more cleverly attention-getting clutter. This dynamic continues today, but in the eighties and nineties the stakes rose dramatically. Cable began to offer the three major networks their first real competition, and every channel had to work harder to differentiate itself. Perhaps more important, the widespread use of remotes for grazing and zapping, and VCRs for time shifting and playing prerecorded tapes, gave viewers more control over what they watch.

The result was what John Caldwell calls televisuality. To keep viewers' attention on the images and their fingers away from remote controls, ads, promotions, even many programs became more stylized and aestheticized.[48] In a culture in which most television remains cheap and devalued compared with feature films, especially to sought-after upper-middle-class viewers, some new series began to look and sound more like Hollywood movies. Shows like *Miami Vice*, *Moonlighting*, and *thirtysomething* beginning in the eighties, and *Northern Exposure* (discussed in chapter 6) and *NYPD Blue* in the nineties, possessed distinctive cinematic visual styles or writing (or both) that many saw as qualitatively superior to most television writing.[49]

However, this cinematic version of televisual stylization remains less visible than the other strategy, the videographic, which often self-consciously flaunts its style and is, more important, cheaper.[50] New computer imaging technology make possible videographic televisuality through the digital compositing of images and graphics from several sources into a single synthetic video image.

Until the early eighties, much of the discourse of television itself, all those network and station identifications, introductory and credit sequences, promotions, and other transitions that became the tacit background frame within which programs and ads were placed—these had been relatively plain and sober, even realist in style. Now the words on the screen shone, whirled, and flew through three-dimensional space, as if the camera were flying through gigantic orbiting letters, the viewer traveling in space rather than sitting in front of the television.[51] Combined with fast, brassy music, this videographic style signified excitement,

FIGURE 5.9

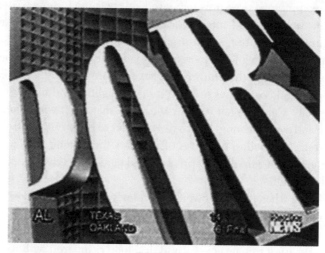

FIGURE 5.10

FIGURE 5.11

FIGURE 5.12

speed, and efficiency. Figures 5.9, 5.10, and 5.11 capture three moments in a single unfolding "shot," the televisual signature of CNN Headline Sports in 1997.[52] Here the illusion of three-dimensional space includes not only the deep space through the screen as window but also the offscreen space on all sides of the viewer as well. The smooth and coordinated movement of all these graphic elements comes to signify not realism but the command and control over space and time, the smooth professionalism of the network itself.

In the eighties and nineties, as channels proliferated and the audience fragmented, more programmers were dividing the same size pie. Budgets were tight. But computer graphics were relatively cheap, so that even public service announcements could make one image seem to peel off, leaving another behind it, as in figure 5.12.[53] Digital compositing could also place a new car into a chariot race in what seemed to be a silent film, as in the Pontiac commercial in figure 5.13.[54] The placement of the new and modern car (in bright green) into the conventionalized ancient setting (in black and white) drew attention to the artificiality of the image itself in a conspicuous display of technical prowess. Even when such stylization emphasized the three-dimensional depth of the image, it still flaunted its synthetic and nonrealist qualities. With televisuality, the flow of commercial television moved decisively away from the relatively serious and temperate realism of its beginnings. Visual style came to the fore at the expense of narrative and argument, and style became playful, self-conscious, and reflexive (about itself), even exhibitionistic.[55] Where these traits had once been outrageous, the province of modernist and avant-garde art, they now became attempts to manipulate viewers' attention.

Television has become increasingly reflexive in a different way as well. In addition to drawing attention to style, even to its own constructedness, television also has begun to refer more and more to itself, with programs and ads referring to other programs and ads, to genre conventions, and generally to information you can only get by watching television.[56]

As noted in chapter 4, we make sense of texts not through comparing them with unmediated reality but largely through comparing them with other texts or culturally conventionalized knowledge. Thus every text makes sense through its

FIGURE 5.13

placement in a network of other texts, through the codes and conventions and references that connect these texts in webs of *intertextuality*. Since the eighties, television's intertextuality has been increasingly limited to its own texts. Vanna White, who appears on *Wheel of Fortune*, shows up on *L.A. Law* to date one of the partners. *Entertainment Tonight* reports gossip about the fictional characters on *Murphy Brown* during an episode of the latter show, treating the characters as if they were real. Characters from *Cheers* appear on *Jeopardy* and *Wings*, while characters from *St. Elsewhere* go for a drink at *Cheers*. Oprah Winfrey and Connie Chung play themselves in brief appearances on several fictional programs.[57]

With these and other intertextual strategies, television rewards us for watching television. The more we watch, the more we "get it." The information we get from watching becomes not just trivia but useful and valuable social currency, connecting us to a larger imaginary television community. It connects us also to those real people with whom conversations about television can become the beginning or sustenance of friendship and the basis of a common culture.[58] Meanwhile people keep watching, the ratings stay high, and the commercial machine keeps rolling.[59]

Television's deliberate confusion of the fictional and nonfictional is only a symptom of larger problems. Through its increasingly dense network of self-references, television becomes an environment rather than a medium. It seems to give us the world, to provide access to whole realms of entertainment, pleasure, and knowledge beyond our immediate life space. But what vital information, what worlds and realities are missing from the world according to television? "Certainly," Robin Andersen notes, "the nonfictions and fictions critical of the corporate practices that dominate the media and the lives of most Americans are omitted."[60] As television selects and translates everything outside itself into its all-consuming and self-referential system, not only information is lost. Alternative frames of reference, public and noncommercial cultures, and ways of living sustainably with the earth are marginalized, made invisible. We need to hear the voice of experience of Peg McIntire, protesting the militarization of space at Cape Canaveral, Florida, as well as the experts and network correspondents. These ways of living, these other frames of reference can make most of television seem a waste of time or worse. Television's fiction and nonfiction "realisms" as well as its nonrealist televisual and reflexive framing discourses work to shut out these alternatives. Respect for biological and cultural diversity demands attention to life beyond commercial culture.

FURTHER READING

Allen, Robert C., ed. *Channels of Discourse, Reassembled: Television and Contemporary Criticism.* 2d ed. Chapel Hill: University of North Carolina Press, 1992.

Andersen, Robin. *Consumer Culture and TV Programming.* Boulder, Colo.: Westview, 1995.

Brook, James, and Iain A. Boal, eds. *Resisting the Virtual Life: The Culture and Politics of Information.* San Francisco: City Lights, 1995.

Caldwell, John Thornton. *Televisuality: Style, Crisis, and Authority in American Television.* New Brunswick, N.J.: Rutgers University Press, 1995.

Fallows, James. *Breaking the News: How the Media Undermine American Democracy.* New York: Pantheon, 1996.

Gerbner, George, Hamid Mowlana, and Herbert I. Schiller, eds. *Invisible Crises: What Conglomerate Control of Media Means for America and the World.* Boulder, Colo.: Westview, 1996.

Grossman, Karl. *The Wrong Stuff: The Space Program's Nuclear Threat to Our Planet.* Monroe, Maine: Common Courage Press, 1997.

Morse, Margaret. "An Ontology of Everyday Distraction: The Freeway, the Mall, and Television." In *Logics of Television: Essays in Cultural Criticism,* edited by Patricia Mellencamp, 193–221. Bloomington: Indiana University Press, 1990.

———. "The Television News Personality and Credibility: Reflections on the News in Transition." In *Studies in Entertainment: Critical Approaches to Mass Culture,* edited by Tania Modleski, 55–79. Bloomington: Indiana University Press, 1986.

Nichols, Bill. *Ideology and the Image.* Bloomington: Indiana University Press, 1981.

CHAPTER SIX

The Flow of Commodities

Northern Exposure debuted on CBS in July 1990 for a summer season of eight episodes. The network brought the show back for another seven in spring 1991 and broadcast first-run episodes through spring 1995, with syndication beginning in fall 1994. Cable distribution began in fall 1997, with a twice-a-day run on the upscale Arts & Entertainment Network. *Northern Exposure*'s producers were alumni from MTM—the television studio that made its mark in the 1970s and 1980s with *The Mary Tyler Moore Show, The Bob Newhart Show, Lou Grant, Hill Street Blues,* and *St. Elsewhere. Northern Exposure* was in the early 1990s likely the leading example on the air of MTM's enduring demographic legacy: "quality television." [1] In chapter 5, we associated quality television with quirkiness. Within the industry, quality means programs whose script and performance design draw particularly affluent viewers, who broadcasters in turn can sell to advertisers at premium rates. To viewers of these shows, the term offers a seal of approval marking their cultural superiority. [2] The characters in such narratives tend to be written and directed with multiple and contradictory traits, more like *Masterpiece Theatre* than *Married . . . with Children.* Accordingly, co-creator John Falsey described the show as "character-driven." To the show's other creator, Joshua Brand, this emphasis on character made the show more "European." Less realist shows from the same period but more in touch with contemporary arts in Europe as well as North America, shows like *Twin Peaks* and *Wild Palms,* tended to put off part of this quality audience. They were derided by some as "boutique programming" with "flat" characters. Although all three shows included bizarre imagery, what made *Northern Exposure* different was that as a character-driven show, such imagery was invariably in service to an ostensible emotional truth about a character, as if the character preexisted the show. One of *Northern Exposure*'s producers, Matthew Nodella, said the difference between *Northern Exposure* and *Twin Peaks* was that "we're real and they're not." [3]

Northern Exposure began as a series about a Jewish doctor from New York assigned to Cicely, a small (and fictional) Alaskan town with its share of colorful characters, to work off his $125,000 medical school debt over four years. The show's similarity with *Twin Peaks,* which was at the height of its initial popularity as *Northern Exposure* was being prepared for debut, gradually diminished. The doctor and his not-feeling-at-home sensibility were decentered in favor of a gentler ensemble "dramedy," industry lingo for sitcoms with heart. In short, it became less like *Twin Peaks* and more like an hour-long, more dramatic version of that multibillion-dollar quality program *M*A*S*H*—only, befitting the change in generations, more multicultural, more fantastic, a bit less male, and with a sense of humor perhaps less visible but certainly more awry.

The affluent, middle-highbrow sensibility of *Northern Exposure* was most explicit in the May 18, 1992, episode, "Cicely," which ended the second full season and was extraordinarily lesbian-friendly and antipatriarchal by the standards of commercial television. Its story was that the town had gained its identity in 1909, guided by Roslyn and Cicely, two upper-class progressive women from Montana, a couple looking for what the Roslyn character calls a haven for the "human spirit," the "freedom to express our love, our art, the freedom to be who we want to be," just before she is shot and killed for her trouble. By fall 1994, advertisers were paying upwards of $225,000 for 30 seconds of *Northern Exposure* (not counting the cost of making the commercial), at the time a bit above the median for a prime-time, major network show.[4]

What do we watch when we watch commercial television? Newspaper TV listings, *TV Guide,* and most critics of the medium present television as a series of programs, one following another. Yet no one encounters commercial television in this way. When we turn on the set, we see a pastiche of materials, each flowing into the next, oblivious of program boundaries. This is especially true at the beginning and end of programs. Chart 6.1 lists some of what happened during the 10 minutes around the opening of *Northern Exposure* on July 4, 1994, as it was broadcast on the CBS affiliate in West Palm Beach, Florida. Each of these moments could be divided further into separate shots, just as we broke down the Cascade commercial in chapter 4. Here we shall show how the seemingly separate elements of this flow work toward the institutional project we outlined in chapters 2 and 3, to bundle audiences for sale to Procter & Gamble and other advertisers. This project has side effects that may be as hazardous to our environmental health as anything programs or commercials accomplish in themselves.

Perhaps we should warn you: *Northern Exposure* and its ads were meant to be seen on television, not read about in a book. Although reading what follows may not be as entertaining as watching it on TV, having these excerpts in print with examples so easily available to review should enable a close analysis not possible as the images go by. Perhaps the devil *is* in the details.

TV Guide in its July 2, 1994, issue described the episode, known as "Heal Thyself" and originally broadcast November 15, 1993, this way: "Shaman-in-training Ed diagnoses a patient (Kimberly Norris) who then falls for him, but his low self-esteem brings a visit from the demon Green Man (Phil Fondacaro). Meanwhile, Holling's tomfoolery gets him thrown out of Shelly's Lamaze class; and Maggie misses the camaraderie of the local coin-laundry after buying a washer-dryer. Leonard: Graham Greene. Phil: Jared Rushton." Other cast information not provided by *TV Guide:* Ed is played by Darren E. Burrows. Holling is played by John Cullum. Shelly is played by Cynthia Geary. Maggie is played by Janine Turner. Dr. Joel Fleischman is played by Rob Morrow.

Our purpose is to make visible the structural patterns within the flow of television, to demonstrate the sorts of connections *available* for viewers to make. These connections have several levels. Here are just a few you might notice as you go through chart 6.1's 10 minutes:

The most obvious:

- The CBS Eye logo (shots 4, 6, 7, 8, 9, and 13).
- The fireworks (shots 5 and 11).
- Rob Morrow's voice (in *Northern Exposure* and the MasterCard International ad).

Less obvious:

- The AT&T character as a soft masculine type, echoed in *Love & War,* *Northern Exposure,* and other ads (shots 1, 2, 4, 7, 35, 36, and, in a Burger King ad later in the show, 54 and 55—Sensitive New Age Guys one and all).
- The doctor as medical authority in the Aleve ad and, in Darren Burrows's, Graham Greene's, and Rob Morrow's characters, in the episode of *Northern Exposure.*[5]

The least obvious:

- Graphic matches between the rough-hewn lettering of *Northern Exposure* and that in ads for Taco Bell and Burger King (shots 16, 22, 51, and 56).[6]

The more abstract:

- The configuration of multiculturalism in *Northern Exposure* and in several ads (MasterCard International, shot 46; Taco Bell, shot 53; and Burger King, shot 57).
- The direct address and voice-over narration in the commercials, which might well resonate with moments on news and talk shows as well as with other ads.

Consider the volume and variety of signifiers involved in these 10 minutes alone. Much happens here, and much wealth rides on it. Although not all of the potential connections are planned, advertisers and broadcasters do limit the range of possible images to those they believe will function effectively with the audience both want to reach and hold. According to Edwin L. Artzt, board chair and CEO of Procter & Gamble at the time of the broadcast, corporations spend $5 billion a year on the spots *between* programs alone. This flow of materials continues throughout *Northern Exposure,* throughout the night and day. Yet this flow, which seems made up of disparate items, is only apparently heterogeneous. The individual items share means as well as aims, as we shall show. It is this similarity of purpose and means, drawing on similar cultural images to reach similar demographic groups, that accounts for the similarities noted above—that and occasional coincidence and idiosyncrasy. What advertisers want is access to our minds for their commercials. In return, they give us commercial television, and, though other effects may vary, we unfailingly give them our limited *time.*

In that sense, commercials do not interrupt programs. Rather, programs exist to position viewers to receive ads. Channel surfing can defeat this, but the way most people watch television most of the time, hands off the remote, might more aptly be likened to tubing a river, leisurely moving through the pleasant parts to be delivered now and then to the commercial rapids, where the real business of

CHART 6.1. FLOW CHART

Program:
- 9:55:00 P.M.

Love & War (a sitcom). Jack (Jay Thomas) and Dana (Annie Potts) fight and flirt over whether to have sex at the end of their first date (shot 1).

Commercials:
- 9:57:00

AT&T offers True Savings and Your True Voice. An animated ad featuring a shaggily dressed, curly-haired, 30something man—not unlike Jack in *Love & War*, or Joel in *Northern Exposure*—wearing earth tones, backed by pop-jazzy music similar to that in *Love & War* (shot 2).

- 9:57:30

McDonald's offers "Super Size Free" (shot 3).

- 9:58:00

A promotional teaser.
"Next! . . . Is Holling comfortable with the facts of life? . . . *Northern Exposure*." *Northern Exposure* theme music heard throughout; a small CBS Eye visible through most (shot 4).

- 9:58:10

A promotion for *Late Night with David Letterman*.
"Tonight! Spend your 4th with an all-new Dave." Fireworks (shot 5).

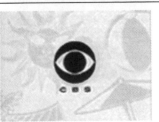

- 9:58:15

CBS Eye billboard (shot 6).

CHART 6.1. (*continued*)

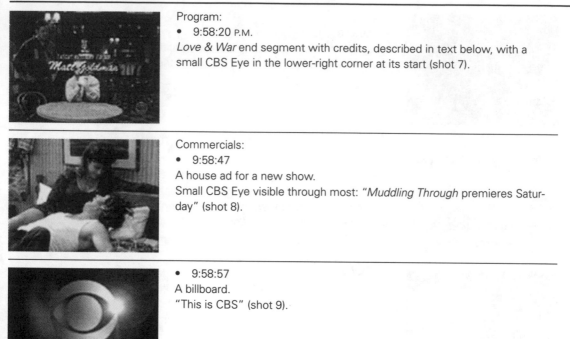

Program:
- 9:58:20 P.M.

Love & War end segment with credits, described in text below, with a small CBS Eye in the lower-right corner at its start (shot 7).

Commercials:
- 9:58:47

A house ad for a new show.
Small CBS Eye visible through most: "*Muddling Through* premieres Saturday" (shot 8).

- 9:58:57

A billboard.
"This is CBS" (shot 9).

- 9:59:00

Local ad: Rooms to Go (shot 10).

- 9:59:30

Local ad: "It's the Dodge 4th of July celebration. . . . Marvel at the power of Dodge Ram. . . . You'll be in awe of Dodge Dakota Sport. So hurry to the Dodge 4th of July celebration." Fireworks explode noisily throughout (shot 11).

- 10:00:00

Local promo: "The Tuesday forecast and the outlook for the week at 11" (shot 12).

Program:
- 10:00:05

Program begins announced only by a high-pitched sound and the CBS surround sound logo, with the small CBS Eye in corner (shot 13).

This is a crucial moment for any program; the threat of channel changing is high.
Non-western Muzak, with flute and drum and maracalike percussion.
Animal noises, wilderness sights, perhaps they are Ed's dream (shot 14).

Inside, Leonard persuades Ed, whom he has awakened, to help heal Bonnie. Leonard (tag line): "No one is ever ready" (shot 15). With that line, viewers interested in the story are presumably hooked.

- 10:01:35

Northern Exposure credits begin.
Music: Westernized World Music, with harmonica, bass, and African drum, could be a lost cut from Paul Simon's "Graceland."
Credit design: floating white letters, as if hand-carved (shot 16).

Shots of town just after dawn, moose walking through (shot 17).

Some shots are from moose's point of view (shot 18).

CHART 6.1. (*continued*)

Shot of wall with side painted "Roslyn's Cafe," with a picture of a camel in the desert and "An Oasis" underneath (shot 19).

Just before the credits end, the moose crosses in front of the sign and at one moment is positioned in the same spot as the camel, which it resembles, as if the moose were the camel, and Cicely, the oasis (shot 20). Credits end with moose walking offscreen left.

Commercials
• 10:02:20
Cut to black and brief silence.
Cut to black with "*Northern Exposure*" filling screen and theme music resuming, but at lower volume, as a male announcer (with deep announcer voice) says: "*Northern Exposure*" (shot 21).

• 10:02:30
Name starts to dissolve.
Same announcer says: "Sponsored by Tide" [a Procter & Gamble product] as dissolve continues into concentric-circled center of Tide box, with several seconds of *Northern Exposure*/Tide overlap (shot 22).

(Shot 23.)

Below the Tide name, it says, "If it's got to be clean, it's got to be Tide" (shot 24).
The announcer continues: "For your tough laundry problems, if it's gotta be clean, it's gotta be Tide."
Northern Exposure theme music, which has continued throughout, rises to volume of credit sequence as Tide fades to black.

- 10:02:45

Another box, along with a bag of Tide.

A different announcer, with a similar announcer voice: "Now Tide comes in a refill bag . . . It's 80 percent less trash, and less money, too. The new Tide refill bag. If it's gotta be clean, it's gotta be Tide."

On-screen appear the words: "If it's got to be clean, it's got to be Tide" (shot 25).

- 10:03:00

Aleve Drug for Pain [a Procter & Gamble product]. A young woman speaks to a camera offscreen, as if she were being interviewed (shot 26).

"She's not your typical mother. Not one to let her pain"—

Cut to shot of her mother in swimsuit, positioned where her daughter was in the frame, goggles around her neck, rubbing her shoulder (shot 27).

Cut to shots of the mother diving and swimming (shot 28).

—"keep her from doing, or swimming, or living her life."

But when other pain remedies don't work, "It's time to call a doctor, time to ask a doctor what you need."

Male voice (more soothing than in previous ads) over picture of hand opening Aleve as images of Aleve and its prescription-only predecessor are graphically matched and intercut (shot 29).

(Shot 30.)

CHART 6.1. (*continued*)

(Shot 31.)

"Introducing Aleve, nonprescription strength of Anaprox . . ."
The daughter and her mother are shown together, with the mother now in the same place she and her daughter had sequentially occupied in earlier shots, looking at and being looked at by her daughter, who is on the left side of the screen, addressing the camera (shot 32; compare with shots 26 and 27).

"She is one tough lady," says the daughter. "I'm not so tough," says the mother, now rubbing her daughter's shoulders as she had earlier rubbed her own, as the mother takes care of the daughter who had earlier worried about her pain. The Aleve logo reappears, then becomes the Aleve box. The announcer has the last word, aural reinforcing visual: "New Aleve. All day strong. All day long" (shot 33).

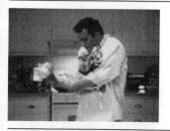

• 10:03:45
Cascade laundry detergent [a Procter & Gamble product]. This ad—analyzed in detail in chapter 4—has a structure similar to that of the last. It opens with another young woman speaking, though here she faces the camera directly: "I think women should share household chores, don't you?" (shot 34).

Cut to shots of husband bumbling in kitchen, almost dropping dishes (shot 35—see how he resembles the males in shots 1, 2, and 4).

"I cook and my husband Bill does the dishes. He's terrific at it. He always scrapes the plates and he never, ever overloads." Bill is pale, unkempt, and inept, licking plates, overstuffing the dishwasher—a far cry from the hints of crisp male professionalism of the doctor, the pharmacist, the voice-over in the previous ad. Or in this one, for no sooner does the woman's speech stop than another male narrator comes in: "No matter who does the dishes, Cascade does the dirty work . . ." The P&G product brings the pair together, as it did in the previous ad (shot 36).

• 10:04:15
MasterCard brings the world together.
The narrator is Rob Morrow, star of *Northern Exposure* but unidentified here. He speaks in the sometimes hesitant voice of his character: "Here's the thing." Whip pan across empty stadium to hand holding MasterCard with World Cup logo, empty stands behind (shot 37).

(Shot 38.)

"It's a credit card. It won't bring the world together."
Swish pan/cut to filled stands (shot 39).

"Actually, maybe it will."
Cut to close shots of soccer played on field (shot 40).
"I mean MasterCard is an official sponsor of the 1994 World Cup."

Cut to shot of three young men with faces painted in black/white that rhymes with soccer ball (shot 41).

"So soccer fans from all over the world will be coming to America."
Cut to shots of fans coded to be read from different continents/countries/ cultures, including three males wearing funny hats shaped like soccer balls. "Nothing brings people together like silly hats" (shot 42).

CHART 6.1. (*continued*)

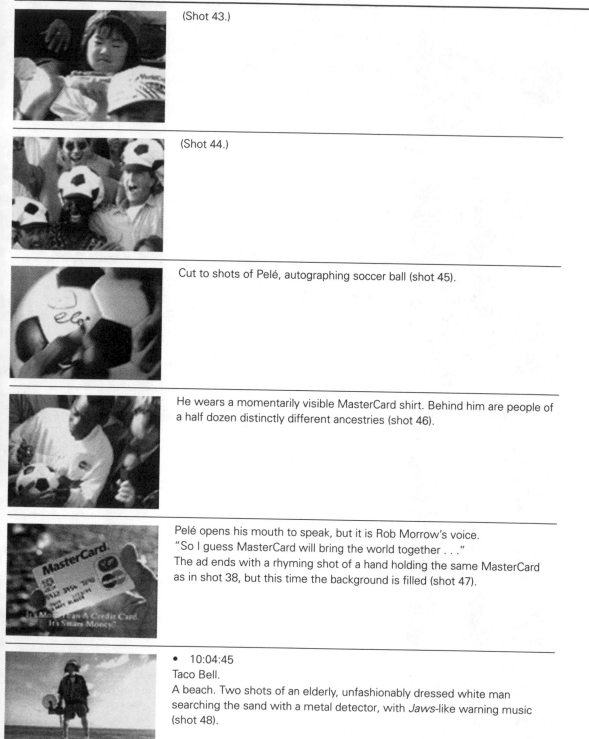

(Shot 43.)

(Shot 44.)

Cut to shots of Pelé, autographing soccer ball (shot 45).

He wears a momentarily visible MasterCard shirt. Behind him are people of a half dozen distinctly different ancestries (shot 46).

Pelé opens his mouth to speak, but it is Rob Morrow's voice. "So I guess MasterCard will bring the world together . . ." The ad ends with a rhyming shot of a hand holding the same MasterCard as in shot 38, but this time the background is filled (shot 47).

• 10:04:45
Taco Bell.
A beach. Two shots of an elderly, unfashionably dressed white man searching the sand with a metal detector, with *Jaws*-like warning music (shot 48).

A gong, as a Taco Bell bag (with a bell in its logo) fills the screen, held by a black man (shot 49).

Cut to a young white man biting into a taco (shot 50).

A loud crunch, and a cut to the elderly man jolted by the sound.
The upbeat music and voice sound as if Cheech Marin were singing a tourist Caribbean version of 1960s beach music.
In tropical yellow, red, and green, value prices fill screen, a computerized imitation of a hand-lettered sign (shot 51; compare with the *Northern Exposure* sign in shot 16 and Burger King sign in shot 56).

The price signs alternate with beach scenes of swim-suited young people, most of them northern European–looking, some eating tacos (shot 52).

A beach buggy moving between two artificial palm trees, under a color-coordinated sign, "Cross the Border" (shot 53).
The singer ends with a shout: "Cross the Border!"
(End of 10-minute segment)

- Later in the program.
Burger King commercial (see text for discussion).
The commercial begins in a crowded Burger King where a staff member begins singing a catchy song ("The Lion Sleeps Tonight") featured in the Disney production of *Lion King,* then in theaters. Other staff and customers join in. Song runs throughout.
Father sings and clowns with kids as they eat. Cups have *Lion King* motif (shot 54).

CHART 6.1. *(continued)*

Customer grabs cashier's microphone and wails out chorus (shot 55).

Close-up of Kid's Meal with *Lion King* motif and free *Lion King* toy (shot 56).

Final scene is of customers and staff joined in line dancing to music. Burger King logo appears in lower right corner (shot 57).

the trip takes place. This flow continues wherever people watch commercial television, altered by the specifics of whatever else people happen to be doing at the time. The different cultural references people bring to television also affect flow.

Flow works in four ways that we shall analyze in this chapter:

- as network practice to gather and hold viewers for sale;
- as one form advanced capitalist society takes, here in the commercial television system;
- as the movement of commercialized meanings within and between television texts and between television and its audiences; but also
- as a site from which can be pulled out texts for critical analysis, analysis that enables members of the audience to understand how commercial culture works. At the right moment, such analysis might also make visible a connection between contesting commercial culture politically and reconstructing a sustainable cultural and natural environment.[7]

Networks try to preserve the flow of audiences. Programmers have no professional interest in the content of individual flows of meaning. Their interest lies in affecting viewer channel changing to their advantage, in defending against other choices and distractions. Susan Eastman has put it well: "They try to maximize the number that *flow through* to the next program on their channel and the number that *flow in* from rival channels or home video, at the same time minimizing the number that *flow away* to competing channels or activities" (emphasis in original).[8] *Flow away* must be avoided at all costs, whether caused by boredom, discomfort, or incoherence. Hence the contradictory drive for so much television to skirt sensation while remaining bland, looking stylish but not too stylized, seeming fresh but not offensive. The networks plan each evening's schedule to emphasize *flow through* and attract *flow in*. This is true as well of such advertising-dependent cable services as Lifetime and A&E.

Although commercial broadcasters uniformly seek to maintain the flow of viewers into their ratings as commodities they can sell, at different times they seek to sell different demographic packages. Consequently, flows differ according to targeted audiences.[9] Monday night on CBS in 1993–1994, for example, was couples situation comedy night (*Evening Shade* to *Dave's World* to *Murphy Brown* to *Love & War* to the dramedy *Northern Exposure*), aimed at viewers (mostly women but also men) uninterested in the more masculine Monday night football on ABC or the heavier TV and theatrical movies or more youth-oriented, gag comedy series on NBC or Fox.[10] Unlike much educational and public television in the world, in which separate programs are scheduled for different groups of viewers across an evening, U.S. commercial television aims to hold its audience as long as it can, ideally habituating people to certain scheduling routines (It's Monday night! *Murphy Brown* and *Northern Exposure*!), all the while advertising its succession of ostensibly separate program experiences.

Barry Diller, head of QVC and a former Fox executive, has made this explicit: "The trick going way up through the '60s, '70s, some of the '80s—even now, to some degree—was flow. Could you get them and keep them?" As more viewers had remote control devices, maintaining flow became more difficult, according to Diller. "What changed was that now you didn't have to get up."[11] So the remote becomes a site of struggle, though within the boundaries of the environment television offers. Spurred by advertisers, the networks wrestle against viewers' potential desire to design flows for themselves. In this, the networks' interests may not always coincide with those of advertisers, who care only that their ads are seen at appropriate times—no matter the network. "The point is to try to keep the viewer's thumb off that remote-control button," says Ted Harbert, president of ABC Entertainment.[12] Promos such as the 10-second *Northern Exposure* spot before the coda of *Love & War* ("Next! Is Holling comfortable with the facts of life?"—an enigma that requires watching the show to solve yet also depends on viewers already caught up in the show, viewers who recognize the name and the story line and in so doing construct themselves as part of the *Northern Exposure* audience)—and the 10-second preview of the Fourth of July Letterman show constitute traditional ways networks try to maintain flow from program to program.

Researchers say the most powerful force shaping audience choice of programs is inertia, for absent compelling reasons to switch, audiences tend to remain where they are. Since, as Diller says, they require less effort than getting up and selecting a new channel, remote control devices lower the threshold of desire necessary for change. Network research shows that as many as one-quarter of all viewers can be lost during a commercial, and industry executives tremble at the thought that credits, theme songs, and station breaks constitute a call to millions of viewers that "surf's up."[13] Recently, the networks have been experimenting with new tactics for organizing material between programs to discourage channel changing.[14] We can see one such strategy at work in the *Northern Exposure* flows outlined above: at 10 P.M. the story begins without credits beyond the opening logos. We get a full 1 minute and 30 seconds of story that sets up another of the show's enigmas: Is Ed ready to heal Bonnie? Only *then* do we get 45 seconds of the standard weekly credits and introduction, and *then,* after this 2 minutes and 15 seconds of program, to pay for this 2 minutes and 15 seconds of program, we get nearly 3 minutes of commercials, seven ads in a row. This is a small-scale version of the decades-old network movie strategy. It involves showing perhaps 20–30 minutes of a movie without commercials to start—as the audience makes up its mind—and then stuffing them in tight as the movie is about to end, viewers already engaged. As viewers' commitment to the movie increases, so does the price TV exacts. Another new strategy shows up in the 27-second coda of *Love & War.* Audiences might be less likely to hit the remote during the half minute of contractually required closing credits if there were a comedy bit to watch at the same time, especially after 60 seconds of commercials and another 20 of previews. Here two characters stage a parody of a film noir police interrogation: Did Jack and Dana have sex? The extra effort put into what the industry calls "living end credits," which sometimes involve split screens, acts as insurance against switching away from the next show. Networks have also experimented with what they call "hot-switching," or the elimination of all ads, promos, and logos between shows. But too much of this may cost the networks more money in lost ad revenue than they might recoup by keeping viewers. There also have been reports that networks are pressuring producers to consider dropping opening title theme music, but this move is meeting with resistance as well.

Flow and the Political Economy

Flow is not only a network practice; it is also part of the culture's political economy—its intersections of state and private power, which structure distribution of opportunity, power, and wealth and define who can legitimately alter the environment and affect its governance. Although corporate executives do not conspire to bind viewers to the system, their separate acts work together in an overall *power flow* that attempts to channel the desires and thoughts of viewers in ways that serve the interests of capitalism and its commodified culture. They accomplish this even with programs that seem indifferent to or critical of this culture. Television does not advertise this power flow, nor is it listed in *TV Guide.* Like the self-conscious network practice of trying to channel viewer flow, its effects vary. Still, the more time people spend in front of the set, the more this flow becomes their cultural environment, leaving aside other potential influences found among friends and family, at the workplace, in the community. To see how flow relates to the political economy, however, we have to look closely at its specific elements and ask how they relate to similar elements in other spheres of life.

Months before the crucial moment of broadcast, the most important monetary exchange has already taken place, the sale of the commodity audience, or at least the image of the expected audience broadcasters market to advertisers. At the broadcast moment, there is an exchange involving time and, as we discussed in chapter 4, an exchange involving subjectivity. This exchange is not just a psychological process. It is an economic one as well. Advertisements add value to products by "reframing" their meanings.[15] Take the Taco Bell ad in the July 4, 1994, *Northern Exposure.* Taco Bell competes with home cooking and other national fast-food restaurants for customers looking for quick, inexpensive meals. Like its more expensive counterparts such as Chi-Chi's, it also surely makes it more difficult for small restaurants owned by people of Mexican descent, reducing diversity. Owned at the time by Pepsi-Cola, Taco Bell originally sold itself on its accessible exoticism: whatever its authenticity, in many towns in the United States, it was for years the only place one could buy prepared Mexican food. In a period in which money has been tight for more than 80 percent of the population, Taco Bell, like its growing number of competitors, has had to cut prices. This ad does more than promise inexpensive exoticism.

Taco Bell appears not as fast food from the cuisine of another country but as a product from that new, imaginary place that since the mid-1990s has increasingly been a part of the national consciousness, the Multicultural Mall. There difference exists for the pleasure of consumers, offering a cornucopia of diverse and international products every day, each item with sufficient marks of a geographic place to appear to be from *someplace* but with enough reassuring familiarity to ensure that it is from *no place* at all. The Multicultural Mall works at "maintaining the particularity of diverse groups while simultaneously unifying such differences" in the similarity of food-court takeout, to borrow Henry Giroux's critique of the United Colors of Benetton.[16]

Since Pepsi-Cola could not give Taco Bell a semiotic facelift by changing its name and destroying its brand value, the company seems to have been determined to relocate it culturally, in Giroux's term, to engage in its "recontextualization."[17] And so we hear Caribbean music, sung with an accent more Jamaican than Mexican. The setting and demographics seem more Orange County than Baja. The colors have nothing to do with the Mexican flag, everything to do with youth, exotic beaches, and tourism. The women and men whose labor creates the Taco Bell food—many from disadvantaged ethnic groups—are nowhere to be seen in the advertising. In this context, to "Cross the Border" can only mean to enter the imaginary space of the Multicultural Mall.[18]

While this usage of "border" may subtract from its meaning as a marker of difference as well as of unjust political and economic division, it adds to the economic value of the product. It is this value on which brand names trade. But it does still more. For any of us who work through the process of making the ad meaningful, it affects not only how we see the object, altering our minds in that sense, but also how we see whatever else might subsequently invoke the magical image: Jamaica, beaches, older people, younger people, the "Border." These changes to what Judith Williamson calls the "referent system" help define how we think of ourselves in the world—indeed, they change the world itself as we experience it.[19] Such changes are by-products of the selling process, taking place regardless of whether we purchase the product. Yet even if they have no immediate economic value, these associations still have cultural significance. As Uma Narayan has said, "Seemingly simple acts of eating are flavored with complicated, and sometimes contradictory, cultural meanings," often to give exotic value to inexpensive food.[20] This might be said of viewing as well, even in the fleeting moments ads pass across the screen. If the commercial does not affect consumption, the mental effects concern the advertisers as little as pollution or waste or any other environmental impact, unless public outrage or the law intervenes.

With its flow between commercials and programs, television introduces another dimension to this process of value creation. It makes possible subtle associations between aspects of the show and the commodity, thus fostering an environment in which favorable associations, or at least recognitions, can take place, can enter the "nation's emotional grammar."[21] Cosmoexoticism flows through the hour, before and after Taco Bell, starting with *Northern Exposure*'s music and invocation of Native American shamanism and culminating in a Burger King ad referring to African music and dance. More precisely, the ad trades on *The Lion King*, in theaters at the time, with its version of "The Lion Sleeps Tonight," an African song originally but then redesigned into an early 1960s U.S. pop hit. *Northern Exposure*'s setting is as mythological geographically as the Border for Taco Bell or the Jungle for Burger King. Yet just as much as the rough-hewn lettering discussed earlier, such commercialized myths link all three, or at least make such linkage possible, adding value, "sign value," wherever they are made.[22] This explains why football players with winning teams, like Deion Sanders of the Dallas Cowboys, can earn millions for appearing in commercials.[23] During the 1996 Super Bowl, Sanders appeared in ads for Nike, Pizza Hut, and Honey Frosted Wheaties. These were shown within minutes (in one case, seconds) of him playing in the game, no doubt enhancing the value of his presence in both.[24]

Such associative value creation was also Procter & Gamble's aim in identifying itself (or, rather, its Tide brand) as the sponsor of *Northern Exposure*.[25] This sponsorship did not require P&G to buy all or even most of the commercial time in the show. The relationship was unlike that of the advertiser-supplied and -sponsored shows of the 1950s, of which only the *Hallmark Hall of Fame* survives. It was also unlike the soap operas that P&G has owned and operated on network television for decades.[26] In this case, rather, before *Northern Exposure* went on the air, P&G agreed to pay part of its production costs during the summer season, leaving CBS with a reduced licensing fee. According to contemporary trade and newspaper reports, P&G also agreed at the outset to buy half the commercials at the going summer rate. In return, the company became a minority partner in the program and secured a guarantee of fixed ad rates, discounted to the original summer rate, for one minute of airtime during the show's entire network run. For P&G, the up-front expenditure constituted a gamble that the show would take off and the price of advertising rise enough above its weekly expense to cover the original premium costs.[27] This package constituted an opportunity neither CBS nor the makers of the show, MCA/Universal and the Brand-Falsey group, could refuse. Indeed, there is evidence that without P&G's subsidy, *Northern Exposure* would never have aired. With ratings lower in the summer, it would have been hard for CBS on its own to afford to pay the producers of *Northern Exposure* anything like the cost of making the show.

For P&G, *Northern Exposure* meant access to women, aged 25–49, whom it has trouble reaching with its extensive daytime programming—those who work outside the home. The company's goal is to reach 90 percent of its target audience for its different brands with reliable frequency, at least six or seven times per month, according to Artzt.[28] This is how P&G, for example, sells 50 million tubes of premium-priced Crest a year.[29] Its fear seems to be that without such reach consumers will switch to other brands or generics. Most threatening of all to the system is the possibility that without the frequency and reach it needs, consumers might shop less altogether or start brushing their teeth with baking soda. Evidently, P&G saw the show as a hospitable environment for its commercials. This provides a documented example of how television programming responds to the needs of advertisers before it responds to those of audiences. In that sense the show is typical—it is advertiser-supported precisely because it provides a suitable environment for the ads. P&G executives picked the proposed *Northern Exposure* to sponsor and in that sense made it happen as a TV program; there is no evidence that they fashioned *Northern Exposure* to their measure, complete with an irregular series of scenes of the characters doing laundry. Indeed, those connected with the show have stressed their independence.[30] The program was not an infomercial, at least not explicitly. After all, no one was shown using Tide.

However, ABC president Robert Iger has said at least once that the producers of *Northern Exposure* made extra money by selling off product placements within the show for fees approaching hundreds of thousands of dollars apiece, in some cases more than the cost of an ad.[31] We could not confirm this with any other source. In any case, there is no doubt that product placement, including paid placements, is becoming more common on television, even if there is an ongoing interest in keeping it unobtrusive. "Whatever we do, we try to look for a natural integration with a show," a Fox vice president told *Time* about his network's openness to placements. "Our main concern is to make sure viewers don't feel everything is overcommercialized."[32]

The makers of *Northern Exposure* risked this on the episode broadcast March 1, 1993. It included a reference to Miller Lite just as CBS was announcing a promotional campaign involving the network, *Northern Exposure,* and Miller beer. CBS officials maintained the product placement was a coincidence.[33] The *Northern Exposure* office had a standard answer for reporters and viewers who complained of increasing numbers of plugs on the show (Advil twice and Nikon in one episode alone): "Nobody pays us to be on the air. We asked them permission to use their names. We use brand names all the time and have the clearance files to prove it."[34] The Center for Science in the Public Interest, the PTA, the American Medical Association, and a range of religious groups have asked the Federal Trade Commission to ban product placements involving alcohol in film and television, so far without success.

Despite the small fortunes to be made in selling product placements, most mentions of goods on TV shows are not hidden ads.[35] As Jerry Seinfeld says, "We like to have real products in the show," presumably to make the programs more realist. *Seinfeld* staff say they are not paid to insert the products (although product placements frequently come with free or discounted samples for staff) and that they vary them to avoid offending advertisers.[36] Whatever the case, from Junior Mints to babka (an Eastern European Jewish coffee cake), mere mention on *Seinfeld* seems to have spiked sales.

For its part, Procter & Gamble had a connection with *Northern Exposure* that no one else had; its efforts can be seen as a way of guaranteeing product placement and its effects, if not inside the program, then within the hour of the show. Not only was P&G's Tide for years the first product plugged once the show started, every week at two minutes after the hour the company displayed its Tide logo and slogan for 15 seconds to the *Northern Exposure* theme, to reinforce and enlarge the sign value of their brand. In the episode we studied, after the first long program segment (10 minutes), P&G had the first word, for Comet. Offscreen, too, the company heightened connections between its brands and TV shows. As the 1994–1995 season began, for example, shoppers could acquire T-shirts with the logos of *Northern Exposure*, *Murphy Brown*, and *Dr. Quinn, Medicine Woman* for a mere $4.95, plus proof of P&G purchases. The company donated $1 per shirt to the Juvenile Diabetes Foundation, up to $150,000.

Corporations have become increasingly active in developing the programming that will envelop and present their ads.[37] This is in part to control product placements. P&G may not have insisted that Cicely's residents use Tide when they washed their clothes, but they hardly would have allowed them to use a competing brand like Arm and Hammer (Advil and Nikon must have passed muster because P&G sells no equivalent products). More to the point, corporations want to make sure programming exists that would sell their products effectively. "In [TV] movies, we're certainly hands on," says one advertising agency programming chief. "In many cases, the ideas start with us."[38] Where advertisers have equity shares, the control tends to be even more intensive. In late 1995, P&G finalized an agreement with Viacom's Paramount and GE's NBC that had P&G and Paramount splitting the cost of developing new programs, NBC receiving guaranteed advertising revenue in return for promoting and scheduling the shows it would want to air, and P&G receiving partial ownership—increasingly attractive in an uncertain media environment—and the right to advertise at favorable rates from network first run through syndication and international sales.[39] P&G's "intent is to form alliances with the major entertainment houses like Viacom, Disney and Sony USA to create programming with some combination of our agencies, the networks and the cable stations involved," says a senior vice president for advertising and services.[40] According to *Business Week*, "Procter says it worries that the flood of new media may wash traditional ad-sponsored programming away, leaving it no place to run its commercials unless it owns some of the shows."[41] Yet even with new media slicing off network audiences, Artzt says "broadcast television is still the best way to achieve the reach and frequency advertisers need to build consumers' loyalty."[42] By becoming involved in producing programs, P&G wants to make sure there will be shows with appeal broad enough to reach its target customers, enabling it to keep selling at the enormous volume it needs to survive and grow. "Television shows are getting more and more fragmented, more and more targeted toward specific audiences," one corporate media buyer said in 1995. "Look what P&G sells—products that just about everybody uses."[43] Not known for its irony, P&G named one of the successful award shows it developed and owns *The People's Choice*.

The Value of Blandness

The flow of meanings moves unevenly through moments of daily life, through the minds of those subject to it. As P&G and other corporate executives know only too well, the media give value by association to otherwise lifeless commodities, linking culture and economics. This interest in value creation explains why the television industry sometimes has difficulty finding sponsors for controversial shows like *NYPD Blue* or the coming-out episode of *Ellen*, with potential for associations that might *reduce* the worth of advertisers' products—at least until controversy proves a good sell. It is also explains why, given the racism still prevalent in the United States, commercial television has yet to come up with any enduring dramatic shows concentrating on African Americans. And it is why just about everything on network TV is screened in advance to make sure it will not offend an advertiser. This is a problem for public as well as commercial television; it explains why so much of the programming on both is so bland. Except for certain shows (such as some on Fox) intended for specific, smaller audiences, "Don't offend" remains the slogan of the age as far as desired viewers are concerned, although perhaps it is nostalgic to think U.S. television was ever basically different. "The key consideration for a network programmer today is whether a program is 'advertiser friendly,'" one successful independent producer told the *Christian Science Monitor*.[44] That means don't challenge any desirable sector of the audience, don't question conventional wisdom, don't risk driving anyone you want away. To the extent this eagerness to please pervades the programming, it becomes another element of flow—a loosely centrist view of the world (running from center-right to center-left). It betrays a "timid majoritarianism" designed to make most viewers feel welcome by prohibiting that which might offend.[45]

Whenever sharply off-center views do appear, they are discounted or softened by show's end (like Maurice's rightist rants on *Northern Exposure*). Or they are balanced, allowing different viewers to identify with the arguments of different characters (as in a discussion of the Star Wars weapons policy on the *Northern Exposure* episode we analyze, a *MacNeil-Lehrer NewsHour* in miniature).[46] A few programs, including *Northern Exposure*, do include rare unanswered critiques of the commercial system and even of absorption with television itself, yet these tend to be cast more in personal terms with which almost anyone might agree, rather than as specific political criticisms that might lead more hidebound defenders of the status quo to reach for their remote control. Again, P&G does not directly control program content. But in both the *Northern Exposure* and Paramount-NBC agreements, it reserved the right to withdraw from any episode it found inappropriate for showcasing its wares.[47] Network and production company executives know the cost of displeasing an early investor and part-owner more than occasionally. They know P&G wants the programming it supports to be simpatico overall. Asked about the company's role in shaping content, one P&G spokesperson told a reporter, "It's safe to say we have an interest in any show we advertise in."[48] In that sense, when the system works well by corporate standards, programming is little different whether it is controlled directly by advertisers or by the networks or outside suppliers.

If viewers regarded programs as gussied-up infomercials, they might well raise their guard and become less susceptible to their power. As it is, popular TV shows reel off magical images of the world, and viewers sometimes incorporate aspects of the programs into their lives. This shows the power of television's fictional realism, its contribution to the irrational. Stores throughout Alaska sell T-shirts of Cicely, and tourists buy them in droves. At the same time, Alaskan tourist advertising cashes in on *Northern Exposure*, much the same way that Princess Cruises capitalized on *The Love Boat* a generation earlier. Tourists also flock to Roslyn, Washington, about 50 miles east of Seattle, where exteriors for the show are filmed. "Like Cicely," Roslyn "has its own bunch of wonderful characters," writes Rob Morrow in his book of *Northern Exposure* photographs.[49] Fans hungry for the favorite recipes of characters they like can buy *The Northern Exposure Cookbook* or read *Letters from Cicely* to learn more about their innermost thoughts.[50]

Even if few of us personally know people *that* taken in by the show, surely all of us have been in conversations in which people talk about television characters as if they were real. Study after study shows that people use material from television's narratives to make value judgments and as evidence for arguments about the world, most notoriously perhaps in the case of some viewers of *The Cosby Show,* who used the success of the program's fictional family as evidence against the need for affirmative action programs.[51] Arjun Appadurai writes of "mediascapes," "image-centered, narrative-based accounts of strips of reality . . . a series of elements (such as characters, plots, and textual forms) out of which scripts can be formed of imagined lives," of "their own as well as [of] those living in other places."[52] In providing an effective sales environment for the ads, then, television shows also help form the mental worlds, the scenarios, in which viewers live. This, too, is normally an unintended by-product of decisions made to sell individual products, not the result of conspiracy or subliminal design.

Karl Marx used the term *fetish* to describe human relations with commodities under capitalism, and his argument can help us understand what it is in goods that reaches out and touches us so effectively. Eighteenth-century anthropologists applied the term to any inanimate object with a magical trace. For Marx, commodities were not fetishes as long as people took them or left them based on their potential for practical use. Indeed, as useful things, commodities testified to the human dexterity and labor they embodied.[53] A car, for example, is glass, metal, petroleum, and other materials that workers have transformed—imaginatively designed, perhaps, but not magic. The magic begins when, as consumers, we see a car in an ad, on a lot, or on the street and find it so evocative that it ceases to appear to be the product of other people's work, produced for a specific use, distributed through specific social relations, and becomes the emotionally charged totem of an imagined lifestyle. (What does it tell us that, if news reports are to be believed, only between 5 and 20 percent of owners of off-road vehicles in the United States actually drive off road?) The car itself is still transformed glass, metal, and petroleum products, only now it has been fetishized—a token of feeling or an image of desire. Marx likened this *mental* transformation, itself an act of what Jean Baudrillard has called "cultural sign labor," to that performed by religious people who believe that a statue, a trinket, a piece of wood, a book, or a building has a sacred character or could be a magic wand able to help people change.[54] Hence the relevance of the anthropological term *fetish* to commodities.[55] Running full tilt, those who fetishize objects have no doubt they are seeing the object *as it really is;* their sign labor is invisible to them. They believe their sense of the object is due to its nature ("It's that because that's what it is."). However, their sense of the object is itself a form of culture, an outcome of social pressures in a specific time and place that corral certain meanings in and zone others out of bounds. The economic system, especially its marketing apparatus, separates us as consumers of commodities from their producers. Unless peddling a romanticized version of industrial craft, advertising generally seeks to block thoughts of conditions of production, for fear they might dispel the magic, or worse (think of the recent campaigns to fight horrendous production conditions outside the United States for some designer clothes sold here). Few product labels list where an object comes from or where it is going: Who made it, and at what cost? How difficult was the work? How well were the workers paid? What energy does the product consume? What pollution will it release? Where will it go and what will it become after it has been used? Without such questions, and answers, the environment itself becomes phantasmagoric.

Why Buy Tide?

Marx could not have foreseen the rise of modern advertising, which since the 1920s has given this fetishization a new cast and pervasiveness, as broadcasters and advertisers have found increasingly sophisticated ways to turn viewers into profitable commodities by fetishizing them as potential consumers of other commodities, and viewers have learned new ways to fetishize themselves and their world. Take the four Procter & Gamble ads, starting with the admonition, "If it's got to be clean, it's got to be Tide." What does "clean" laundry mean? Jokingly, researchers for Consumers Union report that the difference between the least effective laundry detergent they tested and the most was that between "clean" and "cleanest."[56] "Leave aside the puffery," they say. "The truth is that all detergents clean clothes. Most also brighten, remove stains to some extent, and work in a variety of temperatures."[57] In any case, price is not a factor. "You don't have to pay extra for performance."[58] Yet pay extra people do. At one Saint Paul, Minnesota, supermarket in late 1997, 100 ounces of liquid Tide sold for $6.99 while the same container of ERA—also made by P&G—cost $5.59. Who knows what the difference is? Why would anyone buy Tide instead of ERA? How many people stop to think about it, let alone read *Consumer Reports* or call the 800 number P&G offers for those who want more information? The same amount of Ultra Yes costs $4.98. How many people in the United States who buy Tide or ERA have done a blind comparison of the three?

That's why P&G's marketing is so important. If the company wants to maintain or increase sales, the consumers targeted must be hit with those exposures every month, and alternatives must be marginalized, especially generics. Knowing there are price-conscious consumers, P&G does make less expensive alternatives such as ERA, as it aims for multiple markets simultaneously. But larger profits would seem to be in the higher-priced brands, and they get the major advertising push. For a new product, as Aleve was at the time, such exposures are all the more urgent. So P&G crafts them carefully, targeting women yet like most national advertisers grounding the commercials in the wisdom of men, carelessly reinforcing what decades of feminist organizing have yet to eradicate—the power of internalized male authority. However different they are, all four commercials use a deep, measured male voice to make the sale, a voice like the one that announces Tide's sponsorship of *Northern Exposure* and makes the lion's share of announcements on television generally, including network news and identification, a voice with an accent that has been the national standard for so long that for many—in a denial of ethnic difference—it appears to be no accent at all.[59] And in the three ads that follow Tide (including a Comet ad that opens the second pod), the voice, identically, in a fatherly way, offers solutions to a woman in need, just as Leonard and Joel do to the characters in the episode, each a doctor in his own way. Again, this may be a by-product of marketing strategy, rather than a planned backlash against feminism, but the consequences are the same. The similarity of gender, voice, and narrative role is produced by the timid conventionalism of ad and program makers. It is what makes flow structurally likely without deliberate design, which is usually impossible to document in any case. The issue is not the individual morality of workers in the advertising or television industries. Nor is it the degree of political self-consciousness of those who design and profit from advertising or programs. What matters is that this socioeconomic process narrows the range of available cultural forms.[60]

People who buy Tide pay more than a dollar a container in unwitting tribute to this timid conventionalism, here found in the marketing savvy of Procter & Gamble. In fairness, Tide did top the *Consumer Reports* ratings in most categories, but the magazine argued that considering the price differentials "differences may not matter all that much."[61] There is, however, an important difference between laundry detergents and laundry soap—no longer on sale at many supermarkets. Soap, which can be made from animal or vegetable fat, lacks such ingredients as bleach, alcohol, and whitening agents, chemicals called "optical whiteners" that are dyes that help laundry glow in the sun and florescent light by converting ultraviolet to visible blue light, and chemical dirt dissolvers that break down oil and grease and dirt.[62] These constitute detergents' appeal, but they also eventually find their way into water supplies. Marketing, in this case linking Tide to the amicable low-tech (if detergent-using) world of *Northern Exposure,* must also shut out environmental and other social concerns on which it does not want to trade. Whatever branded ads include, these exclusions just as much construct a cultural identity for the product, fetishize it in ways everyone within the cultural mix on which it trades will understand. In many states, particularly in states that have banned phosphates, detergents advertise themselves as phosphate-free. In states and countries where the law allows, many of the same manufacturers include phosphates, which spur the growth of algae in lakes, sometimes making water undrinkable and unswimmable for humans and deadly for fish and other aquatic life. They also make laundry shine.

But who *needs* their clothes to shine? Consumer culture not only makes products to sell but also attaches meanings to them to the same end. Working through those who will tell us what our best friends won't, corporations such as P&G bombard us with a standard of being that requires our bodies and their clothing to appeal to the senses of others according to quite specific (but often changing) rules. This intentional fetishization takes the practice far beyond Marx, who described a largely unconscious system of recast meanings. How much it affects the consciousness of each of us depends on the extent to which, like children, we enlist in the style police of body presentation. Unlike children, who at times enforce conformity viciously on wayward schoolmates, we are taught to make as our most important object of scrutiny the body each of us inhabits. In this sense, our bodies have become texts on which we write our participation in commercial systems of meaning. We have learned to fetishize ourselves.

This is not to say that advertising causes conformity, that if advertising were banned, conformity would disappear. Nor is capitalism alone responsible, nor would a change in economic systems necessarily end waste and commodity desire. Advertising only affects those subject to its appeals, and cultures without advertising likewise enforce strict codes of body furnishings and smells and sounds, often along oppressive lines of ethnicity, gender, or social status, although these codes of presentation are rooted in community history, not the spreadsheets of a marketing mogul. Still, for those within commercial culture's circuits of meaning, these wants can seem to be needs. For many people these perceived needs evolve along with their standard of living. Since few who depend on commodities for identity ever feel whole for very long, the needs can become interminable, their satisfaction limited only by the wealth (or credit) of the consumer and the capacity of the planet to comply.

The Theory of Flow

By analyzing these forms of flow, we can begin to find and question its traces in our ways of seeing ourselves and the world. Such questioning offers us an alternative way of conceiving ourselves: not only as consumers on what increasingly resembles Pinocchio's Pleasure Island (unwittingly transformed and sold to corporate barkers) but also as participants in a planetary environment that is both under attack and worth saving. To be more than just another form of TV consumption, however, such insights need connection to concerted action against the commercial system and its priorities. It was Raymond Williams, in his 1974 *Television: Technology and Cultural Form,* who inaugurated the socially critical analysis of flow, seeing it as a symptom of television's economic and social conditions of existence.[63] Pointing out underlying similarities between program and commercial segments within a San Francisco news show, Williams showed concretely how advertisements and other forms of television (news, entertainment) are not autonomous entities with autonomous effects but interrelated parts of a single text, in Nick Browne's phrase, a Super Text.[64] In doing so, he offered detailed evidence that the cultural economy of capitalism fragments, decontextualizes, and congeals human social relations into abstract equivalents and exchangeable things. Textual elements become fungible as viewers are transformed into commodities bought and sold as market share, based on their promise as buyers in retail markets. Much valuable work has followed these important insights, not all of it directly influenced by Williams.

Against Williams's emphasis on flow's continuity, Jane Feuer in the early 1980s urged that flow be thought of as "segmentation without closure," discrete elements whose relations are left unresolved.[65] The expansion of cable offerings and more sophisticated remotes, VCRs, and game machines in the years since has led her to expand the argument and now speak of "cable flow," a new dimension of alternating material intensified by "zipping, zapping, and channel surfing."[66] Tania Modleski has explored the similarities between the rhythm of household work, with its constant interruptions, and the flow of daytime television aimed at female household workers.[67] Noting that only half the switched-on TV sets are actually watched, Rick Altman has analyzed the role of the sound track in mediating between television flow and what he calls "household flow."[68] Elsewhere, we have examined the ways commercials present problems similar to those constructed by program narratives, solving them through advertised products.[69] While most who write about flow differ with Williams on the fine points of his argument, some critiques are fundamental. Lynn Spigel maintains that Williams's method was flawed by his attention to textual details rather than to the "actual viewing experience."[70] As John Fiske argues, television texts themselves do not make explicit connections between their elements. Making such connections becomes "devolved to the viewer," who may or may not make them, even unconsciously. Viewing, then, "may leave the contradictions between segments active and unresolved."[71]

Let's consider the arguments of Spigel and Fiske by looking at one connection in the July 4, 1994, *Northern Exposure,* that between Rob Morrow's voice in the MasterCard ad and the presence of Morrow as Dr. Joel Fleischman in the show.

Although the frequency of connections visible to one who looks for them may make it seem otherwise, as a rule programs and commercials are not designed as a unit (exceptions include ads prepared to be broadcast during such special occasions as the Super Bowl or the Olympics). Unless they pay to sponsor a program as P&G did *Northern Exposure,* advertisers buy "spots" in specific shows or groups of shows (the more specific the arrangement, the more expensive it is). According to Joan Bogin, vice president for advertising at MasterCard, Morrow was chosen for the ads because of recognition from *Northern Exposure* and because of an "intelligent and street-wise humor that comes through in his voice." He speaks "friend-to-friend," Bogin said. "It's not the booming announcer-type voice."[72] The gimmick of the ads is their substitution of Morrow's voice for all the characters in each commercial—in this case even that of Pelé, who according to Bogin was surprised to learn that the ad would not feature his own voice.

MasterCard bought time for the ad from CBS as part of a package, one large enough that the company would get "some representation" on *Northern Exposure.* It was less interested in viewers connecting MasterCard International and Joel Fleischman ("His character tends to be a little wacky," Bogin said. "That's not something we want") than with them associating the card with Morrow's early nineties soft masculinity. The ad was also designed to connect MasterCard with the upcoming Soccer World Cup, another media event.

While MasterCard does not pick the specific broadcast time or location of its ads to ensure compatible flow, it does ensure that its network ads will not appear in an *incompatible* flow.[73] It does this, along with other major advertisers through their agencies, by hiring Advertising Information Services in New York, a company cooperatively owned by the agencies themselves. AIS attends live tapings such as *The Tonight Show* and *Saturday Night Live* and screens programs with ads inserted for their clients an average of four days but rarely more than two weeks before broadcast. According to Bogin, AIS would alert her if a MasterCard ad was set to run next to, say, one for American Express or in a program containing either "excessive sex and violence," a disparaging remark about credit cards, or a dramatization of credit card theft—in short, anything with which MasterCard did not want to be associated. Equipped with a synopsis of what might be problem areas for its product, an advertiser or its agency can then decide to move to a different location or negotiate to leave the episode entirely. They don't need to read Williams to appreciate the importance of flow.

Still, critics of Williams are right that, to advertisers' regret, no one can know in advance what viewers will do with the signs broadcast through their sets. What happens rests on a complicated mix including physical placement and attention, cultural background and knowledge base, interest, and mood. What can we say, then, of connections here between Morrow's voice in program and ad? Williams argued that program and ad were linked in the text, a montage, connected for viewers watching them together, and perhaps most important connected in that "this is the flow of meanings and values of a specific culture."[74] If he was right, analyzing flow can help us see that culture at work, the power flow discussed above—making meanings available. Of course, it cannot tell us for certain what *effects* television texts have. In part, this is because flow is so present in contemporary life that it cannot be isolated experimentally. "This is the characteristic that sets TV apart—not its ability to transmit sight and sound but its ubiquitousness," writes Bill McKibben. "Here, as a result, we sit, taking in that information and amusement for many hours a day—for most people a fifth of their waking life."[75] As Wendell Speer, a student of ours, pointed out to us in the late 1970s when T-shirts with corporate logos became fashionable, flows are not created by television. They work, they are meaningful, only because they begin elsewhere in a culture saturated with come-ons for products. *Then* they are available to resonate with TV images, billboards, newspaper and magazine ads, radio, and the pamphlets corporate marketers prepare for children in school. They resonate as well in our speech, in those referent systems in our minds, bouncing off the products themselves on display in stores and on bodies.

Yet as linked as commercials and shows can seem to be, nearly everyone, reviewers and academics as well as viewers at large, seems to think and speak of television as a series of discrete programs—like movies in a theater or on a VCR. This indicates the power of the notion that the commercials are not significant except perhaps as annoyance or amusement, that the programs are indeed the free lunch A. J. Liebling warned us decades ago cannot exist in commercial media.[76] Thinking about watching TV as if it had no ads indicates lessons learned well in thinking of commercials as a different sort of text, one that can be seen through, or over, or under to consume the real stuff of TV. Commercials may seem irrelevant because they are irrelevant to most of us most of the time—niche demographics and our own varying circumstances see to that. Ads for cars, for example, are not directed at those who could not qualify to lease or buy them on credit or at those temporarily uninterested in the market (even though they might have effects on others who see them). This explains why ads can seem feeble in their power against us, not requiring the sort of guard an educated consumer might raise against, say, a car salesperson who bullies customers into paying too much. That ads do not directly address us most of the time also disguises the way that TV does constantly address our needs and anxieties in a general sense, including appealing to desires to move "somewhere else" in the social space through the right purchase. We may not be corralled by an individual product pitch. Yet the overall system of turning wants into needs to shop for has become so ubiquitous that it is easy to understand why so many in this culture shape their appearance and behavior accordingly, the symbolic presence of class culture in and on the body. Commercial culture becomes our environment even if we do not consciously attend to it, even if we try not to attend. It becomes *common sense,* in Antonio Gramsci's usage, the "'philosophy of non-philosophers,' or in other words the conception of the world which is uncritically absorbed by the various social and cultural environments in which the moral individuality of the average [person] is shaped."[77]

Then, too, thinking that one can remain above television's economic circuit as one consumes its amusements offers a sense of populist empowerment—of beating TV at its own game. After all, no one is forced to watch television. Sitting in front of the set might understandably produce what Browne has described as the feeling of being a "consumer freely and democratically participating in the free-market distribution of abundant social goods."[78] Precisely this sense of power over television gives television its power over us. Who believes they owe their allegiance to Tide to television or to other advertising? Yet except for those who think higher prices mean better goods, who has a reason for spending the extra dollars on Tide that is not at bottom the product of an ad? Think about Master-Card's relation to *Northern Exposure,* with the program's self-professed, vaguely countercultural, low-consumption, all-cotton connotations of living lightly on the land. It is these connotations that are being used to sell MasterCard, *plastic,* a vehicle for spending money one does not have, often to buy things one cannot afford and does not need. Surely most people know they are watching ads as they do so. They quite reasonably expect ads to be different from the programs and do not apply the same criteria for television realism that we discussed in the last chapter. But the identification of certain broadcast material, ads and infomercials, as commercial relies on the identification of the rest as not-commercial (or at least not commercial in the same sense), making all the more powerful whatever associations can be made by the flow. This seems particularly true as the TV and advertising industries move to connect programs and commercials all the more closely.[79] Coca-Cola, for example, not only spent $30 million running Diet Coke ads with characters from *Friends* during episodes of that and other shows, but it organized a contest around matching actors' names with Diet Coke caps, intensifying flow by giving away *Friends* sunglasses and T-shirts, and sponsored a special one-hour episode after the 1996 Super Bowl that had been filmed before an audience that included 100 contest winners and a special commercial for *Friends*/Diet Coke.[80] "The target market we are aiming at, the 18 to 34 age group, is a perfect match with the *Friends* audience," a Coke executive told reporters. "It's no longer a promotion—it's a lifestyle."[81]

In the last two chapters, we argued that the experience of television includes the process of participating in already constituted meaning systems to make each moment understandable. We also considered the analysis that television at times includes the pleasure of interpellation, being addressed in a way that reinforces an idealized sense of self. ("You are someone special who appreciates this sort of culture," *Northern Exposure* implies to its fans. "You are someone who has an intelligent, street-wise sense of humor but you are not too wacky," says MasterCard International. "You are independent-minded, an outsider who is admired," says commercial culture in general.) This process of address is not one that television announces, although its traces are hardly hidden. It slips into, even constitutes, circuits of meaning in a voice with which one can identify, literally so in the case of the MasterCard ad, making watching television a dialogue with oneself, with a pedagogical twist.

This conversation, this *conscience,* has clear intent: to keep viewers watching and to make the urge to buy seem personal, to have its origins within. Lacking assertive signs that the images on screen are representations, viewers might well pay more attention to the world that seems accessible through TV's "Magic Window" than to the motives of the woman or man behind the curtain.[82] Although the theory of hegemony outlined in chapter 1 was originally developed to explain sociopolitical blocs, it can be used as well to think about the flow of social power through individuals. In that sense, the realist style of television enables hegemony. Ever flexible, realist style provides the veracity required for the available imagery (fictional or nonfictional) to be comfortably consumed. Yet it can do so only if it resonates with the expectations of audiences, developed over years of watching and learning the system's changing conventions and ways of making meaning. So it must track and readjust to the movements of social groups as well as try to lead them.

That explains why considering hegemony theory one of blunt domination misses its utility as a tool for analyzing and thinking through conditions of social change. Hegemony describes the "process of creating and maintaining consensus or of co-ordinating interests."[83] True, having people internalize voices of power as their own (however amusing, however benign or uplifting in spirit) is the surest road to securing their consent. It takes the sting out of overcharging and over-consumption, out of the tension of devoting hour-upon-hour to sitting in front of the set amid a life with too few moments for loved ones and self, out of the risk that we might defetishize commodities and think of their cost to others and to the planet. It makes the harmful desirable, or at least acceptable. Hegemony functions by limiting possibilities, frameworks of production and interpretation, frameworks presented so often they can appear unlimited, or at least the products of shared common sense rather than the operations of a system thoroughly hierarchical and driven by the imperatives of financial markets that demand ever increasing profits. Precisely because there is no conspiracy or central command post, the system can seem more open than it would if analyzed in terms of the similar intentions of competing corporations and the structural imperatives these corporations embody and reproduce. Hegemony need not dominate or "secure active commitment by subordinates to the legitimacy of elite rule"; it needs only to secure people's "disaffection" from revolt.[84]

That advertisers need continuously to bombard people with their specious associations shows their individual corporate hegemony incomplete. Indeed, as hegemony theorists have argued, hegemony needs constantly to be revived, re-produced, and revised to succeed. This is precisely because its constructions, the meaning systems it seeks to diffuse, have such costs (in, say, disease and pollution and inequity) and could not on their own ring true. Without marketing, who would pay 40 percent more for Tide or insist on clothes whiter than white? So the bombardment continues.

As Daniel Hallin has argued, in the commercial media, "a world-view compat-ible with the existing power structure in society is reproduced." This claim has considerable power, allowing us to see the general operations of the system in their specific forms. Still, it may not adequately attend to the complexities of in-dividual experience with such power as television within the commodity system, experience that is "decentralized and open to contradiction and conflict."[85] At the same time, however, this decentralization, this variety of experience, this un-evenness (not unlike that experienced with commercials), may serve the aims of the hegemonic bloc: each of us as subjects of hegemony knows of occasions when it has failed; to the extent that each of us seeks a sense of rational autonomy, these failures may blind us to its success. Within academic institutions in which critical thought has been valued and can itself become a commodity, the hegemonic field may seem more open, at least in theory. One important argument Ernesto Laclau and Chantal Mouffe, Stuart Hall, Lawrence Grossberg, and others have made that draws on social movements since the 1970s has been that theories of hege-mony too often bifurcate social relations into, in Grossberg's words, "two mutually exclusive worlds corresponding to two social groups, each with its own realities, experiences, cultures and politics"—classical Marxism's working class and ruling class. Yet "social differences actually proliferate" through more than a "single di-mension." Power flows "along many different, analytically equal axes: class, gen-der, ethnicity, race, age, etc., each of which produces disturbances in the other," while "those seeking to hold the dominant position do not constitute a single coherent group or class."[86] As a result, hegemony is a "war of position," as Gramsci frequently called it, in which opposing blocs combine, split, and recombine. Individual identities are "never unified and, in late modern times, increasingly fragmented and fractured; never singular but multiply constructed across different, often intersecting and antagonistic, discourses, practices and positions."[87] Neither corporate advertisers nor consumers are unified; indeed, their positions cohere only in moments of economic exchange, across the set or across the sales counter, fragmenting once they have passed. But these moments, and the moments that prepare participants for them, take more and more of our time, draw more and more of the world into their nexus, require more and more production of goods (and consequent materials and work hours) to feed the expanding demands of people globally who want to look like the cultural icons on their screens.

This is a process in which advertisers paradoxically sell individuality en masse. They seek to address consumers as a group, to hail or interpellate them to positions of desire, to what Hall calls "points of temporary attachment."[88] Such positions offer a taste of unified identity, but this in the end is no more than a "fantasy of incorporation" into a durable unit greater than oneself. Individualist identification, like any form of labeling, requires differentiation (masculine/feminine; Europe/Africa; Bloomingdale's/K-Mart; Tide/Brand X).[89] Consequently, it also involves exclusion of other possible positions, ones that might involve commonality, or nonindividualist transcendence, or concern with the costs of goods to the environment, to society, to those whose labor makes them. Advertisers may invoke these communal feelings, as they do in linking purchases with environmental consciousness (Tide in a refill bag), trying to define waste in ways favorable to their specific business. They may even help disseminate environmentalist and other critiques. Nevertheless, such ads indicate how corporate hegemony seeks to co-opt potentially oppositional movements and revulsion against waste in general.[90]

They need to be vigilant, for people are more than the social roles designed for them. They seek more than transient comfort. Just as those who work in advertising or the television industry are not reducible to their jobs, so, too, audiences are neither reducible nor condemned to their positions as consumers. Especially in more politicized times, such identities can conflict with other social positions and desires, causing stress, opening possibility.

From an environmental perspective, it may not matter if anyone identifies wholeheartedly with or feels good about the label "advertiser" as opposed to "consumer," or "polluter" as opposed to "Green activist." What counts is what people do to and in the world they inherit and remake, to the bodies of others as well as to their own. People may engage in contradictory practices, just as they have contradictory identities. They still *act like advertisers,* or polluters, or consumers, or Green activists, if only for moments. They serve definable interests, for example acting "at the behest of capital," or in opposition to it, or both, no matter how they appear to themselves.[91] Consumers *acting like consumers,* individually shopping and thinking about shopping, however judiciously, scarcely have any power compared with corporations, except to disengage. People *acting politically,* to change those they can reach, can organize collectively for power to contest practices (and, yes, identities) that further inequality and cause widespread harm. Such struggles against corporate power neither can nor should subsume those of other groups organized around issues of age, gender, international and interethnic inequality, or sexuality. However, anticorporate environmental activists can make the case that they and others who struggle against powerful blocs are involved in "chains of equivalents between the different struggles against oppression," that together they can organize participants from and within various positions to seek radical democratic change.[92] Information about such work is hard to find on commercial television, or in private malls, no matter how Green or multicultural an image they might project.

This activism would create new possibilities for identity that we can only begin to imagine. New political identities could provide at least as much pleasure and comfort as commercial ones; a "common collective" against corporate control of the environment could hail people to its cause as successfully as Procter & Gamble if it were able to win access to comparable communication outlets.[93] Activists of all stripes have known the pleasure of such solidarity for generations. Working with other people for change in what Kobena Mercer has called an "elective community of belonging" seems more important and could be more appealing than valorization of isolated "oppositional" reactions to commercial texts, the notion, for example, that "those who spent the eighties watching TV could claim to be the true radicals of the decade."[94] We take such arguments seriously in the next chapter but in the end argue for action outside the home theater. Overvaluing spaces of sporadic personal resistance that just might one day shift to social action (for example, hooting at commercials or walking through the mall making critical remarks—as liberating as both may feel) may unexpectedly serve the status quo. It may blind us to possibilities of living differently in a world not ruled by markets, of even *conceiving* of a world in which we were not bound to commercially based conceptions of self. Paradoxically, programs such as *Northern Exposure* offer pleasure in their glimpse of such a world. The residents of Cicely spend little time watching television, doing boring work, or shopping in impersonal stores, almost none on-line or paying bills. They spend their time with one another, sharing one another's lives, exploring the physical space in which they find themselves, building a community of care. But we cannot enter that world as participants in its diegesis—the story space that may fill in for our lives, that may seem to live for us—only as potential participants in the commercial space of the hour in front of our sets. Ironically, it is precisely when we are participants in that space that, unlike the characters in *Northern Exposure*, our viewing is seen by corporations as an object for sale. Our possibilities for an environment that sustains itself and us remain outside the commercial life, outside the flow of commodities, in a world in which "we shall be free to think about what we are going to do,"[95] in which alone and together, we can learn what it means to speak and be heard not in what AT&T defines as "Your True Voice" but in voices that together we make our own.

FURTHER READING

Andersen, Robin. *Consumer Culture and TV Programming*. Critical Studies in Communication and in the Cultural Industries. Boulder, Colo.: Westview, 1995.

Browne, Nick. "The Political Economy of the Television (Super) Text." *Quarterly Review of Film Studies* 9, no. 3 (Summer 1984): 174–182.

D'Acci, Julie, ed. "Lifetime: A Cable Network 'for Women.'" *Camera Obscura: Feminism, Culture, and Media Studies* 33–34 (May–September 1994/January 1995).

Giroux, Henry. "Consuming Social Change: The United Colors of Benetton." In *Disturbing Pleasures: Learning Popular Culture,* 3–24. New York: Routledge, 1994.

Goldman, Robert, and Stephen Papson. *Sign Wars: The Cluttered Landscape of Advertising.* Critical Perspectives. New York: Guilford, 1996.

Houston, Beverle. "Viewing Television: The Metapsychology of Endless Consumption." *Quarterly Review of Film Studies* 9, no. 3 (Summer 1984): 183–195.

Modleski, Tania. "The Rhythms of Reception: Daytime Television and Women's Work." In *Regarding Television: Critical Approaches—An Anthology,* edited by E. Ann Kaplan, 67–74. American Film Institute Monograph Series II. Los Angeles: American Film Institute, 1983.

Morley, David. *Family Viewing.* London: Comedia, 1986.

Williams, Raymond. *Television: Technology and Cultural Form.* 1973. Introduction by Lynn Spigel. Hanover, N.H.: Wesleyan University Press, 1992.

Williamson, Judith. *Decoding Advertisements: Ideology and Meaning in Advertising.* London: Marion Boyars, 1978.

CHAPTER SEVEN

From Consumers
to Activists

Our own voices, unencumbered by commercialism, our places in a sustainable planet—how do we find them, distant as they seem from the environment of profit-driven culture? How do we break out of the world of having into the realm of being? Are any exit signs left?

As more people anger over the coming effects of global warming, the split will widen between those who cannot give up the drive for *more* and those committed to its end. Just as we finished this book, government officials began to hint that it was too late to prevent global warming, because "the world's economic and political systems cannot depart from business as usual rapidly enough." Many scientists maintain that late in the next century, carbon dioxide levels will be double what they were before the Industrial Revolution, raising temperatures worldwide from 3 to 8 degrees Fahrenheit. This would happen even with implementation of the global warming treaty signed in December 1997 in Kyoto, Japan. As one report put it, an implemented treaty might slow down global warming, but even at that slower pace, there would be a "rise in sea levels that would inundate low-lying coastal areas and small island nations, more frequent and severe floods and droughts, a shift in climatic zones, and disruption of natural ecosystems." Some scientists predict that without more radical action than the Kyoto treaty carbon dioxide could reach triple or quadruple preindustrial levels, causing unknowable planetary catastrophe.[1] This leads some experts to abandon hope and counsel acceptance of this preventable catastrophe as if it were a fact of life. Since global warming cannot in practice be stopped or significantly slowed, says one leading government researcher, "we need to pay more attention to adapting to climate change." Of course, in a hierarchical global order, the burdens of adaptation would fall less on the comparatively affluent whose practices fuel global warming and far more on the already poor and disempowered. Environmental groups, from liberal to radical, argue that resources need to be redirected toward equitable solutions.

They say no matter the doomsday warnings, we must not give up fighting to make the economic and cultural changes required to slow global warming down, to the benefit of everyone. The role of television and the commercial culture in this seems clear. Although efforts could be made to advertise conservation and conversion to sustainability, countering normal advertising and its accumulated effects would cost trillions of dollars over time. More thinkable in the short run might be a struggle to outlaw advertising for gas-guzzlers (and eventually the gas-guzzlers themselves). Sport utility vehicles, for example, pollute the air and add to global warming far more than the cars they have displaced on the nation's roads. Indeed, if a legal loophole did not consider them "light trucks" instead of cars, the environmental damage they cause would keep them off the road altogether. Light trucks, which also include pickup trucks and minivans, are the fastest-growing source of global warming gases in the country, contributing nearly twice as much per vehicle as cars, according to a study by the Environmental Protection Agency. Indeed, they are expected to account for more than half of all U.S. global warming gases by 2010, if sales rates continue. Recently announced design modifications would cut pollution from these vehicles and make them much easier on the environment in terms of smog, but they do nothing to cut the gasoline consumption that leads to global warming.[2]

Relatively few light trucks (about a quarter) are used for commercial or farm purposes, just as relatively few large-engine sport utility vehicles are used for towing (15 percent) or by families larger than three (25 percent).[3] Nor are they necessarily safer to drive than cars. So their owners do damage to the planet largely for the usual reasons of style. A political movement organizing individuals to action as members of an interconnected planet might reverse this trend, if it can get legislation passed making unneeded light trucks less accessible and can promote them as unfashionable. Just as the attractiveness of these vehicles has been sold by the irrational associations of advertising (connecting them with the clean outdoors, with families, with friends), so could their unattractiveness be communicated by a combination of person-to-person and mass media arguments and government action, much as has been done with cigarette smoking, especially among the more educated.

Doing so would involve creating new positions for identification—"I recoil from thinking of myself (or having others think of me) as a person who smokes or drives a sport utility vehicle because someone sensitive to other people and the environment would do neither." Of course, on some level this would still be a matter of style. Optimally, however, this would be a style, a comfortable definition of self, not of consumption but of concerted political action. Limiting light trucks would not only require organizing for regulation as well as a rearticulation of the meaning of the vehicles but would also require reaching out to working and small-business people whose livelihoods depend on their manufacture, sale, and repair.

This example shows personal identity to be a matter of Green concern, and it shows how a Green politics would need to reach out to those outside environmentalist cultures. Homi Babha's notion of culture seems relevant here. "Culture reaches out to create a symbolic textuality, to give the alienating everyday an aura of selfhood, a promise of pleasure."[4] A new environmental movement must become culture in that sense, drawing more people to it and in so doing allowing itself to be redefined in ways that keep pleasure's promise. People need to be won over. Initial, limited struggles could spark deeper economic and social critiques and more radical action. Until now in our argument, we have used Antonio Gramsci's concept of hegemony to analyze ways established power blocs win consent from those they harm. Yet the concept applies as much, if not more, to organizing new blocs for radical change.[5] As the environment deteriorates, the ranks are sure to grow of those prepared to commit themselves to getting out of this fix, seeing connection to those already disaffected. This is true no matter how sclerotic the political situation appears at the moment.

What might this new environmental movement look like? If it is of any size and scope in the 21st-century United States, it would require new ways of thinking about diversity. The many categories of diversity were created historically in social formations and are renewed and reformed within relations of power today.[6]

The roots of diversity run deep, connecting the ways groups of people are thought of by outsiders and the ways they think about themselves. Advertisers contribute in their own way to marking out lines of difference through demographic strategies. They construct identification points for the privileged, organize them into "image tribes," groups of people who "gravitate to materials that most closely zero in on their likes and dislikes, their sense of themselves," and "prefer not to confront materials that cause them discomfort." Like real estate entrepreneurs, advertisers create gated communities, if virtual ones, leaving the most disadvantaged homeless in terms of media that articulate their interests.[7] On the other hand, a new environmental movement might seek what Murray Bookchin has called an "ethics of complementarity in which differences enrich the whole," committed "to mutual recognition and care for each other as well as the planet."[8] It would need to dismantle the gates of commercial identity and refashion itself to take into account diverse interests and needs in a nonhierarchical way. And it would have to offer identities more appealing and inclusive than those available on TV and in the stores of the mall. Ella Shohat and Robert Stam speak of a "polycentric multiculturalism," global, dispersed without center, emphasizing "fields of power, energy, and struggle," in which the privilege to define what ideas or forms of living count most would belong to "no single community or part of the world, whatever its economic or political power." This does not mean a "pseudo-equality of viewpoints," they maintain, for in this way of thinking, "sympathies clearly go to the underrepresented, the marginalized, and the oppressed."[9]

Some academics working in media and cultural studies, however, even those otherwise socially critical, have developed an alternative vision. Often cast like polycentric multiculturalism in terms of identification with groups systemically oppressed (because of racism, heterosexism, or economics), this vision offers instead a radical politics of individual empowerment. Such empowerment comes not in rejecting commercial culture but in taking sustenance from against-the-grain readings of commercial images. Chuck Kleinhans has written a helpful overview of this position and its critique, using Madonna's popular 1990 video *Vogue* as an example of commercial culture with important noncommercial meanings.[10] He argues that the video "lavishly expresses the physical beauty of African American men" and that these men "are lovingly presented and endorsed by the camera work, who dance with an astonishing skill."[11] He also argues that the video promotes identification with female empowerment (in centering the Madonna persona's unfettered desire). But if *Vogue* accomplishes these ends, it does so at the cost of validating whiteness and appropriating Harlem drag culture unacknowledged.[12] *Vogue* makes no mention of the origins of its images, the gender-complex performance culture represented in Jennie Livingston's 1991 documentary *Paris Is Burning*—a film with related problems. Unlike MTV or VH-1, this culture developed in the crucible of class/gender/race oppression (and not without its own misogyny). In this sense, *Vogue* constitutes a site of both "appropriation and reappropriation." While offering a sense of empowerment for those outside dominant sexual/racial/class realms, it provides amusement and spectacle for those comfortably inside in one way or another. While providing a space in which the culture of the largely unseen may be heard, it does so in a mediated form.

People spend so much time in front of screens that it is not surprising critical media scholars searching for exit signs have stressed the ways viewers recast media texts in their minds and in conversation with others to meet their needs, including political needs.[13] This recasting, this *performance* of the text shows media institutions are not all-powerful. The argument itself has a context, changes in the world system during the last three decades: the success of nationalist and other social movements in constructing positive identity and of movements around gender and against racism to take apart, multiply, and diversify the meanings of sex and race; and the failure of the democratic Left to establish convincing alternatives to hierarchical capitalism. The result has been the declining visibility *even of claims* that institutional power should and could be radically transformed. As a consequence, aspiration for change becomes limited, exclusively local, tangible, more modest in the number of people it desires to affect. Still, if audiences make their own meanings, they do so under conditions they do not choose. These semiotic glitches may be but moments in a successful industrial-commercial process. No matter what meanings viewers get from television, for example, they are still assembled as audiences for sale to advertisers who buy access to their minds and to their wallets, at least a small but sufficient portion of the time.

Over the last decade, audience-response theory has come to take more seriously some of the claims of political economy (for example, that the process is commercialized), and political economy has in turn thought more about the problems of knowing what texts mean to people and how they work through individuals. There seems to be increasing agreement that spectatorship is informed by gender and sexualities, ancestry and racism, and—although it is the least developed—class. Of course, other aspects of spectator position might be invoked as well: nation, religion, region, local culture. Indeed, positions are themselves constructed categories that are more hybrids of situations than expression of pure identities; there is no mechanical relation between them and points of view.[14] In any case, political economy tends to subsume these into economic categories; cultural studies in practice tends to concentrate on these to such an extent—as in the *Vogue* analysis above—that the economic system fades from view, except as an abstract category.

Not Either/Or but Both/And

We tried to keep the economic in mind in our analysis of the Cascade ad and of *Northern Exposure,* but our analysis was lacking on at least one count. Now it seems useful to explore a vital distinction in thinking about television and the cultural environment, that between "spectators" on the one hand and "audiences" on the other. The distinction may sound all too academic, but it offers a way of reexamining what we so far have said about television's impact: About whom are we talking? What basis do we have for our claims?

The question of spectatorship has been central to film studies for more than two decades, motivated first by concern about gender difference in viewing and later by incisive critiques of the notion that there could be an ideal spectatorship outside fragmented positions. How, for example, can we speak of "the viewer" or generalized "effects" of *The Birth of a Nation* or *Gone with the Wind,* highly racialized films bound to elicit different responses from those who see them, depending on background and politics, historical eras, and the difference between, say, viewing a film in a segregated theater at the time of release or in a nominally integrated college classroom now? One way of dealing with these questions is to say that "spectators" are identified in theory by critics; we shall differentiate them from "audiences" in just a moment. Those who analyze spectatorship assume certain social-psychological links between images and their construction in films and the response of specifiable portions of the audience (for example, black feminist spectators—and others in sympathy with them—offended by the representation of African American women in *Gone with the Wind* or *Deconstructing Harry*). At the same time, as we discussed in chapter 4, such analyses assume that encounters with representations help construct spectators' own subjectivity by addressing them in ways that affect how they conceptualize themselves.[15] And they argue that our subjectivities are hybrids, oscillating between what might be contradictory identifications through viewing experiences that themselves contain contradictions. Our own work on *The Cosby Show* undertook a similar analysis of spectatorship, arguing that the show was popular with racist whites because it flattered their desire to encounter financially successful African Americans who would be neither too different nor confrontational on racism-related issues; yet even this form of "modern" or "enlightened" racism is contradictory, including within it commitment to the ideal of racial equality even if it lacks commitment to equitable outcomes. Although such analysis usually relies on evidence like the demographics of ratings reports, reviews, contemporary commentary, and the shows themselves, it remains bounded by deductive principles of reasoning, seeking to build on assumptions in a logical way.

"Audiences," on the other hand, are the people who consume media. Unlike spectators, they can be studied and measured, but like spectators they can never be known directly, only through a different set of "projection, myth-making, and fabrication," as Ien Ang and Rick Maxwell have demonstrated in their critiques of audience ratings systems and other corporate conceptions of who sees what.[16] Interviews with audiences have much to contribute to critical media studies: they can tell us how people view their own viewing, and they can add insights far more diverse than any critics with their own partial frameworks might conceive. In that sense, audience research democratizes the available voices.

Still, the gap between what people say and what they think or do is easily demonstrated, and the gap between what any of us feel and what language can capture is a commonplace of linguistics and psychoanalysis. In just about every account of audience interviews we have seen, audience members find themselves to be people who think and act logically and independently. Perhaps so. But this ignores larger socioeconomic processes in which they might be involved.

Indeed, political economy and audience activity are connected in practice.[17] Dallas Smythe argued two decades ago that what audiences saw as hours spent being entertained in front of the set was also labor for the corporations that target them (us) for training as consumers. "The work which audience members perform for the advertiser to whom they have been sold is to learn to buy particular 'brands' of consumer goods, and to spend their income accordingly"[18]—and to work producing goods and services to earn the income to spend. Looked at this way, the line between leisure and labor becomes less defined. This is not to say that this process is all that matters when people watch television, as the most extreme political economists might argue. But it is to say that watching television is a process that is multidimensional, and that for an environmental theory of media, unidimensional analysis remains inadequate.

Warnings and Targets

We are back to Edwin Artzt and the strategies of Procter & Gamble, the effort to hit those target audiences so many times a month, with each sale contributing to a change in the nonhuman environment, in production, distribution, use, and postconsumer disposal. But we are also back to spectators of shows like *Northern Exposure,* who would seem to use the show and so many others to fill out their mental maps of the environments in which we live. Think how different consumption would be if every sport utility vehicle and other product had to carry a label listing its environmental consequences. Think how different ads would be if their smooth-toned announcers had to tell us at the end the costs to the planet of the goods they push. Think how different TV shows would seem if they had to announce up front that their purpose was to ensnare as well as entertain, that to watch was to be commodified for advertisers, to labor for them, to learn to think their way, if only occasionally and in pieces at a time. For even if we are not targets of a specific ad, we are constantly targeted by commercial television to think well of ourselves as beings who buy. Think how different our lives would be if we spent less time with *Friends* and more time with friends, less time with *Baywatch* and more time watching bays. Think of the hours spent in solitary shopping, of the hours working in order to buy. Try adding up how many hours of labor are embodied in your car.

Few would dispute that in the United States and elsewhere more people are working more hours to maintain what they honestly believe to be a necessary standard of living—one that nevertheless would seem royal by the standards of most people in the world. How much overconsumption do we need? What about the rest of the world? What about the poor right at home? As more become able to overconsume, what right do the earlier consumers have to limit later ones' consumption in the name of environmentalism? This has been a particularly thorny issue in negotiating international agreements on global warming. Why should the more recently industrialized and industrializing zones of the world forswear what the West throughout the century has presented as an improved standard of living so that the already industrialized can continue to pollute? How can the planet possibly survive efforts by multinational corporations to hook everyone possible into circuits of want and waste? How can we afford to give up more and more of our time to work and learn the brands and jingles and to consume to meet corporate priorities, when as a consequence our social and family lives become less abundant by the year?

According to one labor economist, Juliet Schor, working people in the United States added nine hours of paid labor a week during the 1970s and 1980s, reversing nearly a century's trend toward more available time. With growing job requirements for home cellular phones, e-mail, fax machines, and voice mail, the workweek has no doubt increased substantially in the 1990s, at least in some sectors of the economy, and much of it has been unpaid. This is not a worldwide phenomenon; probably because of stronger union movements, in France and Germany during the last half century the average workweek has dropped significantly below that in the United States. Suffering most in this country have been working women with children who do more than their share of the unpaid housework and child care.[19] Advertisers trade on this suffering, as we saw in the appeal demonstrated by the Cascade ad analyzed in chapter 4.

Declining productivity (worker hourly output) is not the cause of the increasing workweek. As Schor points out, from 1948 through the 1980s, productivity more than doubled, even taking inflation into account. This means that if we were able to live at a 1948 level of consumption, *"every worker in the United States could now be taking every other year off from work—with pay"* (emphasis in original). Yet the time dividend was swept away by corporate employers and marketers as deftly as the elusive "peace dividend" promised at the end of the Vietnam War. In 1990, the average person owned and consumed "more than twice as much as he or she did in 1948, but also [had] less free time." U.S. consumers do, however, spend more time shopping, save less, and owe more than anyone else in the world. As a result of these trends, people spend less time eating and sleeping. The effects are as profound as they are familiar, especially for women: "Parents are devoting less attention to their children. Stress is on the rise, partly owing to the 'balancing act' of reconciling the demands of work and family life." At least as stressed, of course, is the portion of the labor force unable to find enough work, even as others are "subjected to mandatory overtime and are suffering from overwork." Such paradoxes result from deliberate elite policy to keep unemployment and underemployment high enough to preserve the value of their bonds. "The rational, and humane, solution—reducing hours to spread the work—has practically been ruled out of court."[20]

Combining Schor's and Smythe's analyses produces a bleak picture indeed of life in the commercialized environment. No wonder the Berkeley Media Studies Group looks at the situation as a problem of public health.[21] Yet for some (more so among the more affluent), such a negative critique may seem at odds with the agreeable experience of being in this culture. That is where political economy and audience research come together: commercial television may be pleasantly consumed, offering a cornucopia of choice, but devoting hours to it is *in practice* to participate in a system of unfreedom and waste. An environmental perspective becomes useful here, for such a perspective asks what sort of rearrangements of nonhuman nature are demanded by overconsumption. What sort of life is human life when it is stretched out and stressed and literally less healthy as a result, when "satisfaction is . . . tied to destruction" and "technical progress is tied to progressive manipulation and control of human beings?"[22]

This trajectory may not be sustainable, but an environmental movement sensitive to the harm of corporate culture must even now envision life after the fall, must begin to think through possibilities of interconnection without domination. It needs to press the common interest in a world without hierarchies, without privilege. Although the elimination of all conceptual distinctions between the nonhuman and the human seems neither possible nor necessarily desirable, a social ecology could break with thinking of nature as an object, an Other, and instead start to *"differentiate* ourselves from nature, that is, to recognize it in ourselves, as body, and to recognize ourselves in it, as those who care for the earth" (emphasis in original).[23] Much feminist environmentalism rightly argues that the domination of nature and the domination of women flow from patriarchal structures and ideas.[24] There are indeed commonalities in the exploitations of capitalism, heterosexist patriarchy, racism, and, not least of all, the sort of human chauvinism that views the nonhuman as its preserve. A social ecology would seek institutional change for the purpose of ending these destructive ways of life and in doing so release desires for interconnection.

That this seems to have little to do with commercial television, even "quality" television like *Northern Exposure,* points to the importance of rejecting the intrusiveness of television, of commercial culture generally, in the moments of one's life. Looking at screens may seem to connect us to others in the world, *but it does not.* Mostly it connects people only to the low-definition images they can have of one another across the set. Think of the alternative: it is there for us to seize if only we can learn to let go of our virtual connections in favor of ones in which bodies meet and touch and struggle together for a new world. Such a struggle would "serve to protect and enhance life itself. The drive for painlessness, for the pacification of existence, would then seek fulfillment in protective care for living things. It would find fulfillment in the recapture and restoration of our life environment, and in the restoration of nature, both external and within human beings."[25] Such a revolution will not be televised. No corporation has an interest in sponsoring it. It cannot be displayed in a show window. It can only be lived, with others, in the spaces our bodies and hearts so deeply desire to reclaim.

Alternatives

Clearly, we need to find the exit signs—and to help build the exits. To begin, we've got to turn off the television and get out of the consumer rat race, reduce our needs, and pay attention to things that matter. Fortunately, millions of Americans seem to be doing just that. They are "downshifting," choosing "voluntary simplicity" and "sustainable consumption." This movement is still relatively small but seems to be growing rapidly. The grassroots organizations mentioned below are part of it. The *Trends Journal* predicts it will attract 15 percent of baby boomers by the year 2000, and more younger people are sure to follow. Many Americans are dissatisfied with the consumer treadmill, working more to buy more, repeating the cycle endlessly.[26] Most don't yet know how to get off, though. But a book called *Your Money or Your Life: Transforming Your Relationship with Money and Achieving Financial Independence* by Joe Dominguez and Vicki Robin has sold more than 400,000 copies with a message of reducing material needs and reasserting the values of frugality and sustainability. A related volume, Duane Elgin's *Voluntary Simplicity,* promotes ecological awareness, noncommercial personal growth, and living with balance.[27] New organizations, magazine articles, and Web sites support this nascent transformation in the American Dream. New alternatives are developing.

Democracy itself depends on knowledgeable choices among radically different possibilities, in culture and the economy as much as in political candidates. Here we shall survey some concrete alternatives to commercialized television, from individual changes to collective action and organizations, from small to major projects. There are hundreds of grassroots organizations, publications, Web sites, local, national, and global alternative media production and distribution organizations. Some are well established, others short lived. Our survey is necessarily selective and incomplete, but the sources we discuss below are generally among the most valuable and will lead you to other options. At the end of this chapter are addresses for organizations and lists of other resources to help you explore these alternatives further.

Organizations and Publications

Perhaps the best place to start is by gathering information about publications and organizations that help provide and sustain alternative views of television as well as alternative media. The Institute for Alternative Journalism, dedicated to strengthening independent and alternative journalism, publishes the valuable *MediaCulture Review* and other documents on-line, organizes conferences, and provides links to a variety of noncommercial and anticommercial media. In 1996 and 1997 IAJ sponsored well-attended Media and Democracy Congresses, which brought together journalists, academics, and media activists to develop responses to the crisis in public interest journalism caused by the rapid concentration of media ownership and control, privatization, technological changes, and threats from the Right.

Fairness and Accuracy in Reporting (FAIR) is a national media watch group that documents bias and censorship in the media through its bimonthly magazine *Extra!*. In 10 years, *Extra!* has published important exposés such as "The 26 Corporations That Own Our Media" (1987—it's fewer now); the overwhelmingly white, male, establishment guest lists on *Nightline* and the PBS *NewsHour;* Pentagon censorship and journalists' self-censorship in coverage of the Gulf War; and "Rush Limbaugh's Reign of Error." FAIR maintains a continuous dialogue with journalists at dozens of news outlets and makes recommendations to media professionals on how to expand, diversify, and improve coverage of a wide range of issues, including Green marketing, racism, sexism, and prejudice against the young. FAIR spokespersons discuss media issues on national and local TV and radio programs, publish op-ed columns, and lecture at universities and community forums around the country. FAIR is also developing a network of local affiliates to link community activists with national campaigns. One of its projects involves making public broadcasting more responsive to the public and less to corporate underwriters and conservative politicians.

On-line, the Institute for Global Communications provides and develops accessible computer networking tools for environmental and other movements. EcoNet, PeaceNet, LaborNet, WomensNet, and ConflictNet are among their communities of activists.

Adbusters, Journal of the Mental Environment specializes in humorous parodies and critiques of advertising. Bright and lively in format, and appealing especially to an audience of young adults, the magazine consistently makes the natural environment central to its critique of commercial culture. It is published by the Media Foundation, whose "Culture Jammer's Video" includes award-winning parodies of commercials like *American Excess, Autosaurus, Ecological Economics,* and *Talking Rainforest.* The Media Foundation promotes Buy Nothing Day, held since 1993 on the first shopping day after U.S. Thanksgiving, traditionally the busiest shopping day of the year. Now celebrated in eight countries and receiving increasing attention in commercial media, Buy Nothing Day invites residents of the affluent West to join a 24-hour moratorium on consumer spending.[28]

Other groups concentrate less on publications than on organizing people to critique and change the media environment. Perhaps the most important of these is the Cultural Environment Movement, initiated by George Gerbner and others, which held its founding convention in 1996. A coalition of independent organizations centered in the United States but worldwide, CEM represents a wide range of social and cultural concerns and works for freedom, diversity, responsibility, respect for cultural integrity, and democratic decision making in media and cultural environments. Building a coalition of more than 6,000 individuals in over 150 social, political, religious, labor, media, and environmental organizations, CEM is dedicated to media reform through both grassroots organizing and transformations of public policy.

One of the most ominous developments in the media today is the commercial invasion of the public schools. Corporate propaganda disguised as teaching materials, lunch programs run by McDonald's or Pizza Hut, school bulletin boards and buses plastered with advertising, and underpaid and overwhelmed teachers resorting increasingly to commercial videos during class time—these are symptoms of a pervasive commercial colonization of public space as surely as the brand names on students' clothing. Spearheading this invasion is Channel One, a nationwide project of Whittle Communications, Inc., in which Whittle contracts with schools to provide video monitors and other equipment in exchange for 15 minutes of news and commercials, *which all the students in the school are required to watch.* In an era when major corporations report record profits, lay off workers, and constantly shift their share of the total tax burden onto hard-pressed individual taxpayers, causing tax rebellions, public schools are chronically underfunded. Forced to turn for revenues to the private corporations whose selfishness squeezed them in the first place, they often can only obtain audiovisual equipment through Whittle. Thousands of schools have done so. Channel One's "news" hardly deserves the name, and its commercials are so much more interesting that students often respond to and remember them over the ostensibly educational material. In some schools the 15 minutes of Channel One is the only time in the day when all students must be in their seats doing the same thing at the same time.[29]

However, there have been organized protests, resistance, and successful rollbacks of Channel One's campaign. These are often sparked by the Center for Commercial-Free Public Education, a national coalition of students, parents, teachers, and community members based in Oakland, California. The center provides assistance to communities, publishes materials, and tracks classroom commercialism around the United States.

Television is not just invading the schools; it is out of control in many homes. Take an inventory of your own relation to television by considering what and how much you watch in a week. What is television's place in your life and the lives of your family and friends? Since commercial television is designed to encourage continuous viewing for hours at a time, most people watch more than they realize.

Perhaps the best way to measure the place of television in your life is to try turning it off for a week. This salutary exercise, used in scattered families and media studies classes for years, has been developed into the beginnings of a national movement by a small but growing nonprofit organization, TV-Free America. Founded in 1994, the group held its first national TV-Turnoff Week April 24–30, 1995. More than 4,000 schools participated, and over a million people turned off their TV sets for a week. By 1997 more than 25,000 schools and community groups participated, and an estimated 4 million people turned off their sets.

TV-Free America wisely argues that, sure, there are good things on television, but that's not the point. It "focuses attention not on the *quality* of TV programming but on the excessive *quantity* of television that most Americans watch. . . . TV-Free America encourages Americans *to reduce,* voluntarily and dramatically, the amount of television they watch in order to promote richer, healthier and more connected lives, families and communities. . . . Instead of watching a documentary about birds, go out (with binoculars if you have them) and see how many live birds you can identify in your neighborhood. . . . Turn off the Discovery Channel and make your own discoveries."[30] Like the other grassroots citizens' organizations mentioned above, TV-Free America is a small national office linked to a growing network of community activists. The group's excellent *Organizer's Guide* shows how to organize a TV Turnoff and includes testimonials from those who've done it, helpful hints, 101 activities to substitute for watching television, news articles, book lists, and more. New projects include a school-based "More Reading, Less TV" program to encourage children's reading for pleasure and reduce their television viewing for extended periods; an international TV Turnoff Week extended to the English-speaking countries of Canada, Great Britain, Australia, and New Zealand; and a conference on television as a public health problem that may well be contributing to violence and aggressive behavior, obesity, eating disorders among girls, and other health problems.

TV-Free America has clearly begun to catalyze a deep dissatisfaction with television among many Americans. But you don't have to follow their route or wait until April to try this out yourself. You can start turning off the television, at least more often, right now. These folks are right: for most of us, regardless of the quality of what we watch, television is what it is designed to be, a habit. Kicking that habit is a positive step. In the process, you may find time for more valuable things to do. This is hardly an immediate solution for the massive problems of commercial culture, but if enough people do it . . .

Media Advocacy in the Public Interest

Many groups try to influence the U.S. media through government media policy, but most of them are self-interested, promoting well-funded corporate agendas. Among the Washington, D.C., groups are two that work in the public interest. The Center for Media Education fosters telecommunications policy making and regulation through research, lobbying, education, publicity, and coalition building. Its primary focus is on children, and it effectively spearheaded a national campaign that resulted in a 1996 Federal Communications Commission decision to require television stations to air a minimum of three hours of educational children's programs each week. It works to expand access of poor and minority children to new educational technologies, exposes manipulative advertising on the World Wide Web targeting children, and organizes nonprofit groups to become involved in the policy debate over the "information superhighway."

The Media Access Project is a nonprofit public interest law firm that defends our First Amendment rights on current and future electronic media. It promotes diversity of ownership of electronic media, equal access to the Net as a basic right, and freedom of speech on the Net.

Media Literacy

Media literacy is not a publication or a single organization but a whole movement in itself, a growing, loosely organized, and diverse group of individuals and institutions dedicated to educating viewers in the critical skills needed for a ubiquitous, overwhelming media environment. Burgeoning in the eighties and nineties in response to growing public alarm over media violence and commercialism, media literacy is centered in the schools but also works through churches, families, and other institutions.

Elizabeth Thoman of the Center for Media Literacy has defined three aspects of media literacy, from beginning to more advanced:

1. Managing television time and the choices involved.
2. Developing critical viewing skills—understanding media frames.
3. Looking behind the frames—political, economic, and social analysis of the media.[31]

In the broadest sense, then, this book is part of the media literacy movement.

Video Production and Distribution

One of media literacy's strengths is its diversity and grassroots shape. It uses the publications and organizations described above to help demystify television and other media. One of the best ways to do this, with or without the analyses of media literacy, is for people to make and distribute their own videos. Since we mostly experience television and other mass media as distant, powerful forces, one-way communications beyond our control, planning, shooting, and editing our own videos can be empowering. Through public access cable, schools and colleges, unions, environmental organizations, community groups, and other institutions, people around the country and the world are using camcorders and inexpensive editing decks to contribute to what Frances Moore Lappé and Paul Martin Du Bois call public talk. "By *public talk* we mean people expressing their views, hearing different views, weighing the differences—we mean all that goes into forming public judgment. Public judgment is not just public opinion—the undigested, knee-jerk reactions to the questions of pollsters. Instead, public judgment requires that we ourselves help shape the questions and frame the issues. It means we have the opportunity to reflect, to weigh alternative solutions, perhaps even create some ourselves."[32] In their valuable book *The Quickening of America: Rebuilding Our Nation, Remaking Our Lives,* dedicated to showing how Americans are revitalizing community and political organizations, Lappé and Du Bois show how citizens are making television and video work for them.

> With just a half-dozen people sitting in her living room, Dorothy Green started an organization in 1985 to protest the impending death of the Santa Monica Bay caused mostly by the dumping of raw sewage in the Pacific Ocean just west of Los Angeles. Heal the Bay now has nine staff members and a half-million-dollar budget. The organization was instrumental in the passage of ordinances promoting conservation and linking growth to sewage treatment capacity. They also got a commitment from the Los Angeles City Council for $3.4 billion to expand the inadequate existing system.

Heal the Bay produced public service announcements to appear in movie theaters before the main feature. . . .

The success of this approach spurred the organization to try more ads at theaters and on late-night TV.[33]

The approach is working—the ocean is getting cleaner. Dolphins, starfish, pelicans, and other marine life are returning. Using television and film to publicize their campaign, citizens took the initiative in cleaning up their environment.

Indigenous peoples like the Inuit of North America, the Kayapo of the Amazon Basin in Brazil, and Aboriginal Australians are using camcorders and VCRs to battle ecological and economic degradation, cultural destruction, and geographic encroachment. Using inexpensive, small-scale technology to communicate with one another, neighbors, and the outside world, these groups face a "'Faustian dilemma': on the one hand, they use new technologies for cultural self-assertion, on the other they spread a technology that might ultimately only foster their own disintegration."[34] Without romanticizing these peoples or their technology, we can see how video and other media can bring new voices into the public conversations of the entire planet.

Closer to home, we can refunction entertainment and news through family discussions. One of the first lessons for parents concerned about television is to talk with their children about specific programs and commercials. Mediate television before it mediates you. Expand the conditions of reception—watch more as a citizen activist, less as a consumer. Expand the conditions of distribution as well—rather than accepting what your local video store, library, or PBS station already has available, ask for more diversity, more documentaries, independent and foreign films, whatever you like. Write to your senator or congressperson about the concentration of media ownership and control in the hands of a few multinational corporations and how it promotes violence and commercialism and undermines diversity and public accountability. Remember that a single intelligent and reasonable letter—preferably handwritten—from a constituent is typically taken in Washington to represent 5,000 potential voters.

In New York City, media activists experienced in video production for local cable access channels founded Paper Tiger Television in the early eighties. Working cheaply and without the slickness of most professional television and video, Paper Tiger has produced and distributed scores of programs to public access channels, universities, and museums around the country. These include a popular and sardonic series in which media critics "read" *TV Guide,* various television series, and other commercial media products.

Another exemplary institutional model for video production and distribution is the Media Education Foundation. In 1990 Sut Jhally, a professor of communication at the University of Massachusetts, released to a small group of educational and community institutions his critique of music videos, *Dreamworlds: Desire/Sex/Power in Rock Video.* It demonstrated not only the sexist imagery in music videos but also how these videos often link sexual pleasure and desire with violence toward women and how this can affect attitudes toward rape. When MTV saw the video, it threatened to sue. But when the *New York Times, Newsweek,* the *Boston Globe,* and other media covered the story, MTV realized it could be hurt more by negative publicity and suspended legal action. The publicity generated vastly increased sales for *Dreamworlds,* making possible the founding of the Media Education Foundation in 1991. *Dreamworlds* has now been shown in hundreds of high schools, colleges, women's centers, and rape crisis centers and seen by more than a million people to date. The Media Education Foundation now distributes more than a dozen educational videos, including *Pack of Lies: The Advertising of Tobacco, The Killing Screens* with George Gerbner on television violence, and *No Rewind,* on preventing the spread of HIV and AIDS among teenagers. An updated version of *Dreamworlds* was released in 1995. Aided by foundation grants and individual memberships, MEF has donated copies of its video *Date Rape Backlash* to rape crisis centers and women's groups. As it expands, the foundation plows its resources back into new projects of critical media literacy. One of its recent videos, *Advertising and the End of the World* clearly demonstrates the connections between advertising and environmental destruction.[35]

The Internet and the World Wide Web are opening whole new worlds of possibility, including decentralizing and democratizing communication on a global scale. In these worlds, production and distribution of culture and information take on new meanings, since we can all make works and put them on the Net. The freedom, even anarchy, of the Internet is valuable and important to protect. In some ways it is a pure marketplace of ideas, enormously more open and egalitarian than commercial television. But as in other markets, entry is limited—in the case of the Net, to those who can afford computers, printers, modems, and the leisure to develop computer skills. The working poor and the impoverished have largely been excluded from this "revolution." So far it is mostly the professional middle class who uses the Net, and since the attention of that group is one of the most highly prized commodities in the world, Web sites and other venues on the information superhighway have rapidly been colonized by marketers.

Developed in the 18th century at a time of absolutist rulers and state power, the U.S. Constitution and Bill of Rights were designed to protect citizens against a powerful central government. Although the federal and state governments have grown enormously since then, their power is increasingly dwarfed by multinational corporations, institutions whose power and global reach the framers of our Constitution could scarcely have imagined. Although paying lip service to conservative ideas of the "free market" and "free enterprise," these corporations must dominate and control all aspects of the markets for raw materials, labor, expertise, and customers in order to compete against other global giants. Presenting television as a "free marketplace of ideas" in which viewers vote with their remotes, these corporations equate democracy with the market they control. Thus if truth supposedly emerges from the free competition of ideas, then our media environment has also emerged from the ratings, neutral record of the free choices of millions of viewers. It may not be the best of all possible media environments, but it's a democratic choice.

The problems with this reasoning are two. First, as we have demonstrated, the choices of viewers are made from alternatives already largely—though not entirely—controlled by the media giants. Their choices condition our choices in a thousand ways, known and unknown. Second, the "marketplace of ideas" has less and less become a place where ideas or stories compete for consideration. More and more now the "marketplace of ideas" is a literal one, where ideas and stories—and the attention of their audiences—are bought and sold. In a situation in which the consideration of affluent viewers sells to advertisers for considerably more than the consideration of poorer viewers, it's not one person, one vote, but one dollar, one vote. As George Orwell put it, everyone is equal, but some are more equal than others.

Beyond Television and Media: Green Directions

Ultimately, solutions to the crisis of our media environment are not primarily personal or individual but collective. As the best of contemporary post-poststructuralist thought has argued, subjectivity is not centered in individuals but decentered in social action, including discourse. Character is action. The Internet can create another synthetic media environment around us, or it can help us make time and priorities for reconnection to the natural one. Technologies like television and the Net can make life more convenient and provide access to information and entertainment, but they are not intrinsically emancipatory. Look for alternatives, and, with others, make your own.

Beyond the media-oriented groups discussed above are important environmental and Green groups. The mainstream environmental movement includes the Sierra Club, the Audubon Society, the Natural Resources Defense Council, Friends of the Earth, the Environmental Policy Institute, the Izaak Walton League, the Wilderness Society, the Environmental Defense Fund, the National Wildlife Federation, the Union of Concerned Scientists, Zero Population Growth, the World Resources Institute, and Greenpeace. These groups have largely focused their attention and resources on influencing government policy and have had significant successes. As a result, however, they have mostly neglected grassroots organizing and direct action for "inside-the-beltway" lobbying and Washington politics, making more and more compromises on the environment as they became political insiders. With intermittent exceptions, their failure to nourish their local roots has made them less accountable to their members, less democratic, and less activist. While still sometimes effective at influencing public policy, they need to decentralize, to *organize* in addition to fund-raising.[36]

Much smaller but more activist are the grassroots Green organizations. The Student Environmental Action Coalition provides information and strategies for current environmental campaigns by student groups around the country and coordinates the networking of these groups through programs and conferences. Youth for Environmental Sanity helps organize young people around environmental issues through camps, performances, and direct action.

The Greens are a decentralized grassroots organization of local activists, and "are not just an environmental movement. They are a movement of diversity and empowerment. The Greens see domination of the environment by people as intimately related to the domination of people by people. Thus environmentalism is a cornerstone, but not the sole component, of the Greens."[37] Associated with the Green Party USA, which is working to elect local and state Green candidates, and with Green Parties in Europe, Latin America, and around the world, the Greens demonstrate the potential to become a transformative force. Their magazine, *Synthesis/Regeneration*, reflects the sometimes chaotic diversity of the Green movement in the United States and globally.

Following is information about organizations and other resources for media activism.

Institute for Alternative Journalism
77 Federal St., 2d floor
San Francisco, CA 94107
415-284-1420
415-284-1414 FAX
http://www.igc.org/an/
71362.27@compuserve.com

FAIR
130 W. 25th St.
New York, NY 10001
212-633-6700
212-727-7668 FAX
http://www.fair.org/
fair@fair.org

Independent Press Association
P.O. Box 191785
San Francisco, CA 94119-1785
415-896-2456
indypress@igc.org
http://www.hues.net/ipa

Institute for Global Communications
(IGC)
Presidio Building (D12, 1st floor)
Torney Ave., P.O. Box 29904
San Francisco, CA 94129-0904
415-561-6100
415-561-6101 FAX
http://www.igc.org/igc/

Adbusters Magazine
The Media Foundation
1243 West 7th Ave.
Vancouver, BC
V6H 1B7 Canada
604-736-9401
604-737-6021 FAX
http://www.adbusters.org
adbusters@adbusters.org

Z Net
18 Millfield St.
Woods Hole, MA 07543
508-548-9064
zsysop@zbbs.com
http://www.lbbs.org/

Cultural Environment Movement
CEM@libertynet.org
P.O. Box 31847
Philadelphia, PA 19104

The Center for Commercial-Free Public
Education
360 Grand Ave., #385
Oakland, CA 94610
510-268-1100
510-268-1277 FAX
unplug@igc.org

TV-Free America
1611 Connecticut Ave. NW, Suite 3A
Washington, DC 20009
202-887-0436
202-518-5560 FAX
http://www.essential.org/orgs/tvfa
tvfa@essential.org

Center for Media Literacy
4727 Wilshire Blvd., #403
Los Angeles, CA 90010
1-800-226-9494 (orders)
213-931-4474 FAX
http://www.medialit.org

Center for Media Education
1511 K St. NW, Suite 518
Washington, DC 20005
202-628-2620
202-628-2554 FAX
cme@cme.org
http://tap.epn.org/cme/intro.html

Alliance for Community Media
666 11th St. NW, Suite 806
Washington, DC 20001
202-393-2650
202-393-2653 FAX
alliance@aol.com

Media Access Project
1707 L St. NW
Washington, DC 20036
202-232-4300
http://www.essential.org/map/index.html

Paper Tiger Television
339 Lafayette St.
New York, NY 10012
212-420-9045
212-420-8223 FAX
http://www.papertiger.org
tigertv@bway.net

Media Education Foundation
26 Center St.
Northampton, MA 01060
413-584-8500
1-800-897-0089 (video orders)
http://www.igc.org/mef
mediaed@mediaed.org

Association of Independent Video and
    Filmmakers
304 Hudson St.
New York, NY 10013
212-807-1400
212-463-8519 FAX
aivffivf@aol.com
http://www.virtualfilm.com/AIVF/

The Student Environmental Action
    Coalition
1-800-700-SEAC
http://www.rpi.edu/dept/environ/pubs/
    enviRenss/Issue 1/SEAC.html

Youth for Environmental Sanity
420 Bronco Rd.
Soquel, CA 95073
888-937-6946
408-662-0793
408-662-0797 FAX

Yes & Know
P.O. Box 3816
Santa Cruz, CA 95063
408-477-4151
yes@yesworld.org

Campus Alternative Journalism Project
Center for Campus Organizing
Box 748
Cambridge, MA 02142
Te/Fax 617-354-9363
cco@apc.org

Synthesis/Regeneration
A Magazine of Green Social Thought
WD Press
P.O. Box 24115
St. Louis, MO 63130
314-727-8554
jsutter@igc.apc.org

FURTHER READING

Cronon, William, ed. *Uncommon Ground: Rethinking the Human Place in Nature.* New York: Norton, 1996.

Dominguez, Joe, and Vicki Robin. *Your Money or Your Life: Transforming Your Relationship with Money and Achieving Financial Independence.* New York: Penguin Books, 1992.

Dowie, Mark. *Losing Ground: American Environmentalism at the Close of the Twentieth Century.* Cambridge: MIT Press, 1995.

Elgin, Duane. *Voluntary Simplicity.* Rev. ed. New York: William Morrow, 1993.

Hay, James, Lawrence Grossberg, and Ellen Wartella, eds. *The Audience and Its Landscape.* Cultural Studies. Boulder, Colo.: Westview, 1996.

Hazen, Don, and Julie Winokur, eds. *We the Media: A Citizen's Guide to Fighting for Media Democracy.* New York: New Press, 1997.

Jacobson, Michael F., and Laurie Ann Mazur. *Marketing Madness: A Survival Guide for a Consumer Society.* Boulder, Colo.: Westview, 1995.

Jagtenberg, Tom, and David McKie. *Eco-Impacts and the Greening of Postmodernity: New Maps for Communication Studies, Cultural Studies, and Sociology.* Thousand Oaks, Calif.: Sage, 1997.

List, Peter. *Radical Environmentalism: Philosophy and Tactics.* Belmont, Calif.: Wadsworth, 1993.

Schor, Juliet. *The Overworked American: The Unexpected Decline of Leisure.* New York: Basic Books, 1991.

Shohat, Ella, and Robert Stam. *Unthinking Eurocentrism: Multiculturalism and the Media.* London: Routledge, 1994.

Smythe, Dallas. "Communications: Blind Spot of Western Marxism." *Canadian Journal of Political and Social Theory* 1, no. 3 (1977): 1–27.

Warren, Karen J., ed. *Ecological Feminism.* Environmental Philosophies. London: Routledge, 1994.

Notes

One. Television and the Environment: An Introduction

1. John P. Robinson, "As We Like It," *American Demographics* 15 (February 1993): 47.
2. For a study attuned to the complexities of local narrowcast television as well as to those of audience response, a study that implicitly raises questions about oversimplified conceptions of any television programming and responses to it, see Hamid Naficy, *The Making of Exile Cultures: Iranian Television in Los Angeles* (Minneapolis: University of Minnesota Press, 1993).
3. Robert Stam, Robert Burgoyne, and Sandy Flitterman-Lewis, *New Vocabularies in Film Semiotics: Structuralism, Post-Structuralism, and Beyond* (London: Routledge, 1992), 142–146.
4. Newton N. Minow, *How Vast the Wasteland Now?* (New York: Freedom Forum, 1991), 10. Includes the title speech, made May 9, 1991, in New York at the Gannett Foundation Media Center at Columbia University, as well as the original "vast wasteland" address of May 9, 1961, to the National Association of Broadcasters in Washington. Available from the Gannett Foundation Media Center, 2950 Broadway, New York, NY 10027.
5. John P. Robinson, "I Love My TV," *American Demographics* 12 (September 1990): 27.
6. Michael Morgan and Nancy Signorielli, "Cultivation Analysis: Conception and Methodology," in *Cultivation Analysis: New Directions in Media Effects Research,* ed. Nancy Signorielli and Michael Morgan (Newbury Park, Calif.: Sage, 1990), 13.
7. "Media Usage and Consumer Spending: 1984 to 1997." *Statistical Abstract of the United States, 1996* (Washington, D.C.: GPO, 1996), 562. Source cited: *Communications Industry Forecast Report* (New York: Veronis, Suhler & Associates, n.d.).
8. For one recent comprehensive study of viewing habits, emphasizing the impact of channel switching and including a valuable methodological critique by Horst Stipp of NBC, see *Channels* (magazine), *How Americans Watch TV: A Nation of Grazers,* foreword by Merrill Brown (New York: C.C. Publishing, 1989).
9. Nielsen Media Research, "Weekly TV Viewing by Age," *Information Please Almanac, Atlas and Yearbook* (Boston: Houghton Mifflin, 1997), 747.
10. Nielsen Media Research, "Hours of TV Usage per Week by Household Income," *Information Please Almanac, Atlas and Yearbook* (Boston: Houghton Mifflin, 1997), 747; *Channels, How Americans Watch TV,* 69–70.
11. This largely explains why John Robinson's figures tend to be lower than the others: he counts only "primary" viewers, those who "give television their undivided attention." Adding in "secondary" and "tertiary" viewers, those who eat or read or do something else while watching and those who have the set on but pay little attention to it, raises average viewing to about three hours a day. See Robinson, "I Love My TV," 24–25. According to *TV Guide,* almost two-thirds of viewers say they watch TV while eating dinner; 29 percent "often" fall asleep in front of the set, with parents of young children most likely to do so. Forty-two percent routinely turn on the set when, at home, they walk into a room where it is off. Three percent have a TV in the bathroom. *"TV Guide*

Poll: Would You Give Up TV for a Million Bucks?" *TV Guide,* October 10, 1992, 11–13.

12. Ien Ang, *Desperately Seeking the Audience* (London: Routledge, 1991).

13. Adam Snyder, "I Can't Get No . . . ," in *Channels, How Americans Watch TV,* 21.

14. Ibid., 83; "*TV Guide* Poll: Would You Give Up TV for a Million Bucks?," 11–13. On the other hand, 93 percent in *TV Guide'*s poll did say that, stranded on a desert island, they would prefer the company of a loved one to a television set.

15. Althea C. Huston et al., *Big World, Small Screen: The Role of Television in American Society* (Lincoln: University of Nebraska Press, 1992).

16. Michael Schudson, *Advertising, the Uneasy Persuasion: Its Dubious Impact on American Society* (New York: Basic Books, 1984), 209–233.

17. Robert Bocock, *Consumption* (London: Routledge, 1993), 93.

18. Few know this better than parents of small children, who can be forbidden direct contact with a media product and still become expert in its details. One way to chart TV's influence is to keep a diary of all references to television advertising and programming encountered in conversation during a given day of normal activities. Another way to see television's part in one's life is to chart viewing for a few weeks, while trying not to let the record keeping affect behavior. How rapidly the hours accumulate!

19. For detailed accounts of the condition of the environment, see the joint report of the World Resources Institute Staff, United Nations Environment Programme Staff, United Nations Development Programme Staff, and World Bank Staff, *World Resources, 1996–97* (Washington, D.C.: World Resources Institute, 1996) [a trade paperback edition is available from Oxford University Press]; studies produced by the United Nations Environment Programme (such as *Environmental Data Report, 1993–94 Edition: A Report for the Global Environment Monitoring System within Earthwatch* [Cambridge, England: Blackwell, 1994]); and the annual reports of the Worldwatch Institute (such as Lester R. Brown, Michael Renner, and Christopher Flavin, *Vital Signs, 1997: The Environmental Trends That Are Shaping Our Future* [New York: Norton, 1997], and Lester R. Brown, Christopher Flavin, and Hilary F. French, *State of the World, 1997: A Worldwatch Institute Report on Progress toward a Sustainable Society* [New York: Norton, 1997]).

20. Christopher Flavin, "The Legacy of Rio," in Brown, Flavin, and French, *State of the World, 1997,* 19.

21. World Resources Institute (in collaboration with the United Nations Environment Programme and the United Nations Development Programme), *World Resources, 1994–95* (New York: Oxford University Press, 1994), 321.

22. "A Little Good News," *ULS Report,* July–August 1997, based on U.S. Environmental Protection Agency findings. On the World Wide Web, September 1997, http://www.cygnusgroup.com/ULS/Current_ULS_Reports/ No.21_JA97. html#SR.

23. Bedřich Moldan, "Transition and Environment," remarks to Macalester College Faculty Development Seminar, "Transition and Globalization," Budapest, July 11, 1995; revised version published in *Macalester International* 2 (Autumn 1995): 76–96.

24. William Leach, *Land of Desire: Merchants, Power, and the Rise of a New American Culture* (New York: Pantheon, 1993), 386–387.

25. Neil Smith, *Uneven Development: Nature, Capital, and the Production of Space,* 2d ed. (Oxford: Basil Blackwell, 1990).

26. Brown, Renner, and Flavin, *Vital Signs, 1997,* 20.

27. Lester R. Brown, "Facing the Prospect of Food Scarcity," in Brown, Flavin, and French, *State of the World, 1997,* 23–41.

28. Brown, Renner, and Flavin, *Vital Signs, 1997,* 19–20.

29. Ibid., 17–18; William K. Stevens, "Ever-so Slight Rise in Temperatures Led to a Record High in 1997," *New York Times* (national ed.), January 9, 1997, sec. A, 8.

For a more optimistic view regarding the United States, see Gregg Easterbrook, *A Moment on the Earth: The Coming Age of Environmental Optimism* (New York: Viking, 1995), discussed below. For summaries of environmentalist critiques of Easterbrook, including ways antienvironmentalists have used his arguments, see Ron Nixon, "Limbaughesque Science: 'Eco-Realism' vs. Eco-Reality," *Extra!* (July/August 1995): 25–26 [copies available from FAIR (Fairness and Accuracy in Reporting), 130 W. 25th St., New York, NY 10001], and Will Nixon, "The Forest for the Trees," *In These Times,* July 24, 1995, 17–19.

30. Bill McKibben, *The End of Nature* (New York: Anchor/Doubleday, 1989).
31. Bill McKibben, *Hope, Human and Wild: True Stories of Living Lightly on the Earth* (Boston: Little, Brown, 1995).
32. Easterbrook, *Moment on the Earth,* xviii.
33. Brown, Renner, and Flavin, *Vital Signs, 1997,* 15.
34. Ibid., 16.
35. On the burning of fossil fuels, see ibid., 17; quotation from Easterbrook, *Moment on the Earth,* xviii.
36. Schudson, *Advertising,* 20–23.
37. For one history, see Erik Barnouw, *The Sponsor: Notes on a Modern Potentate* (Oxford: Oxford University Press, 1978).
38. Economic growth does not necessarily lead to environmental harm, however. Because of stricter environmental regulation, for example, new cars pollute much less than those from the 1970s. The replacement of old cars by new ones, a policy the state of California, for one, has subsidized, both improves the environment and adds to the gross national product (although investment in public transportation might do both even better). This also applies to refrigerators and industrial retooling designed to reduce pollution and waste. Gary Krueger, Comments on Bedřich Moldan's "Transition and Environment," Macalester Faculty Development Seminar, "Transition and Globalization," Budapest, July 11, 1995. In parts of the world where pollution control has lagged, such as Eastern Europe, opportunities for economic growth tied to a cleaner environment are considerable, and industries on their own might decide to invest in waste reduction to cut ongoing costs. However, private investment in pollution controls seems more often to require political action by environmentalist movements as a spur, since aggregate private investment in a market economy would seem structurally indifferent to environmental costs and effects. For an opposing argument, that "there isn't . . . any basic conflict at all, between macroeconomists, financiers, and environmentalists," see Jeffrey Sachs, "Economies in Transition: Some Aspects of Environmental Policy," in *Economic Instruments for Sustainable Development,* ed. Bedřich Moldan (Prague: Ministry of the Environment of the Czech Republic, 1995), 27–34.
39. Stuart Ewen, *Captains of Consciousness: Advertising and the Social Roots of the Consumer Culture* (New York: McGraw-Hill, 1976).
40. Leach, *Land of Desire,* 386–387.
41. Ibid., 7.
42. Ibid., 3. For more on the democratization of desire and its relation to political democracy, see Stuart Ewen, *All Consuming Images: The Politics of Style in Contemporary Culture* (New York: Basic Books, 1988), 24–40, 57–77.
43. Leach, *Land of Desire,* 9.
44. Stuart Ewen, "Advertising and the Development of Consumer Society," in *Cultural Politics in Contemporary America,* ed. Ian Angus and Sut Jhally (New York: Routledge, 1989), 82–95.
45. Simmel quoted in Bocock, *Consumption,* 16–17.
46. Bocock, *Consumption,* 49–50.
47. T. J. Jackson Lears, "From Salvation to Self-Realization: Advertising and the Therapeutic Roots of the Consumer Culture, 1880–1930," in *The Culture of Consumption:*

Critical Essays in American History, 1880–1980, ed. Richard Wightman Fox and T. J. Jackson Lears (New York: Pantheon, 1983), 9.

48. Leach, *Land of Desire,* 40–43.

49. See Schudson, *Advertising,* 168–177, and Roland Marchand, *Advertising the American Dream: Making Way for Modernity, 1920–1940* (Berkeley: University of California Press, 1985), 1–110. For the impact of advertising on newspapers during this period, see Ben H. Bagdikian, *The Media Monopoly,* 5th ed. (Boston: Beacon Press, 1997), 118–207; on magazines, see Christopher P. Wilson, "The Rhetoric of Consumption: Mass-Market Magazines and the Demise of the Gentle Reader," in Fox and Lears, *Culture of Consumption,* 39–64.

50. Leach, *Land of Desire,* 67.

51. Anne Friedberg, *Window Shopping: Cinema and the Postmodern* (Berkeley: University of California Press, 1993), 65.

52. Quoted in Leach, *Land of Desire,* 70.

53. Ibid., 62–63.

54. Friedberg, *Window Shopping,* 65.

55. Leach, *Land of Desire,* 63.

56. Friedberg, *Window Shopping,* 3.

57. Ibid., 35. Friedberg here develops Walter Benjamin's treatment of the Parisian *flâneur/flâneuse,* included in "Paris, Capital of the Nineteenth Century," in *Reflections: Essays, Aphorisms, Autobiographical Writings,* ed. Peter Demetz, trans. Edmund Jephcott (New York: Harcourt, 1978), 146–162, and other writings. For an introduction to Benjamin, see Susan Buck-Morss, *The Origin of Negative Dialectics: Theodor W. Adorno, Walter Benjamin, and the Frankfurt Institute* (New York: Free Press, 1977), or Margaret Cohen, *Profane Illumination: Walter Benjamin and the Paris of Surrealist Revolution* (Berkeley: University of California Press, 1993).

58. Edwin L. Artzt, speech to the American Association of Advertising Agencies Convention, White Sulphur Springs, W.Va., May 12, 1994. All quotations from Artzt in the text are from this speech. To request a copy, write to the Public Affairs Division, Procter & Gamble, 1 Procter & Gamble Plaza, Cincinnati, OH 45202–3315.

59. Leach, *Land of Desire,* 386. However complex this process is for the privileged, it is far more tricky, and more difficult, for everyone else. This is particularly true for those involuntarily stigmatized as different, in terms of ethnicity, national origin, race, or sexuality but also for just happening to be physically unusual. For the classic statement on the problem of living with "double consciousness" in a world that marks one different, see W.E.B. Du Bois's *The Souls of Black Folk* (1903) in several editions, including *The Norton Anthology of African American Literature,* ed. Henry Louis Gates Jr. and Nellie Y. McKay (New York: Norton, 1997), 613–740. "The problem of the twentieth century is the problem of the color line," writes Du Bois. "How does it feel to be a problem?" (620, 614).

60. "Audience interests are exceedingly difficult to measure meaningfully by the usual techniques of social and marketing research." W. Russell Neuman, *The Future of the Mass Audience* (Cambridge: Cambridge University Press, 1991), 120–121. Yet even to talk about measuring audience interests is to assume that the institutions that shaped television cared what the public wanted, unless such knowledge would be profitable. At this writing, some broadcasters are considering breaking their pledge to use the additional spectrum space loaned to them by the government for high-definition television. Instead, they would use it for more pay channels. Audience desires are hardly the issue, whatever their relation to HDTV. "We have yet to see how anyone makes money as an HDTV broadcaster," said the president of the Sinclair Broadcasting Group, which owns or programs 29 stations. The president of Disney-ABC observed, "Our share of the viewing audience will continue to erode as long as we remain a single channel in an expanding multi-channel universe." He says "view-

ing audience," but he means money. For in saying his network was abandoning HDTV, he noted that U.S. viewers spend $30 billion dollars a year on pay-TV services and said ABC wants a share of that. Joel Brinkley, "A Gulf Develops among Broadcasters on Programming Pledge," *New York Times* (national ed.), August 18, 1997, sec. C, 1, 9.

61. Lynn Spigel, *Make Room for TV: Television and the Family Ideal in Postwar America* (Chicago: University of Chicago Press, 1992), 7.

62. Cheryl Russell and Thomas G. Exter, "Mad Money," *American Demographics* 15 (July 1993): 26–30.

63. This sensitivity's limit point might be found in a clothing company ad that appeared in the July/August 1990 *Utne Reader*. The ad asked readers of the magazine (whose cover advertised articles such as "Rethinking TV" and "What Now? After Earth Day"): "We can buy for vital needs, not frivolous ego-gratifying needs. We do need clothes, yes, but so many?" Spend less consuming, it said, and send what you save to "one of the thousands of social and environmental organizations that are working to correct, repair, preserve or halt the damage to which our consumptive ways and economic system have led us." It was signed, "ESPRIT[,] A COMPANY THAT IS TRYING." Few other companies have had the nerve to identify buying their brand with buying less, but commercial culture increasingly declares itself to have environmental well-being on its mind, to the point where it has become a standard packaging strategy. Yet why buy branded pants at all? How many hours of labor does one have to devote to earning enough to pay for them? Who makes the pants? How are they paid? How does their oppression relate to local systems of ethnicity, gender, and class? How are the pants sold? What are the environmental costs involved in manufacture, distribution, and sales? See also Michael X. Delli Carpini and Bruce A. Williams, "'Fictional' and 'Non-Fictional' Television Celebrates Earth Day: Or, Politics Is Comedy Plus Pretense," *Cultural Studies* 8, no. 1 (January 1994): 74–98.

64. For a helpful empirical analysis of environmental reporting, see Christine R. Ader, "A Longitudinal Study of Agenda Setting for the Issue of Environmental Pollution," *Journalism and Mass Communication Quarterly* 72 (1995): 300–311.

65. Jay Letto, "TV Lets Corporations Pull Green Wool over Viewers' Eyes," *Extra!* (July/August 1995): 22. Copies available from FAIR (Fairness and Accuracy in Reporting), 130 W. 25th St., New York, NY 10001.

66. Vincent Mosco, *The Political Economy of Communication: Rethinking and Renewal* (London: Sage, 1996), 63.

67. Unfortunately, the word *environment* may be part of the problem, to the extent that its usage assumes an artificial separation between humans and what surrounds them. For more on the critique of Enlightenment, see David Harvey, *The Condition of Postmodernity* (Cambridge, England: Blackwell, 1989), and Max Horkheimer and Theodor Adorno, *Dialectic of Enlightenment* [1944], trans. John Cumming (New York: Continuum, 1972).

68. The turning of historically bound relations and practices into what appear to be immutable things, reification had its forms in earlier societies but was, for Karl Marx and later Georg Lukács, characteristic of modern capitalism with its press to render everything, including human labor, a product for sale (see, e.g., Karl Marx, "Economic and Philosophical Manuscripts" [1844], trans. T. B. Bottomore, in *Marx's Concept of Man,* ed. Erich Fromm [New York: Ungar, 1966], 119–140, and Georg Lukács, *History and Class Consciousness: Studies in Marxist Dialectics* [1918–1930], trans. Rodney Livingstone [Cambridge: MIT Press, 1971], 83–209); for an overview, see Gajo Petrović, "Reification," in *A Dictionary of Marxist Thought,* ed. Tom Bottomore (Cambridge: Harvard University Press, 1983, 411–413). We apply the term to television advertising in chapters 4 and 5. Of course, capitalist societies are not alone in suffering from reification or in inflicting it on others, as residents of once Soviet-Communist societies attest as they struggle with decades of environmental negligence.

69. Slavoj Žižek, "Eastern Europe's Republics of Gilead," in *Dimensions of Radical Democracy: Pluralism, Citizenship, Community,* ed. Chantal Mouffe (London: Verso, 1992), 195.

70. In August 1995, the Associated Press reported that a National Academy of Sciences panel had announced that radioactive wastes would pose their greatest contamination risks to future generations 50,000 to 250,000 years from now, long after the disintegration of the containers holding them. "At least some potentially important exposures might not occur until after several hundred thousand years," the 15-member panel said, following a three–year study. Antinuclear scientists have been making similar claims for years. In a continuing example of reification of the planet and its beings, U.S. government officials have insisted that 10,000 years was long enough for concern. H. Josef Hebert, "Scientists See Exposure Risk of Radioactive Waste beyond 10,000 Years," Associated Press Dispatch, Washington, PM Cycle, August 2, 1995. An edited version appeared in the "Away from Politics" column, *International Herald Tribune,* August 3, 1995, 3.

71. Bagdikian, *Media Monopoly,* ix–xxxvii.

72. To request the prospectus and other information on the Cultural Environment Movement, write to Cultural Environment Movement, P.O. Box 31847, Philadelphia, PA 19104, or go to http://www.cemnet.org. From the CEM Prospectus:

> The Cultural Environment Movement is concerned with [commercial media's] distortions of the democratic process. They include the promotion of practices that drug, hurt, poison, and kill thousands every day; portrayals that dehumanize and stigmatize; cults of violence that desensitize, terrorize and brutalize; the growing siege mentality of our cities; the drift toward ecological suicide; the silent crumbling of our infrastructure; widening resource gaps and the most glaring inequalities in the industrial world; the costly neglect of vital institutions such as public education, health care, and the arts; make-believe image politics corrupting the electoral process.
>
> How can we *heal the wounds* of all the stories that hurt and tear us apart? How can we put culture-power to liberating ends? The new cultural environment challenges us to mobilize as public citizens as effectively as commercials mobilize us to act as private consumers and to address these questions.

73. George Gerbner, "Television Violence: The Art of Asking the Wrong Question," *World & I* 9 (July 1994): 390.

74. George Gerbner, "Television Violence: The Power and the Peril," in *Gender, Race, and Class in Media: A Text-Reader,* ed. Gail Dines and Jean M. Humez (Thousand Oaks, Calif.: Sage, 1995), 548.

75. Marsha Kinder, *Playing with Power in Movies, Television, and Video Games: From Muppet Babies to Teenage Mutant Ninja Turtles* (Berkeley: University of California Press, 1991), 1–38.

76. Quoted in Minow, *How Vast the Wasteland Now?,* 14.

77. Jerry Mander, *Four Arguments for the Elimination of Television* (New York: Morrow, 1978), 24.

78. Ibid., 254.

79. Richard Dyer, "Charisma," in *Stardom: Industry of Desire,* ed. Christine Gledhill (London: Routledge, 1991), 57–59. This is an excerpt from Dyer's *Stars* (London: British Film Institute, 1979).

80. Jane Feuer, "The Concept of Live Television: Ontology as Ideology," in *Regarding Television,* ed. E. Ann Kaplan (Frederick, Md.: University Publications of America–American Film Institute, 1983), 12–22.

81. Charlotte Cornelia Herzog and Jane Marie Gaines, "'Puffed-Sleeves before Tea-Time': Joan Crawford, Adrian, and Women Audiences," in Gledhill, *Stardom,* 74–91.

82. Mander, *Four Arguments*, 25.

83. Joshua Meyrowitz, *No Sense of Place: The Impact of Electronic Media on Social Behavior* (New York: Oxford University Press, 1985), 36.

84. Antonio Gramsci, *Selections from the Prison Notebooks* [1929–1935], ed. and trans. Quintin Hoare and Geoffrey Nowell-Smith (New York: International, 1971), 12. For a brief introduction to the term, see John Hartley, "Hegemony," in *Key Concepts in Communication and Cultural Studies*, 2d ed., ed. Tim O'Sullivan et al. (London: Routledge, 1994), 133–135, or Anne Showstack Sassoon, "Hegemony," in Bottomore, *Dictionary of Marxist Thought*, 201–203. We consider the concept again in chapter 6.

85. Raymond Williams, *Keywords: A Vocabulary of Culture and Society*, rev. ed. (New York: Oxford University Press, 1983), 145.

86. Dick Hebdige, *Subculture: The Meaning of Style* (London: Methuen, 1979), 16 (punctuation altered).

87. Stuart Hall, "Culture, the Media, and the 'Ideological Effect,'" in *Mass Communication and Society*, ed. James Curran, Michael Gurevitch, and Janet Woollacott (Beverly Hills: Sage, 1977), 332.

88. Ibid., 333.

89. Ibid., 334; see also Todd Gitlin, "Media Sociology: The Dominant Paradigm," *Theory and Society* 6 (1978): 205–253, and Gaye Tuchman, "The Topic of the Women's Movement," in *Making News: A Study in the Construction of Reality* (New York: Free Press, 1978), 133–155.

90. Gerbner, "Television Violence: The Power and the Peril," 549.

91. One of many examples would be the June 12, 1995, *Time* Special Report, "Are Music and Movies Killing America's Soul?" A recent *New York Times* poll also found 56 percent of adult respondents believing that "portrayals of violence in popular culture contribute a lot" (as opposed to "some," "little," or "none") "to whether teen-agers are violent." Elizabeth Kolbert, "Americans Despair of Popular Culture," *New York Times* (national ed.), August 20, 1995, sec. 2: H1 ff. For a more careful view that nevertheless sounds an important alarm about the nation's children, see the American Psychological Association report *Violence and Youth: Psychology's Response*, 2 vols. (Washington, D.C.: American Psychological Association Public Interest Directorate, 1993). Less cautious is the American Medical Association's 1996 *Physician's Guide to Media Violence* (available from the AMA at 515 North State St., Chicago, IL 60610, and http://www.ama-assn.org).

92. "Cultivation" here means the "specific independent (though not isolated) contribution that a particular consistent and compelling symbolic stream makes to the complex process of socialization and enculturation." George Gerbner, "Epilogue," in Signorielli and Morgan, *Cultivation Analysis*, 249. Not everyone who studies this material is convinced that the work of Gerbner and his colleagues can withstand rigorous, social-scientific scrutiny. On the surface, the arguments about the findings tend to be technical, to raise questions about validity as empirical researchers define it, and to revolve around distinctions between, for example, "causation" and "cultivation," or concerns about statistical controls. Morgan and Signorielli, "Cultivation Analysis," 24. See, for example, the detailed critiques by Paul M. Hirsch and the replies by Gerbner and associates as well as more recent work by W. James Potter and John Tapper. Paul Hirsch, "The 'Scary World' of the Nonviewer and Other Anomalies: A Reanalysis of Gerbner et al.'s Findings on Cultivation Analysis, Part I," *Communication Research* 7 (1980): 403–456; Paul Hirsch, "On Not Learning from One's Mistakes: A Reanalysis of Gerbner et al.'s Findings on Cultivation Analysis, Part II," *Communication Research* 8 (1981): 3–37; George Gerbner, Larry Gross, Michael Morgan, and Nancy Signorielli, "A Curious Journey into the Scary World of Paul Hirsch," *Communication Research* 8 (1981): 39–72; Paul Hirsch, "Distinguishing Good Speculation from Bad Theory:

Rejoinder to Gerbner et al.," *Communication Research* 8 (1981): 73–95; George Gerbner, Larry Gross, Michael Morgan, and Nancy Signorielli, "Final Reply to Hirsch," *Communication Research* 8 (1981): 259–280; W. James Potter, *Cultivation Theory and Research: A Methodological Critique,* Journalism Monographs 147 (Columbia, S.C.: Association for Education in Journalism and Mass Communication, 1994); John Tapper, "The Ecology of Cultivation: a Conceptual Model for Cultivation Research," *Communication Theory* 5, no. 1 (February 1995): 36–57. At root, the arguments concern the role and value of critical theory in scientific research, whether verifiable empirical knowledge can ever adequately comprehend the complexity of the world, and whether there may be other useful ways of knowing that traditional empirical research cannot encompass. For discussions of these matters from socially critical perspectives, see Max Horkheimer, "Traditional and Critical Theory" and "Postscript," in *Critical Theory: Selected Essays,* trans. Matthew J. O'Connell (New York: Continuum, 1972), 188–252; Paul Lazarsfeld, "Remarks on Administrative and Critical Communications Research," *Studies in Philosophy and Social Sciences* 9 (1941): 2–16; and Gitlin, "Media Sociology."

93. Gerbner, "Television Violence: The Power and the Peril," 553.

94 Minow, *How Vast the Wasteland Now?,* 12.

95. Morgan and Signorielli, "Cultivation Analysis," 26.

96. Minow, *How Vast the Wasteland Now?,* 13.

97. Gerbner, "Television Violence: The Power and the Peril," 553.

98. Ibid., 554.

99. Mark Jurkowitz, "Scared Witless," *MediaCulture Review* 3, no. 3 (Summer 1994): 1 ff. Originally published in the *Boston Phoenix*. Copies available from the Institute for Alternative Journalism, 77 Federal St., San Francisco, CA 94107.

100. "On TV News, Survey Finds an Electronic Crime Wave," *Washington Post* dispatch, *Minneapolis Star Tribune,* August 13, 1997, sec. A, 1, 8. One-fifth of the stories concerned O.J. Simpson. According to the study reported by the *Post,* conducted by Robert Lichter and the Center for Media and Public Affairs, since 1993, network news about the entertainment industry and commercial culture has eclipsed that about education, the environment, and Japan combined.

101. Spigel, *Make Room for TV,* 7.

102. Fredric Jameson, "Introduction to T. W. Adorno," *Salmagundi* 10–11 (Winter 1969–1970): 140.

103. Ruthanne Kurth-Schai, "Ecology and Equity: Toward the Rational Reenchantment of Schools and Society," *Educational Theory* 42, no. 2 (Spring 1992): 147–163.

104. For "nature-as-self," see Neil Evernden, "Nature in Industrial Society," in Angus and Jhally, *Cultural Politics in Contemporary America,* 151–164.

105. Andrew Ross, *The Chicago Gangster Theory of Life: Nature's Debt to Society* (London: Verso, 1994), 13; Herbert Marcuse, *An Essay on Liberation* (Boston: Beacon Press, 1969), 91.

106. Mosco, *Political Economy of Communication,* 65.

107. We use "determine," as Raymond Williams advises, not to designate an effect as inevitable or inherent in a cause or "absolutely settled or fixed," not in the sense of a physical science model, in which specific effects can be reproduced as if by general law, but in the sense of to "set certain limits or exert certain pressures" within which actions occur that are "unpredictable or voluntary." *Keywords,* 98–102. And we would add Vincent Mosco's admonition that social relations are so layered and complicated that determinations are always multiple. As he says, quoting Aijiz Ahmad, "determination refers not to 'entrapment' but rather 'to the givenness of the circumstances within which individuals *make* their choices, their lives, their histories'" (emphasis in original). Mosco, *Political Economy of Communication,* 5. The quotation

from Ahmad can be found in his *In Theory: Classes, Nations, Literatures* (London: Verso, 1992), 6.

108. Robert W. McChesney, *Telecommunications, Mass Media, and Democracy: The Battle for the Control of U.S. Broadcasting, 1928–1935* (New York: Oxford University Press, 1995).

109. Schudson, *Advertising*, 232.

110. John Fiske has argued against cultural criticism that characterizes media audiences in this way ("cultural dupes"). See, for example, his "Popular Television and Commercial Culture: Beyond Political Economy," in *Television Studies: Textual Analysis,* ed. Gary Burns and Robert J. Thompson (New York: Praeger, 1989), 22. Stuart Hall, "The Rediscovery of 'Ideology': Return of the Repressed in Media Studies," in *Culture, Society, and the Media,* ed. Michael Gurevitch, Tony Bennett, James Curran, and Janet Woollacott (London: Methuen, 1982), 76.

111. Hall, "Rediscovery of 'Ideology,'" 76.

112. John Thornton Caldwell argues that the look of television since the 1980s constitutes a new form of representation that breaks with the classical Hollywood system, an argument we consider in the chapters that follow. See his *Televisuality: Style, Crisis, and Authority in American Television* (New Brunswick, N.J.: Rutgers University Press, 1995). Building on Jean Baudrillard's notion of a "hyperreality" self-conscious of its own cultural production, Robert Goldman and Stephen Papson write of "hypersignification" in advertising, in which advertisers take commercial imagery as the basis for making meaning. See their *Sign Wars: The Cluttered Landscape of Advertising* (New York: Guilford, 1996).

113. Raymond Williams, *Television: Technology and Cultural Form* [1974], intro. Lynn Spigel (Hanover, N.H.: Wesleyan University Press, 1992), 78–118.

114. For an introduction, see David Morley, "Active Audience Theory: Pendulums and Pitfalls," *Journal of Communication* 43, no. 4 (1993): 13–19.

115. Mosco, *Political Economy of Communication,* 5.

116. This seems odd in terms of traditional market ideology, which argues that competition and unfettered investment secure a marketplace of ideas. Yet the evidence regarding U.S. media hardly supports this. That it does not would not be so surprising if the growing number of channels were seen as a consequence of increased capital investment. Ben Bagdikian (in *The Media Monopoly,* cited above) and others have long argued that increased investment tends to drive out diverse entrepreneurs in favor of well-capitalized multinationals. As W. Russell Neuman puts it, "The economics of mass communications do not promote diversity." *Future of the Mass Audience,* 129.

117. William Julius Wilson, *When Work Disappears: The World of the New Urban Poor* (New York: Knopf, 1997), xxi.

118. An alternative is the bimodal audience, in which the audience divides into two distinct groups, one comfortable with what seems to be the show's favorable presentation of the lead character and one comfortable with what seems to be the show's unfavorable representation of the lead character. The most successful example of this was Norman Lear's *All in the Family* in the 1970s. See Neil Vidmar and Milton Rokeach, "Archie Bunker's Bigotry: A Study in Selective Perception and Exposure," *Journal of Communication* 24 (1974): 36–47. We discuss this argument in more detail in chapter 4. In the 1980s, *The Cosby Show* attracted a bimodal audience along a different axis: those for whom the show was a source of African American pride and—startling to us—those for whom the show's main characters were so familiar in the imaginary world of sitcom affluence that they seemed to have no ethnicity at all. See Sut Jhally and Justin Lewis, *Enlightened Racism: The Cosby Show, Audiences, and the Myth of the American Dream* (Boulder, Colo.: Westview, 1992); Mike

Budd and Clay Steinman, "White Racism and *The Cosby Show*," *Jump Cut* 37 (July 1992): 5–14; and Carlos Nelson and Hermon George, "'White Racism and *The Cosby Show*': A Critique," *Black Scholar* 25, no. 2 (Spring 1995): 59–61.

119. Chris Hikawa, quoted in Heather Joslyn, "Maddie, You #%!°&~#!: In a War against Cable and Videos, Network Censors Decide to Lighten Up," *Special Report on Family* (August–October 1989), 12. ABC itself lost more than $1 million in advertising when it broadcast two gay-identified men talking in bed during *thirtysomething* in 1989. "Not Always Ready for Prime Time," *Time,* April 14, 1997, 81.

120. Ellen DeGeneres, quoted in Bruce Handy, "He Called Me Ellen Degenerate?" *Time,* April 14, 1997, 86.

121. For a demonstration of how fans have creatively used material from such commercial shows as *Star Trek* and *Beauty and the Beast* to develop interpersonal relations that are mostly noncommercial, see, e.g., Henry Jenkins, *Textual Poachers: Television Fans and Participatory Culture* (New York: Routledge, 1992).

122. For a brief discussion between academics and activists of the politics of new information technologies, see Barry Yeoman, "Lost in Cyberspace." *MediaCulture Review* 3, no. 3 (Summer 1994): 3 ff. Originally published in the *North Carolina Independent.* Copies available from the Institute for Alternative Journalism, 77 Federal St., San Francisco, CA 94107.

123. Eileen Meehan, "Why We Don't Count: The Commodity Audience," in *Logics of Television: Essays in Cultural Criticism,* ed. Patricia Mellencamp (Bloomington: Indiana University Press–BFI Publishing, 1990), 117–137.

124. Neuman, *Future of the Mass Audience,* 90.

125. Robert D. Putnam, "Bowling Alone: America's Declining Social Capital," *Journal of Democracy* 6, no. 1 (January 1995): 65–78. Online at http://128.220.50.88/demo/journal_of_democracy/v006/putnam.html. For a later version of the argument, see Putnam's "The Strange Disappearance of Civic America," *American Prospect* 24 (Winter 1996): 34–48. For Jane Jacobs's work, see *The Death and Life of Great American Cities* (New York: Random House, 1961).

126. Putnam, "Bowling Alone," 67.

127. Ibid.

128. Ibid., 68.

129. Ibid., 69. To this Putnam adds, "I should note that nearly 80 million Americans went bowling once during 1993, *nearly a third more than voted in the 1994 congressional elections* and roughly the same number as claim to attend church regularly" (emphasis in original). Ibid., 70.

130. Ibid., 75.

131. Michael Shapiro argues that Putnam and others with similar critiques cannot see the democratic vibrancy within contemporary culture because, in the manner of 19th-century analysts, their viewpoint "restricts political action to influence on government decision makers." This makes them blind to postmodern practices "creating different modalities of civic engagement." As an alternative mode of analysis, Shapiro calls for "post-liberal discourses . . . occupied with the present forces of social and political containment and the counter-forces of resistance." The essay provides a helpful application and extension of the theoretical work of Michel Foucault, Ernesto Laclau, and Chantal Mouffe in tune with the contemporary U.S. political scene. As Shapiro says, Putnam "presumes the existence of a unitary national society," ignoring problems of differentially constructed subjectivities and "the variety of different kinds of political enactment within different social venues." Shapiro also points to the lack of political-economic analysis in Putnam's work and its focus "on mentalities rather than material forces," leaving out how and why "opportunity spaces" for action are enabled for some but eviscerated for others. In addition, for Putnam, technology

too often seems self-generating yet with enormous, unavoidable consequences, as if it were like the weather.

Shapiro advocates appreciation of new forms of community organization against oppression, including cultural practices involving religion, music, prison and street life, and watching television, which for some critical viewers fosters the circulation of new meanings. His argument about African American struggles in this regard makes sense, but it falters when he calls such practices a "paradigm," for it is unclear to what percentage of the population in the United States (or even of African Americans) his description applies. The always partial and differentiated world Shapiro presents is surely not without crucial zones and practices that in complicated ways fit Putnam's characterizations. Indeed, these zones likely outnumber the "configurations of oppositional civic engagement" Shapiro rightly values. In addition, Shapiro's argument that we should in significant measure "recognize an aspect of civic engagement in persistent struggles to maintain workable identities" remains unconvincing until these struggles engage issues of resource allocation, conservation, and public health. See Michael J. Shapiro, "Bowling Blind: Post Liberal Civil Society and the Worlds of Neo-Tocquevillean Social Theory," *Theory and Event* 1, no. 1 (1997) (on-line). Shapiro's article can be found at http://128.220.50.88/journals/theory_&_event/v001/1.1shapiro.html. For a critique of the unfortunate (and idealist) tendency in much U.S. cultural studies to take undeniable acts of individual critical engagements as typical, see Mike Budd, Robert M. Entman, and Clay Steinman, "The Affirmative Character of U.S. Cultural Studies," *Critical Studies in Mass Communication* 7, no. 2 (1990): 169–184.

132. Mander, *Four Arguments*, 189.

Two. An Overview of Television Economics

1. *International Television and Video Almanac, 1998* (New York: Quigley, 1998), 21A.
2. Discussion groups on USENET provide a wonderful opportunity for the television researcher to eavesdrop on television fans as they discuss programs they like and dislike. The apparent importance of these programs in the lives of the Internet writers and their seemingly close relationship with the stars and fictional characters are striking. Most of these discussions can be found in groups beginning with alt.tv or rec.arts.tv.
3. End-of-season ratings figures are reported in trade publications such as *Broadcasting* and *Electronic Media* each year in April or May. A 28.2 rating means that an average of 28.2 percent of U.S. television homes tuned in to one of the big three during prime time, and this represented 47 percent of all television homes that were watching any channel at that time. For an explanation of how ratings and shares are calculated, see chapter 3.
4. The 1997–1998 season prime-time average ratings were NBC, 10.2; CBS, 9.6; ABC, 8.4, Fox, 7.1; WB, 3.1; and UPN, 2.8. See Michael Schneider, "Low and Behold, NBC Wins," *Electronic Media,* May 25, 1998, 4.
5. Some industry observers are not yet prepared to write the obituaries for the big three networks. They point out that deregulation has allowed them to enter into promising new production and distribution deals that may mean a rosy future. See "Who is Watching America's TV Networks?" *Economist,* March 31, 1990, 63–64, and Gene Jankowski and David Fuchs, *Television Today and Tomorrow: It Won't Be What You Think* (New York: Oxford University Press, 1995).
6. The satellite is carefully positioned high enough above the earth that it orbits at precisely the same rate as the earth's rotation. As a result, both earth and satellite move

together in such a way that the satellite is "fixed" or "parked" in relation to a given point on the ground.

7. By the end of 1997, DBS was in approximately 6 million U.S. households. Although this is far below the 65 million homes with cable, two of the largest DBS programmers, DirecTV and USSB, predict subscribership could reach 25 million homes (or about one-fourth of the U.S. total) by the year 2000. See Price Coleman, "No Laurel-Resting for DirecTV's Hartenstein," *Broadcasting and Cable,* November 3, 1997, 52–53, and Jim McConville, "Big Numbers Are Music to DBS Ears," *Broadcasting and Cable,* September 25, 1995, 46.

8. Johnnie L. Roberts, "Marketing & Media: Cable Firms' Venture May Be Challenged," *Wall Street Journal,* July 1, 1991, sec. B, 4A.

9. Eben Shapiro, "Entertainment: New HBO Honcho Must Hone Pay Network's Creative Edge," *Wall Street Journal,* March 19, 1996, sec. B, 1.

10. See Bryan Gruley and Kyle Pope, "Television: So What Exactly Is Digital Television?" *Wall Street Journal,* April 3, 1997, sec. B, 1, and Kyle Pope and Mark Robichaux, "Waiting for HDTV? Don't Go Dumping Your Old Set Just Yet," *Wall Street Journal,* September 12, 1997, 1.

11. Jim McConville, "HBO Goes HDTV; Now Who's Next?" *Electronic Media,* June 16, 1997, 4, 37.

12. Bruce Orwall and John Lippman, "Entertainment: Lawsuit Casts Tim Allen TV Series as Victim of Synergy," *Wall Street Journal,* March 17, 1997, sec. B, 1.

13. Joshua Hammer, "The Myth of Global Synergy," *Newsweek,* June 26, 1989, 54.

14. Orwall and Lippman, "Entertainment."

15. Charles W. Fries, "The Dynamics of Mega-Mergers and Their Effect on Creativity and the Marketplace," *Caucus Quarterly* 14, no. 1 (Spring 1997): 5–7.

16. For example, to gain the approval of the Federal Trade Commission for the 1996 purchase of Turner, Time Warner had to agree that its cable systems would carry one 24-hour news channel in addition to its own CNN. Despite this, a dispute arose over Time Warner's refusal to carry the competing Fox News Channel over its Manhattan cable system. For an analysis, see Lawrence K. Grossman, "Bullies on the Block," *Columbia Journalism Review* 35, no. 5 (January/February 1997): 19–20, and Elizabeth Jensen and Eben Shapiro, "It's a Thin Line . . . Time Warner's Fight with News Corp. Belies Mutual Dependence," *Wall Street Journal,* October 28, 1996, sec. A, 1.

17. As of the date of this writing, at least two companies were offering Web surfers free demonstration versions of video streaming software. These were Progressive Networks' *RealPlayer,* at www.real.com, and VDOnet's *VDOLive,* at www.vdo.net. The software allows crude real-time video and audio to be received by computers over regular telephone lines. Progressive Networks lists 38 "content partners" as providers of its "programming," including ABC News, CBS Sportsline, Fox News, and ESPN. Other Web video programmers include the American Film Institute, which uses *VDOLive* to transmit films from its archives (www.afionline.org). As explained below, Microsoft's financial interest in Progressive will likely make its system the industry standard.

18. Diane Mermigas, "Is Comcast Deal a Watershed?" *Electronic Media,* June 16, 1997, 1, 36.

19. See "Video on the Internet: Webbed," *Economist,* January 20, 1996, 82–83; "What's News—Business and Finance," *Wall Street Journal,* April 7, 1997, sec. A, 1; and Stacy Perman, "Bill Gates' Pipe Dream," *Time,* June 23, 1997, 54–55.

20. John Markoff, "Microsoft Takes a Stake in Progressive Networks," *New York Times,* July 22, 1977, sec. C, 6, and "Microsoft Steps Up Bid for Internet Standard on Audio and Video," *Wall Street Journal,* September 11, 1997, sec. B, 7.

21. David Bank, "Microsoft Raises Stakes in Set-Top Battle," *Wall Street Journal,* September 16, 1997, sec. B, 6.

22. Raymond Williams, *Television: Technology and Cultural Form* (New York: Schocken, 1975).

23. A fascinating case study in technological innovation as a socioeconomic practice in American broadcasting can be found in the development of FM radio. Although the technology of FM was clearly superior to that of existing AM radio as early as 1936, powerful corporate forces—in the form of RCA—saw the new service as an economic threat and successfully delayed FM's adoption for years. See Erik Barnouw's *Tube of Plenty*, 2d ed. (New York: Oxford University Press, 1990).

24. For a good overview of the changing nature of production financing in the 1990s, see "Fear Stalks the Small Screen," *Economist*, April 25, 1992, 81.

25. Time Warner, Disney, and News Corp each own major league sports franchises—a source of relatively cheap programming. Although it is true that professional athletes earn hefty salaries, so do some TV stars (comedian Jerry Seinfeld reportedly received $1 million per 30-minute episode during the 1997–1998 season, and his three supporting cast members each got $600,000). The costs involved in owning a professional sports team compare favorably with the cost of producing traditional prime-time TV programs, especially when one considers that a typical game lasts three hours or more and delivers a fairly narrow demographic. Then, too, the team brings in revenue from sources other than television and provides box seats to the corporation's executives.

26. Eileen Meehan, "Why We Don't Count: The Commodity Audience," in *Logics of Television: Essays in Cultural Criticism*, ed. Patricia Mellencamp (Bloomington: Indiana University Press–BFI Publishing, 1990), 117–137.

27. The figure is from 1995 and includes all major media. See *International Television and Video Almanac, 1997*, 18A.

28. Stuart Elliott, "Reebok's Suit over 'Jerry Maguire' Shows Risks of Product Placement," *New York Times*, February 7, 1997, sec. D, 1.

29. Ibid.

30. The film also carried a surgeon general's warning in the closing credits. Mark Crispin Miller, "End of Story," in *Seeing through Movies*, ed. Mark Crispin Miller (New York: Pantheon, 1990), 194, 259.

31. As PPV expands, one unknown factor is the reaction of regulators. Some members of Congress have already expressed concern about the number of sporting events that have moved to cable and would probably threaten to take action if it were proposed that such an American institution as the Super Bowl be made PPV. However, many millions of dollars could be at stake, and the PPV interests, coupled with the professional and collegiate sports industry, would represent a powerful lobby. See "Broadcasters Hold Ground in Contest to Cover Sports," *Wall Street Journal*, June 9, 1994, sec. B, 8.

32. For a fascinating analysis of both the mechanics and the psychology behind one home shopping channel (QVC), see Elizabeth Kaye, "The New Phone Sex," *Esquire* (May 1994): 78–83.

33. August E. Grant, K. Kendall Guthrie, and Sandra J. Ball-Rokeach, "Television Shopping: A Media System Dependency Perspective," *Communication Research* 18, no. 6 (1991): 773–798.

34. Debra Lynn Stephens, Ronald Paul Hill, and Karyn Bergman, "Enhancing the Consumer-Product Relationship: Lessons from the QVC Home Shopping Channel," *Journal of Business Research* 37 (1996): 193–200.

35. Meg Cox, "Corporate Focus: Newhouse Family Starts to Peer into Electronic Future," *Wall Street Journal*, October 21, 1993, sec. B, 4.

36. "Meet the New Media Monsters," *Economist*, March 11, 1989, 65–66.

37. Sue Karlin, "The New Producers," *Mediaweek*, October 14, 1991, 18.

38. John Lippman, "Television: Hollywood Studios' Growing Clout Scares Big Networks,"

Wall Street Journal, February 13, 1995, sec. B, 1; "Television Production: Fear Stalks the Small Screen," 81.

39. Based on figures from Neilsen Media Research reported in *Broadcasting and Cable Yearbook,* 1997, C–238.

40. "Viewing Figures," *Economist,* March 18, 1995, 56.

41. Information compiled from various sources. The *Nation* periodically publishes articles and charts by Professor Mark Crispin Miller containing extensive, detailed, and updated information of this sort. See, for example, the June 8, 1998, special issue "Who Controls TV?"

42. Eben Shapiro, "Ted's Way: Brash as Ever, Turner Is Giving Time Warner Dose of Culture Shock," *Wall Street Journal,* March 24, 1997, sec. A, 1. For a fuller analysis of how the major media corporations (including Microsoft) are economically intertwined, see Ken Auletta, "American Keiretsu," *New Yorker,* October 20 and 27, 1997, 225–227.

43. The technology of UHF television was in its infancy, and UHF frequencies were considered so undesirable in the early days that broadcasters only sought them as a last resort (and sometimes not even then). In fact, it was not until 1963 that U.S. TV sets were even required to be able to tune UHF channels. It was with technical improvements in the 1970s and the expansion of cable that UHF really began to flourish.

44. This explains why it was not until 1987 that a fourth broadcast television network (Fox) appeared. Until the expansion of cable and the renewed growth of UHF, most in the industry believed there simply were not enough unaffiliated broadcasting stations on the air to distribute a fourth network's programming at a profit.

45. Lucas A. Powe Jr. has documented some of the history of the political and legal struggles that constitute U.S. broadcast and cable regulation. See Lucas A. Powe Jr., *American Broadcasting and the First Amendment* (Berkeley: University of California, 1987).

46. Consumers can have an impact on Congress. The 1992 Cable Television Act was primarily a response to cable subscribers who thought their rates were too high. Likewise, it was pressure from some parents' groups that saw the enactment of the Children's TV Act of 1990 and, later, the provision for the V-chip.

47. Similarly, increased cable deregulation may come as the result of a successful DBS technology if it can offer local cable subscribers a genuine alternative to the local cable monopoly. Yet as was mentioned earlier, competitive DBS was made possible only after government intervention forced cable network owners to provide programming on an equal basis.

48. FCC rules restricting economic activities defined a "network" by the number of hours of programming it supplied per week. Fox, WB, and UPN supplied fewer than this number and so were not technically considered "networks" by the FCC.

49. Mark Robichaux, "Dishing It Out: Once a Laughingstock, Direct-Broadcast TV Gives Cable a Scare," *Wall Street Journal,* November 7, 1996, sec. A, 1.

50. The laws are Sections 312 and 315 of the Communication Act of 1934. This requirement makes broadcasters quite unlike newspapers, which can legally refuse to sell ads to or provide coverage of a particular candidate or party.

51. See Quality Time?: *The Report of the Twentieth Century Fund Task Force on Public Television* (New York: Twentieth Century Fund Press, 1993).

52. CPB was the body established by the Public Broadcasting Act of 1967 to provide national leadership for public broadcasting. CPB then established the Public Broadcasting Service (PBS) as a separate entity to operate the national network.

53. Steve Craig, "Public Broadcasting," in *History of the Mass Media in the United States: An Encyclopedia,* ed. Margaret A. Blanchard (Chicago: Fitzroy Dearborn, in press).

54. For the politically conservative perspective on public television, see Laurence Ariel Jarvik, *PBS: Behind the Screen* (Rocklin, Calif.: Prima, 1997).

55. William Hoynes, *Public Television for Sale: Media, the Market, and the Public Sphere* (Boulder, Colo.: Westview, 1994), ch. 4.

56. Documentary film maker B. J. Bullert has analyzed the struggles of producers in getting these and other controversial documentaries on the air. See B. J. Bullert, *Public Television: Politics and the Battle over Documentary Film* (New Brunswick, N.J.: Rutgers University Press, 1997).

57. James Day, *The Vanishing Vision: The Inside Story of Public Television* (Berkeley: University of California, 1995), 348.

Three. Advertisers and Their Audience

1. *International Television and Video Almanac, 1997* (New York: Quigley, 1997), 18A.

2. Some of the data in table 3.1 and elsewhere in this chapter were found at *Advertising Age* magazine's "Dataplace" on the *Ad Age* World Wide Web site. Dataplace contains a large quantity of constantly updated information concerning the advertising industry (www.adage.com).

3. For one perspective on how modern advertising is used to promote fast-moving consumer goods (FMCGs), see "Assault on the Heartland," in "The Advertising Industry," a special supplement to the *Economist,* June 9, 1990, 5–7.

4. "The Party's Over," in "The Advertising Industry," 1.

5. Ibid.

6. Michael Schudson, *Advertising, the Uneasy Persuasion: Its Dubious Impact on American Society* (New York: Basic Books, 1984).

7. Raymond Williams, *Problems in Materialism and Culture* (London: Verso, 1980).

8. Steve Craig, "Women as Home Care Givers: Gender Portrayal in OTC Drug Commercials," *Journal of Drug Education* 22, no. 4 (1992): 305–314.

9. Attributed to Britain's William Lever (Lord Leverhulme), one of the founders of Lever Brothers (later Unilever), one of P&G's major competitors on the world market. Lever, a former grocer, helped build an empire in FMCGs relying heavily on advertising. See Charles Wilson, *Unilever, 1945–1965* (London: Cassell, 1968), 92, and "Looking for a Man with a Dog," in "The Advertising Industry," 15.

10. Sometimes, rates can go even higher. Thirty-second ads for the *Seinfeld* finale show fetched $1 million. Michael Schneider, "Seinfeld Masters His Own Demise," *Electronic Media,* January 5, 1998, 1, 64; Joe Mandese, "Top Shows Lose Luster for Buyers," *Electronic Media,* September 15, 1997, 10.

11. Although the prices for ads have been going down, the cost to reach 1,000 homes has increased. For example, in 1990, the average prime-time 30-second spot cost $122,200, or $9.74 per 1,000 homes tuned in. In 1997, the cost of the spot had fallen to $106,500, but the price per 1,000 homes had increased to $11.18. See *International Television and Video Almanac, 1998* (New York: Quigley, 1998), 22A.

12. Figures from 1993. *Advertising Age,* July 4, 1994, 3.

13. Rick Wartzman, "Making TV Commercials, Los Angeles's Quiet Giant," *Wall Street Journal,* January 8, 1997, sec. C, 1.

14. Almost all of the other one-third are 15 seconds. *International Television and Video Almanac, 1997,* 18A.

15. The programs and ads used in this example were recorded in one of the nation's largest markets, Dallas–Fort Worth. In the biggest markets, prime-time commercial time is much in demand by national spot advertisers, and all the locally originated commercials in this example are national spot ads. Small-market NBC stations running the same shows on the same evening would almost certainly have sold and broadcast local ads in these slots. For reasons discussed below, small-market stations must rely much more heavily on local advertising revenue.

16. Based on Neilsen Media Research estimates. All times apply to Eastern or Pacific time zones. Patterns in the Central and Mountain time zones are similar, but prime time is from 7 to 10 P.M.

17. Precise market descriptions vary slightly among research companies and from year to year. Nielsen identified 211 "Designated Market Areas" (DMAs) for use in its 1996–1997 reports.

18. *International Television and Video Almanac, 1997,* 17A.

19. For a list of the 30 day parts Nielsen reports in its "Viewers in Profile" (VIP) Report, see *Nielsen Station Index Reference Supplement,* published yearly.

20. The industry defines "prime time" as 8–11 P.M. (Eastern Time) on weekdays and 7–11 P.M. on weekends, or an hour earlier in the Central Time Zone. Time differences mean a separate feed is usually necessary for the Pacific and Mountain time zones.

21. Curt Schleir, "Survival of the Soapiest," *Fort Worth Star-Telegram,* May 27, 1997, sec. D, 1–2.

22. Interestingly, the sexist implications of this term—implying that women who stay home *don't* work—seems lost on the industry.

23. For example, Nielsen prime-time ratings taken during February 1996 indicate that *Home Improvement* was the fifth most-watched show among men 18–49, and the sixth most-watched among women in that age group. Similarly, it was seventh most-watched for men 25–54 and eighth most-watched for women 25–54. See "Demographic Ratings: Prime-Time: February 5–11," *Electronic Media,* February 19, 1996, 30, and "Demographic Ratings: Prime-Time: February 12–18," *Electronic Media,* February 26, 1996, 39. For an analysis of the program's strategies for appealing to both men and women, see Steve Craig, "More (Male) Power: Humor and Gender in *Home Improvement,*" *Mid-Atlantic Almanack* 5 (1996): 61–84.

24. "Game Plans," *Economist,* March 19, 1994, 108.

25. Ibid.

26. Bernice Kanner, "The Secret Life of the Female Consumer: What General Foods Has Learned about Women Sells a Lot of International Coffee," *Working Woman* (December 1990): 68–71.

27. See Steve Craig, "The Effect of Television Day Part on Gender Portrayals in Television Commercials: A Content Analysis," *Sex Roles* 26, no. 5/6 (1992): 197–211.

28. Betty Friedan, *The Feminine Mystique* (New York: Dell, 1963), 218–219.

29. Naomi Wolf, *The Beauty Myth* (New York: Morrow, 1991), 66.

30. Quoted in Eric Schmuckler, "A Small World, After All," *Mediaweek,* January 27, 1997, 30–40.

31. "Kids and Teens TV—Special Report: Shows—Season to Date," *Electronic Media,* February 9, 1998, 30.

32. Jim McConville, "Kids and Teens TV—Special Report: Can the Kids Market Stay This Hot?" *Electronic Media,* February 9, 1998, 30.

33. Joseph Pereira, "Playground Safety: Toy Business Focuses More on Marketing and Less on New Ideas," *Wall Street Journal,* February 29, 1996, sec. A, 1.

34. Ibid.; Time Warner owns Warner Brothers with its stable of classic cartoon characters such as Bugs Bunny.

35. Schmuckler, "Small World."

36. Michael Schneider, "NBC to Pay $13 Million a Week for *ER* Elixir," *Electronic Media,* January 19, 1998, 1A, 122.

37. At the time *Home Improvement* was created, the fin-syn rules were still in effect (see chapter 2), and ABC was not permitted to participate financially in the ownership of the show. Instead, it could only contract for the rights to run episodes for a limited time. In the years that ensued, fin-syn was done away with, and Disney purchased ABC. With that merger, Disney owns both a substantial interest in *Home Improvement* and the network on which it runs. In chapter 2, it was pointed out how this has led to legal difficulties between Wind Dancer and Disney. See Bruce Orwall and John

Lippman, "Entertainment: Lawsuit Casts Tim Allen TV Series as Victim of Synergy," *Wall Street Journal,* March 17, 1997, sec. B, 1.

38. John Lippman, "Stations Make Room for 'Improvement,'" *Los Angeles Times,* June 22, 1993, sec. D, 5.

39. Elizabeth Jensen, "New Market Rules Help Make 'Friends' Quick Syndication Hit," *Wall Street Journal,* January 15, 1996, sec. B, 1.

40. Bruce Orwall, "Sports: Field Is Crowded, but Sports Still Score on TV," *Wall Street Journal,* January 13, 1997, sec. B, 1.

41. Jon LaFayette, "CBS Gets Back in the Game with the NFL—For a Price," *Electronic Media,* January 19, 1998, 1A, 120.

42. "Quinn's Clan Too Old?" *Fort Worth Star-Telegram,* June 21, 1998, sec. A, 5.

43. While a portion of these complaints can be placed in the category of "killing the messenger who brings the bad news," at least some of them are well founded. See Steve McClellan, "Broadcasters Lash Out at Nielsen," *Broadcasting and Cable,* October 16, 1995, 18.

44. Ien Ang, *Desperately Seeking the Audience* (New York: Routledge, 1991), 27, 48, 50, 57.

45. Several books have been written about P&G. The most useful is The Editors of *Advertising Age, Procter & Gamble: The House That Ivory Built* (Lincolnwood, Ill.: NTC Business Books, 1988).

46. "Business Brief—Renaissance Cosmetics Inc.: Eleven Fragrance Brands to Be Bought from P&G," *Wall Street Journal,* October 31, 1996, sec. B, 4.

47. This and some of the other information reported here was found on the company's Web page at www.pg.com.

48. John R. Dorfman, "Shareholder Scoreboard: America's Best—and Worst—Performing Companies," *Wall Street Journal,* February 27, 1997, sec. R, 1. According to the company's Annual Report, 1997 earnings were $3.42 billion, up 12 percent from 1996. The Annual Report is available on the company's Web site at www.pg.com.

49. In a 1996 effort at consolidation, P&G sold off a number of "minor" brands. Those sold included Lestoil cleaner, Aleve pain reliever, Bain de Soleil, Fisher Nut, and 11 fragrance brands, including NaVy, Le Jardin, and Toujours Moi. See "Business Brief—Renaissance Cosmetics Inc.," sec. B, 4.

50. "Procter & Gamble," *Standard & Poor's Corporation Records,* March 1997, 6441–6442.

51. Joseph Kahn, "Cleaning Up: P&G Viewed China as a National Market and Is Conquering It," *Wall Street Journal,* September 12, 1995, sec. A, 1.

52. See, for example, the uncritical 1981 history of the company by Oscar Schisgall, *Eyes on Tomorrow: The Evolution of Procter & Gamble* (Chicago: Doubleday, 1981).

53. Alecia Swasy, *Soap Opera: The Inside Story of Procter & Gamble* (New York: Times Books, 1993), 110.

54. The Editors of *Advertising Age, Procter & Gamble,* 18.

55. Swasy, *Soap Opera,* 111.

56. "Marketing and Media: P&G Programming Pact," *Wall Street Journal,* March 12, 1997, sec. B, 6.

57. P&G research data cited in Swasy, *Soap Opera,* 107.

58. Interesting exceptions, of course, are the models featured in ads for P&G's cosmetic and fragrance brands, all of whom must have the glamour "look."

59. Craig, "Women as Home Care Givers."

Four. Signification, Discourse, and Ideology

1. Speech at Florida Atlantic University, March 27, 1995.

2. See Benjamin Barber's unfortunately titled *Jihad vs. McWorld: How Globalism and Tribalism Are Reshaping the World* (New York: Ballantine Books, 1996).

3. Stephanie Coontz, *The Way We Really Are: Coming to Terms with America's Changing Families* (New York: Basic Books, 1997), 37. Coontz points out that in the fifties, "people didn't watch those shows to see their own lives reflected back at them. They watched them to see how families were *supposed* to live—and also to get a little reassurance that they were headed in the right direction" (38).

4. Tamar Liebes and Elihu Katz, *The Export of Meaning: Cross-Cultural Meanings of 'Dallas'* (Cambridge, England: Polity Press, 1993).

5. Modified from Tim O'Sullivan et al., *Key Concepts in Communication and Cultural Studies*, 2d ed. (New York: Routledge, 1994), 281–283.

6. Modified from ibid., 284–285.

7. Modified from ibid., 288.

8. Ibid., 317.

9. Margaret Morse, "An Ontology of Everyday Distraction: The Freeway, the Mall, and Television," in *Logics of Television: Essays in Cultural Criticism*, ed. Patricia Mellencamp (Bloomington: Indiana University Press, 1990), 193–221.

10. Modified from O'Sullivan et al., *Key Concepts*, 43–45, 64–65.

11. Ibid., 286–287.

12. Andrew Wernick, "Vehicles for Myth: The Shifting Image of the Modern Car," in *Cultural Politics in Contemporary America*, ed. Ian Angus and Sut Jhally (New York: Routledge, 1989), 207. See also Andrew Wernick, *Promotional Culture: Advertising, Ideology, and Symbolic Expression* (London: Sage, 1991).

13. Judith Williamson, *Decoding Advertisements: Ideology and Meaning in Advertising* (New York: Marion Boyars, 1984).

14. Coontz, *Way We Really Are*, 57, 126–128; Barbara Ehrenreich, "The Decline of Patriarchy," in *Constructing Masculinity*, ed. Maurice Berger et al. (New York: Routledge, 1995), 288; Robin Andersen, *Consumer Culture and TV Programming* (Boulder, Colo.: Westview, 1995), 55–56; R. W. Connell, *Masculinities* (Berkeley: University of California Press, 1995), 226. See also Cynthia Fuchs Epstein, *Deceptive Distinctions: Sex, Gender, and the Social Order* (New Haven: Yale University Press, 1988), ch. 7.

15. O'Sullivan et al., *Key Concepts*, 127–129.

16. David Bordwell and Kristin Thompson, *Film Art: An Introduction*, 5th ed. (New York: McGraw-Hill, 1997), 92, 478. Our close textual analyses in chapters 4 and 5 have been facilitated by the neoformalist conceptual framework provided by this valuable textbook. Here we have adapted this framework to television and given more emphasis to placing texts within larger social, historical, and ideological contexts.

17. Ibid., 478.

18. Ibid., 65.

19. Ibid., 66.

20. Ibid., 90.

21. Raymond Williams, *Marxism and Literature* (New York: Oxford University Press, 1977).

22. Juliet B. Schor, *The Overworked American: The Unexpected Decline of Leisure* (New York: Basic Books, 1991), 161; Robert D. Putnam, "Bowling Alone: America's Declining Social Capital," *Journal of Democracy* 6, no. 1 (January 1995): 65–78.

23. Schor, *Overworked American*, 161.

24. Modified from O'Sullivan et al., *Key Concepts*, 92–95.

25. Mimi White, "Ideological Analysis and Television," in *Channels of Discourse, Re-*

assembled: Television and Contemporary Criticism, 2d ed., ed. Robert C. Allen (Chapel Hill: University of North Carolina Press, 1992), 161–202.

26. Bordwell and Thompson, *Film Art,* 102–104.
27. Bill Nichols, *Ideology and the Image: Social Representation in the Cinema and Other Media* (Bloomington: Indiana University Press, 1981), 174–178. See also Nichols, *Representing Reality: Issues and Concepts in Documentary* (Bloomington: Indiana University Press, 1991), 34–38.

28. Bordwell and Thompson, *Film Art,* 68–70.
29. John Berger, *Ways of Seeing* (London: Penguin Books/BBC, 1972), 131.
30. This is a slightly modified version of the definition of style in the glossary of Bordwell and Thompson, *Film Art,* 482; see also 355–360. Our linking of this use of the term with the more everyday meaning of style is influenced by the very different approach of Stuart Ewen, *All Consuming Images: The Politics of Style in Contemporary Culture* (New York: Basic Books, 1988).
31. Bordwell and Thompson, *Film Art,* 93–94.
32. Ibid., 479.
33. Ibid., 277–278. The analysis of style in the Cascade commercial draws generally on part 3 of *Film Art.*
34. O'Sullivan et al., *Key Concepts,* 310.
35. This section generally is indebted to Williamson, *Decoding Advertisements.* See also Jim Collins, "Postmodernism and Television," in Allen, *Channels of Discourse, Reassembled,* 327–353.
36. Murray Smith, "Altered States: Character and Emotional Response in the Cinema," *Cinema Journal* 33, no. 4 (Summer 1994): 34–56. Although much television viewing is more intermittent and distracted than film viewing (especially in a theater), nevertheless people often identify as intensely with television and its characters, in large part because of the sheer quantity of time involved.
37. Mark Crispin Miller, "Introduction: The Hipness unto Death" and "Big Brother Is You, Watching," in *Boxed In: The Culture of TV* (Evanston, Ill.: Northwestern University Press, 1988), 1–27, 309–335.
38. Sut Jhally, *The Codes of Advertising* (New York: St. Martin's Press, 1987).
39. Miller, *Boxed In,* 17.
40. Annabel Patterson, "Intention," in *Critical Terms for Literary Study,* 2d ed., ed. Frank Lentricchia and Thomas McLaughlin (Chicago: University of Chicago Press, 1995), 135–146.
41. Neil Vidmar and Milton Rokeach, "Archie Bunker's Bigotry: A Study in Selective Perception and Exposure," *Journal of Communication* 24 (1974): 36–47.
42. Sut Jhally, "The Political Economy of Culture," in Angus and Jhally, *Cultural Politics in Contemporary America,* 65–81, 365–366.
43. Miller, *Boxed In,* 16–17.
44. Vincent Mosco, *The Political Economy of Communication: Rethinking and Renewal* (London: Sage, 1996), esp. ch. 6.
45. Modified from O'Sullivan et al., *Key Concepts,* 139–143.
46. Ibid., 198–199.
47. Valerie Fahey, "TV by the Numbers," *In Health* (December/January 1992): 35; "Harper's Index," *Harper's* (June 1996); cited in "Television Statistics," *1997 TV-Turnoff Organizer's Kit* (Washington, D.C.: TV-Free America, 1997). See chapter 7 for more about TV-Free America.

Five. Television Realisms

1. Tim O'Sullivan et al., *Key Concepts in Communication and Cultural Studies,* 2d ed. (New York: Routledge, 1994), 257.

2. Ibid.

3. Much of the conceptual framework for this chapter is adapted from Bill Nichols, *Ideology and the Image: Social Representation in the Cinema and Other Media* (Bloomington: Indiana University Press, 1981), especially ch. 6, "The Documentary Film and Principles of Exposition."

4. John Fiske and John Hartley, *Reading Television* (London: Methuen, 1978), 162.

5. Annette Kuhn, *Women's Pictures: Feminism and Cinema*, 2d ed. (London: Verso, 1994), 128.

6. O'Sullivan et al, *Key Concepts*, 139.

7. David Bordwell and Kristin Thompson, *Film Art: An Introduction*, 5th ed. (New York: McGraw-Hill, 1997), 108.

8. Kuhn, *Women's Pictures*, 137.

9. Sarah Kozloff, "Narrative Theory and Television," in *Channels of Discourse, Reassembled: Television and Contemporary Criticism*, 2d ed., ed. Robert C. Allen (Chapel Hill: University of North Carolina Press, 1992), 90–91.

10. Bordwell and Thompson, *Film Art*, 77, 170.

11. David Bordwell, Janet Staiger, and Kristin Thompson, *The Classical Hollywood Cinema: Film Style and Mode of Production to 1960* (New York: Columbia University Press, 1985), 155–240.

12. See, for example, David Bordwell, "Convention, Construction, and Cinematic Vision," in *Post-Theory: Reconstructing Film Studies*, ed. David Bordwell and Noâl Carroll (Madison: University of Wisconsin Press, 1996), 87–107.

13. Bordwell and Thompson, *Film Art*, 284.

14. For a different version of this comparison of film and television, see Sandy Flitterman-Lewis, "Psychoanalysis, Film, and Television," in Allen, *Channels of Discourse, Reassembled*, 203–246. Her account emphasizes the differences between the two media. Watching a film in a theater and watching television at home are indeed very different experiences, with different consequences. This chapter argues that there are both similarities and differences in the textual organization and viewing experiences of television and film.

15. Episode broadcast July 6, 1994, on ABC.

16. Bordwell and Thompson, *Film Art*, 481.

17. Ibid., 285–288, 481.

18. Ibid., 481, 288–289.

19. Figures 5.2 and 5.3 from episode broadcast October 30, 1995, on Fox.

20. Bordwell and Thompson, *Film Art*, 289.

21. Ibid.

22. Ibid., 290–291, 480.

23. Kuhn, *Women's Pictures*, 127.

24. Ibid., 129.

25. Oliver Stone and Zachary Sklar, *JFK: The Book of the Film* (New York: Applause Books, 1992).

26. John Thornton Caldwell, *Televisuality: Style, Crisis, and Authority in American Television* (New Brunswick, N.J.: Rutgers University Press, 1995).

27. Bill Nichols, *Representing Reality: Issues and Concepts in Documentary* (Bloomington: Indiana University Press, 1991), 268.

28. In the 1930s, Walter Benjamin argued that the mass production and mechanical reproduction of images contributed to the erosion of the quasi-sacred aura of the unique work of art in the modern era. The erosion of the credibility of the photographic/film/video image and sound because of the social uses of digital technologies can be seen as characteristic of our own more recent postmodern era. Walter Benjamin, "The Work of Art in the Age of Mechanical Reproduction," in *Illuminations*, ed. Hannah Arendt (New York: Schocken, 1969), 217–251.

29. This section is based on Nichols, *Ideology and the Image,* 174–178. See also William Gibson, "Network News: Elements of a Theory," *Social Text* 3 (Fall 1980): 88–111, and Robert Stam, "Television News and Its Spectator," in *Regarding Television: Critical Approaches—An Anthology,* ed. Ann Kaplan (Frederick, Md.: University Publications of America, 1983), 23–43.

30. *ABC World News Tonight with Peter Jennings,* September 4, 1997.

31. Miles Harvey, "The Alonzo Awards," *In These Times,* April 17, 1995, 15.

32. "5–4–3–2–1 Liftoff," produced by Richard Greenberg. *60 Minutes,* October 5, 1997. Karl Grossman, *The Wrong Stuff: The Space Program's Nuclear Threat to Our Planet* (Monroe, Maine: Common Courage Press, 1997). The militarization and nuclearization of space, as exemplified by Cassini, was the most censored news story of 1996 according to Peter Phillips, *Censored 1997: The News That Didn't Make the News—The Year's Top 25 Censored News Stories* (New York: Seven Stories Press, 1997).

33. There are significant exceptions to the rule against using others' tape, including the videotape of Rodney King being beaten by Los Angeles police.

34. David Croteau and William Hoynes, "Men and the News Media: The Male Presence and Its Effect," in *Men, Masculinity, and the Media,* ed. Steve Craig (Newbury Park, Calif.: Sage, 1992), 154–168.

35. Nichols, *Ideology and the Image,* 178.

36. James Fallows, *Breaking the News: How the Media Undermine American Democracy* (New York: Pantheon, 1996), 3 and passim.

37. Robert M. Entman, *Democracy without Citizens: Media and the Decay of American Politics* (New York: Oxford University Press, 1989).

38. Fallows, *Breaking the News,* 24.

39. Leon Friedman, "The Scary Shift toward Corporate News," *Miami Herald,* December 3, 1995, sec. M, 6; Robin Andersen, *Consumer Culture and TV Programming* (Boulder, Colo.: Westview, 1995), 26.

40. Andersen, *Consumer Culture,* 147.

41. "Most of the stories about people, life, and the world are told no longer by parents, schools, churches, or others in the community who have something to tell, but increasingly by a handful of global conglomerates that have something to sell." *Viewer's Declaration of Independence,* quoted in Daniel Hellinger, "Media Conclave Seeks to Reform Corporate Dominance," *Cultural Environment Monitor* 1, no. 1 (Fall 1996): 2. For more information on the Cultural Environment Movement, see chapter 7.

42. Margaret Morse, "An Ontology of Everyday Distraction: The Freeway, the Mall, and Television," in *Logics of Television: Essays in Cultural Criticism,* ed. Patricia Mellencamp (Bloomington: Indiana University Press, 1990), 193.

43. Ibid., 197.

44. Ibid., 203, quoting "cosmallogist" William Severini Kowinski, *The Malling of America: An Inside Look at the Great Consumer Paradise* (New York: Morrow, 1985), 339.

45. Ibid., 205.

46. Ibid., 197, paraphrasing Charles Kuralt.

47. Howard Besser, "From Internet to Information Superhighway," in *Resisting the Virtual Life: The Culture and Politics of Information,* ed. James Brook and Iain A. Boal (San Francisco: City Lights, 1995), 59–70; Edward S. Herman and Robert W. McChesney, *The Global Media: The New Missionaries of Global Capitalism* (London: Cassell, 1997), esp. 106–135.

48. Caldwell, *Televisuality.*

49. Ibid., 14–15.

50. Ibid., 134–159.

51. Ibid., 6 and passim.

52. Figures 5.9–5.11, CNN Headline Sports, September 24, 1997.

53. Figure 5.12, PSA by Florida State Controller, Entertainment Channel, September 27, 1997.

54. Figure 5.13, Entertainment Channel, September 27, 1997.

55. Caldwell, *Televisuality,* 67 and passim.

56. Andersen, *Consumer Culture,* 258–264.

57. Ibid., 260–263.

58. Ibid., 260–262.

59. Ibid., 262.

60. Ibid., 264.

Six. The Flow of Commodities

1. Jane Feuer, Paul Kerr, and Tise Vahimagi, *MTM: 'Quality Television'* (London: BFI Publishing, 1984).

2. This is made possible by years of training in the equation of quality in narrative with a form of psychological realism similar to that developed in the 19th-century novel. Mike Budd and Clay Steinman, "*M°A°S°H* Mystified: Capitalization, Dematerialization, Idealization," *Cultural Critique* 10 (1988): 59–75; Noël Burch, "Porter, or Ambivalence," trans. Tom Milne, *Screen* 19, no. 4 (Winter 1978/1979): 91–105; Kristin Thompson, "From Primitive to Classical," in *The Classical Hollywood Cinema: Film Style and Mode of Production to 1960,* by David Bordwell, Janet Staiger, and Kristin Thompson (New York: Columbia University Press, 1985): 157–173; Christopher Williams, ed., *Realism and the Cinema: A Reader* (London: Routledge, 1980); Raymond Williams, "Realism, Naturalism, and Their Alternatives," in *Explorations in Film Theory: Selected Essays from Ciné-Tracts [1976–1983],* ed. Ron Burnett (Bloomington: Indiana University Press, 1991), 121–126.

3. Scott Nance, *Exposing Northern Exposure* (Las Vegas: Pioneer Books, 1992), 17. Brand and Falsey had not only worked at MTM on such quality programs as *St. Elsewhere,* but they had also produced *A Year in the Life* and *I'll Fly Away,* a show about the civil rights movement that concentrated on a European American family and, secondarily, the African American woman who worked for them. PBS executives deemed *I'll Fly Away* appropriate enough for their audiences to take it on in rerun after it was dropped by NBC (and to produce one new episode that concentrated on African Americans).

4. "The 10 Most Expensive Prime-Time Ad Buys," *Advertising Age,* September 9, 1994; on-line, Lexis-Nexis, June 1, 1996.

5. Here we can see "multiaccentuality" at work. Attributed to Mikhail Bakhtin, this concept refers to the variability of a sign's meaning when used in different contexts. Rob Morrow's character can seem at home lined up with the soft masculine images listed above yet can also be linked with images of therapeutic wisdom and authority. One of the signs of the racializing hierarchies of the show is that Graham Greene's Native American character is not given sufficiently layered traits to be multiaccentual in the same way (just as a Jewish character like Morrow's would not have in U.S. films before World War II). An introduction to multiaccentuality can be found in Robert Stam, Robert Burgoyne, and Sandy Flitterman-Lewis, *New Vocabularies in Film Semiotics: Structuralism, Post-Structuralism, and Beyond* (London: Routledge, 1992), 12–14 and 219. An incisive overview of the construction of "Indians" in U.S. history with its alternately venomous and romanticizing imagery can be found in Robert F. Berkhofer Jr., *The White Man's Indian: Images of the American Indian from Columbus to the Present* (New York: Vintage-Random, 1978). Jim Stewart alerted us to the importance of this book. For more on ethnicity and *Northern Exposure,* see Diana George with Susan Sanders, "Reconstructing Tonto: Cultural Formations and American Indians in 1990s Television Fiction," *Cultural Studies* 9, no. 3 (October 1995): 427–452.

6. Paradoxically, such "natural" lettering, called "grunge fonts" by typographers, requires the latest in computer technology. Ruthann Godollei pointed this out to us.

7. For an argument linking global flow to postmodern theory, see Arjun Appadurai, *Modernity at Large: Cultural Dimensions of Globalization* (Minneapolis: University of Minnesota Press, 1996). Michal McCall directed us to this source.

8. Susan Tyler Eastman, *Broadcast/Cable Programming* (Belmont, Calif.: Wadsworth, 1993), 12.

9. Even within each network, flows and target audiences vary across the day. See Steve Craig, "The Effect of Television Day Part on Gender Portrayals in Television Commercials: A Content Analysis," *Sex Roles* 26, no. 5/6 (1992): 197–211. Across networks they differ considerably. For an important collection on the Lifetime cable network, see Julie D'Acci, ed., "Lifetime: A Cable Network 'for Women,'" *Camera Obscura: Feminism, Culture, and Media Studies* 33–34 (May–September 1994/January 1995), especially the articles by Jackie Byars and Eileen Meehan and by Carolyn Bronstein. For more on gendered flows, see Clay Steinman, "Gaze out of Bounds: Men Watching Men on Television," in *Men, Masculinity, and the Media,* ed. Steve Craig (Newbury Park, Calif.: Sage, 1992), 199–214. For more on television's postfeminist "hegemonic masculinity" since the 1980s, see Robert Hanke, "Redesigning Men: Hegemonic Masculinity in Transition," in the Craig anthology, 185–198, as well as J. D. Tankel and B. J. Banks, "The Boys of Prime Time: An Analysis of 'New' Male Roles in Television," in *Communication and Culture: Language, Performance, Technology, and Media: Selected Proceedings from the Sixth International Conference on Culture and Communication, Temple University, 1986,* ed. Sari Thomas, Studies in Communication 4 (Norwood, N.J.: Ablex, 1990), 285–290. For more on advertisers and demographics, see Joseph Turow, *Breaking Up America: Advertisers and the New Media World* (Chicago: University of Chicago Press, 1997).

10. Acting on sexist stereotype as if it were the essence of sexual difference, NBC quite consciously designed its 1996 Olympic coverage to attract women, emphasizing a soap opera model of individualistic narratives of "idealism" over results, what David Remnick called a "sentimental, highly elastic narrative style designed to bring a tear to the eye and bullion to the coffers." During the Olympics, Nicholas Schiavone, director of research at NBC Sports, mused: "I wonder if the appeal of the Olympics to women the way we do it, 'inside out,' is that life itself comes from inside out, whereas men take a more externalized approach. You could say we dwell in the tension between male and female, the external and the internal. . . . Anyway, the way I see our version of the Olympics is that it's about—with apologies to Jane Austen—it's about sense and sensibility. It really is." We can expect more of this to seep into news coverage as well: "The Olympics is the model by which the rest of television ought to be done," said Schiavone. David Remnick, "Inside-Out Olympics: The NBC Strategy That Made the Games a Hit," *New Yorker,* August 5, 1996, quotations on 27, 26, 27, 28.

11. Quoted by Edwin L. Artzt, "The Future of Advertising," speech to the American Association of Advertising Agencies Convention, White Sulphur Springs, W.Va., May, 12, 1994.

12. Bill Carter, "As Cliff and Norm Drink Up, In Walks Seinfeld," *New York Times,* March 21, 1993, sec. H, 31. Quoted in Susan Tyler Eastman, Jeffrey Neal-Lunsford, and Karen E. Riggs, "Coping with Grazing: Prime-Time Strategies for Accelerated Program Transitions," *Journal of Broadcasting and Electronic Media* 39 (1995): 92.

13. Daniel Cerone, "Networks Won't Give You Much of a Break," *Los Angeles Times,* September 5, 1994; on-line, Lexis-Nexis, October 27, 1997.

14. Ibid., and Eastman, Neal-Lunsford, and Riggs, "Coping with Grazing." For an overview of recent research on remote control and mute devices and television, including industry responses (such as designing commercials to be effective even if zapped through on VCRs and developing "pregrazed spots" that contain within them

sufficient changes to discourage zapping), see Robert V. Bellamy Jr. and James R. Walker, *Television and the Remote Control: Grazing on a Vast Wasteland* (New York: Guilford, 1996). For an illuminating ethnographic study of male domination of the remote control in household practice (generally supported by other studies cited by Bellamy and Walker), see David Morley, *Family Viewing* (London: Comedia, 1986).

15. Robert Goldman, *Reading Ads Socially* (London: Routledge, 1992), 5. See our discussion of Raymond Williams's complementary analysis of magic and advertising in chapter 3.

16. Henry Giroux, "Consuming Social Change: The United Colors of Benetton," in *Disturbing Pleasures: Learning Popular Culture* (New York: Routledge, 1994), 15. Diversity in television advertising is a complex matter, but it is at the least problematic. According to one study, while African Americans, for example, appear in television advertising roughly in proportion to their share of the U. S. population, they appear almost exclusively in ads for inexpensive products, especially food. They rarely appear in ads for luxury goods or for products whose sales heavily depend on fantasy associations created by marketing, like cars. What is more, when they do appear, they are rarely allowed to show intimacy with other characters on screen, black or white. See Robert Entman, Address, "Race and Intimacy in Television Advertising," North Carolina State University, March 26, 1996 (available from the author at the university in Raleigh, N.C.). That African Americans appear more than they did in the past is largely a testament to their disproportionate television watching and the relatively recent decision by ratings companies to count them (and not undercount them) as a distinct market. All but the most racist and antiracist whites seem happy to see blacks on television as long as they act in ways that do not threaten white viewers and their prejudices. See Mike Budd and Clay Steinman, "White Racism and *The Cosby Show*," *Jump Cut* 37 (1992): 5–14. For more on the "commodification of ethnicity," see Coco Fusco, "About Locating Ourselves and Our Representations," *Framework* 36 (1989): 7–15.

17. Giroux, "Consuming Social Change," 19.

18. Of course, "Mexico" as associated with commercial restaurants outside Mexico is a cultural concept—indeed, it is so domestically as well. The linking of food and nation or people is mythological in any context, a "fabrication." See Uma Narayan, "Eating Cultures: Incorporation, Identity, and Indian Food," *Social Identities* 1, no. 1 (1995): 63–86. Sandy Schram found this source for us. What differs here is the construction of an ersatz culinary identity specifically to increase restaurant receipts.

19. Judith Williamson, *Decoding Advertisements: Ideology and Meaning in Advertising* (London: Marion Boyars, 1978).

20. Narayan, "Eating Cultures," 64.

21. Leslie Savan, "On That Chart," *Nation,* June 3, 1996, 22.

22. This is a central concept in Robert Goldman and Stephen Papson, *Sign Wars: The Cluttered Landscape of Advertising* (New York: Guilford, 1996).

23. According to Leola Johnson and David Roediger, Hertz began ads featuring O.J. Simpson running in slow motion through airports only after Roone Arledge at ABC sports had begun using slow-motion instant replays featuring Simpson and other players on the football field. "'Hertz, Don't It?': Becoming Colorless and Staying Black in the Crossover of O.J. Simpson," in *Birth of a Nation'hood,* ed. Toni Morrison and Claudia Brodsky Lacor (New York: Pantheon, 1997), 221–223.

24. Chad Rubel, "Marketers Were Real Winners in the Super Bowl," *Marketing News,* February 26, 1996, 4; on-line, Lexis-Nexis, May 15, 1996. Paradoxically, consumers tend to discount celebrity endorsements even as they are influenced by them. According to Wagner Kamakura, most research shows that celebrity endorsements usually improve sales "because of the transfer of imagery from celebrity to ad and from ad to brand." Consumers deny this takes place, says Kamakura, "because they don't

believe celebrities are endorsing products for anything but the money." Yet "consumers don't necessarily do what they say." See Stuart Elliott, "The Media Business: Advertising: A Study Shows That Celebrity Endorsements of Products Can Help a Company's Stock Price. A Little," *New York Times,* August 16, 1994 (national ed.), sec. C, 6.

25. Contemporary marketing tries to link products with intellectual styles. "You have to find a product that represents a point of view, that becomes a badge of what you think," says the chief marketing strategist for Rockport shoes (a division of Reebok International), Angel R. Martinez. Without links to the culture, he says, "products will be passionless and consumers will be bored." See Glenn Rifkin, "Does This Shoe Fit? Reebok Marketing Ace Stamps His Style on Rockport," *New York Times,* October 14, 1995 (national ed.), 20.

26. In 1995, P&G Productions created and broadcast 765 hours of *The Guiding Light, Another World,* and *As the World Turns.* Zachary Schiller et al., "And Now, a Show from Your Sponsors," *Business Week,* May 22, 1995, 100; on-line, Lexis-Nexis, March 1, 1996.

27. Accounts of the deal's specifics vary slightly. Here is how one of the most detailed reports put it:

> Procter & Gamble chipped in to cover the deficit of a quirky summer tryout series. P&G ended up with an equity stake in a major hit, plus a discounted minute of ad time for the run of the show.
>
> The leverage for P&G was unbelievable. According to industry sources, P&G kicked in some $40,000 per episode for the first six shows in the summer of 1990. That may not sound like much, said one source, "but it bridged the gap. The deal just couldn't get made without P&G.
>
> What did P&G get? It depends [on] the discount. If P&G gets 10 percent off an estimated $175,000 unit cost (figure half that for repeats), then its quarter-million-dollar, one-time investment is yielding $1.3 million a year in discounts. And that doesn't include syndication. (Eric Schmuckler, "And Now a Show from Our Sponsor . . . ," *Mediaweek,* August 17, 1992, 14–15.

Within a year, however, P&G severed its production ties to the show, including its ownership stake but not its advertising rights, as company strategy temporarily abandoned direct involvement in series production. John Kiesewetter, "P&G Hopes to Clean Up with TV Deal," *Cincinnati Enquirer,* March 26, 1995, sec. F, 1; on-line, Lexis-Nexis, June 1, 1996. Still, overall, "The deal" was "great for P&G." Joe Mandese, "In a Twist on the '50s Golden Age of Advertiser's Link with Programming, Profit-Savvy Current-Day Marketers 'Are Seeking a Little Control over Their Own Destiny,'" *Advertising Age,* February 28, 1995, 52; on-line, Lexis-Nexis, June 1, 1996. For a detailed discussion of how the agreement was planned and anticipated within the industry, see N. R. Kleinfeld, "The Networks' New Advertising Dance," *New York Times,* July 29, 1990, 1 ff; on-line, Lexis-Nexis, March 1, 1996.

28. Artzt, "The Future of Advertising."

29. Schiller et al., "And Now, a Show from Your Sponsors," 100.

30. P&G executives have been notoriously secretive about their corporate operations, and as far as we know, no journalist has reported further on the company's relationship to the show. Asked about it, P&G spokespeople refused comment. "We share information where we think it's to the advantage of P&G," said a representative of P&G in a 1994 telephone interview.

31. Robin Andersen, *Consumer Culture and TV Programming* (Boulder, Colo.: Westview, 1995), 1–2.

32. Leslie Savan, "Your Show of Shills," *Time,* April 1, 1996, 70; on-line, Lexis-Nexis, May 15, 1996.

33. Ira Teinowitz and Joe Mandese, "Miller Gains Some Early 'Exposure' on CBS Show," *Advertising Age,* March 8, 1993, 46; on-line, Lexis-Nexis, March 1, 1996.

34. "Focus Forum," *New Orleans Times-Picayune,* March 28, 1993, sec. T, 10; on-line, Lexis-Nexis, March 1, 1996.

35. Adrienne Ward Fawcett, "Free TV 'Ad Plugs' Are on the Rise," *Advertising Age,* July 12, 1993, 21; on-line; Lexis-Nexis, March 1, 1996.

36. Nancy Magiera, "As If Having a Hit TV Show Isn't Enough . . . ," *Advertising Age,* August 10, 1992, 3; on-line, Lexis-Nexis, June 9, 1996; for a case study of how products land on *Seinfeld,* even resulting in script revisions, see Damon Darlin, "Junior Mints, I'm Gonna Make You a Star," *Forbes,* November 6, 1995, 90; on-line, Lexis-Nexis, June 9, 1996.

37. Mandese, "Twist on the '50s."

38. Schmuckler, "And Now a Show from Our Sponsor . . . ," 15.

39. Scotty Dupree, "And NBC Makes Three," *Mediaweek,* November 20, 1995, 6; on-line, Lexis-Nexis, May 15, 1996; see also Karen Kaplan, "Company Town: The Following Is a Paramount–Procter & Gamble Presentation," *Los Angeles Times,* March 3, 1995, sec. D, 1; on-line, Lexis-Nexis, March 15, 1996; and Schiller et al., "And Now, a Show from Your Sponsors."

40. Steve Yahn, "Advertising's Grave New World: P&G Chief Artzt Rocks 4A's with Specter of TV without Ads," *Advertising Age,* May 16, 1994, 1; on-line, Lexis-Nexis, June 1, 1996.

41. Schiller et al., "And Now, a Show from Your Sponsors."

42. Scott Donaton and Pat Sloan, "'Control New Media': Artzt Spurs Advertisers to Seek Greater Role in Programming," *Advertising Age,* March 13, 1995, 8.

43. Kaplan, "Company Town," sec. D, 1.

44. Fred Hift, "The Tough Path to Prime Time," *Christian Science Monitor,* August 5, 1993, 12; on-line, Lexis-Nexis, May 12, 1996.

45. Jackson Lears, Review of *Adcult USA: The Triumph of Advertising in American Culture,* by James B. Twitchell, *In These Times,* April 15, 1996, 29.

46. Now called *The NewsHour with Jim Lehrer,* the nightly PBS show specializes in appearing to present diverse ideas while generally limiting comment to points of view normally considered responsible and worth hearing by the elite audience the show and its sponsors seek. See David Croteau and William Hoynes, *By Invitation Only: How the Media Limit Political Debate* (Monroe, Maine: Common Courage Press, 1994).

47. Dupree, "And NBC Makes Three," 6.

48. John Kiesewetter, "P&G Hopes to Clean Up with TV Deal," *Cincinnati Enquirer,* March 26, 1995, sec. F, 1; on-line, Lexis-Nexis, June 1, 1996.

49. Rob Morrow, *Northern Exposures* (New York: Hyperion, 1994), n.p.

50. Ellis Weiner, *The Northern Exposure Cookbook: A Community Cookbook from the Heart of the Alaskan Riviera* (Chicago: Contemporary Books, 1993), and Ellis Weiner, *Letters from Cicely* (New York: Pocket Books, 1992).

51. Sut Jhally and Justin Lewis, *Enlightened Racism: The Cosby Show, Audiences, and the Myth of the American Dream* (Boulder, Colo.: Westview, 1992), 135–136; see also Andrea Press, *Women Watching Television: Gender, Class, and Generation in the American Television Experience* (Philadelphia: University of Pennsylvania Press, 1991); Andrea Press and Elizabeth Cole, "Women Like Us: Working-Class Women Respond to Television Representations of Abortion," in *Viewing, Reading, Listening: Audiences and Cultural Reception,* ed. Jon Cruz and Justin Lewis (Boulder, Colo.: Westview, 1994), 55–80; Michael X. Delli Carpini and Bruce A. Williams, "Methods, Metaphors, and Media Research: The Uses of Television in Political Conversations," *Communication Research* 21, no. 6 (December 1994): 782–812; and, on people's use in discussions of what they have seen in the news, William A. Gamson, *Talking Politics* (Cambridge: Cambridge University Press, 1992).

52. Appadurai, *Modernity at Large,* 35.

53. Contemporary theorists of commodity fetishism tend to argue that it is no longer possible, if it ever was, to separate what Marx, following Adam Smith, called "use value," a product's apparent worth as a helpful object, from its "exchange value," its economic meaning in a market, because meanings have become so saturated by commercialism. For an overview of this work, see Robert Miklitsch, "The Commodity-Body-Sign: Toward a General Economy of 'Commodity Fetishism,'" *Cultural Critique* 33 (Spring 1996): 5–40.

54. Ibid., 6–7.

55. Karl Marx, "The Fetishism of the Commodity and Its Secret," in *Capital,* vol. 1 [1866–67], trans. Ben Fowkes, (Harmondsworth, England: Penguin, 1976), 163–177.

56. "Laundry Detergents," *Consumer Reports* (February 1991): 104.

57. Ibid., 100.

58. Ibid., 102.

59. Kate Kane, in her research on feminine authority and commercials for body products, argues that the most important exception to male voice-over predominance on television may be ads aimed at women for products that control personal emissions. See her "The Ideology of Freshness in Feminine Hygiene Commercials," in *Feminist Television Criticism,* ed. Charlotte Brunsdon, Julie D'Acci, and Lynn Spigel (New York: Oxford University Press, 1997), 290–299.

60. Mike Budd, R. Stephen Craig, and Clay Steinman, "Fantasy Island: The Dialectic of Narcissism," in *Aspects of Fantasy: Selected Essays from the Second International Conference on the Fantastic in Literature and Film [1981],* ed. William Coyle (Westport, Conn.: Greenwood, 1986), 87–93.

61. "Laundry Detergents," 104.

62. Experts disagree on how harmful such chemicals are to the environment. What testing there has been concentrates on short-term exposure. Since many clothes manufacturers include optical whiteners in their garments, it is difficult to say that their inclusion in detergents constitutes in itself a major source of harm. Consumers Union says there are "no convincing studies to suggest that the surfactants [the dirt-dissolvers] in major-brand detergents contain toxic or environmentally harmful ingredients." Ibid., 106.

63. Raymond Williams, *Television: Technology and Cultural Form* [1974], intro. Lynn Spigel (Hanover, N.H.: Wesleyan University Press, 1992).

64. Nick Browne, "The Political Economy of the Television (Super) Text," *Quarterly Review of Film Studies* 9, no. 3 (Summer 1984): 174–182.

65. Jane Feuer, "The Concept of Live Television: Ontology as Ideology," in *Regarding Television: Critical Approaches—An Anthology,* ed. E. Ann Kaplan (Los Angeles: American Film Institute, 1983): 15–20.

66. Jane Feuer, *Seeing through the Eighties* (Durham, N.C.: Duke University Press, 1995), 8.

67. Tania Modleski, "The Rhythms of Reception: Daytime Television and Women's Work," in Kaplan, *Regarding Television,* 67–74.

68. Rick Altman, "Television/Sound," in *Studies in Entertainment: Critical Approaches to Mass Culture,* ed. Tania Modleski (Bloomington: Indiana University Press, 1986), 44); see also Jane Feuer, "Concept of Live Television," 15.

69. Mike Budd, Steve Craig, and Clay Steinman, "'Fantasy Island': Marketplace of Desire," *Journal of Communication* 33 (1983): 67–77. Perhaps the most unpleasant experience commercial TV creates for its viewers is its interruption of desired programming with commercials. If so, commercial breaks themselves present a problem that the resumption of programming solves, mirroring those commercials with problem/solution structures. The resumption of programming after the ad, sometimes set up by an announcement that "we'll be right back," brings a solution after all, the

"pleasure of the return after disruption," reassurance after threat, after the bald appearance of TV economics, an announcement that "American television works!" Beverle Houston, "Viewing Television: The Metapsychology of Endless Consumption," *Quarterly Review of Film Studies* 9, no. 3 (Summer 1984): 186.

70. Lynn Spigel, introduction to Williams, *Television,* xxvi; see also John Ellis, *Visible Fictions: Cinema: Television: Video,* 2d ed. (London: Routledge, 1992): 116–126.

71. John Fiske, *Television Culture* (London: Methuen, 1987), 101.

72. Phone interview with Clay Steinman, August 24, 1994.

73. While we do not know how widespread the practice is, industry sources confirm that at least some network and local news staffs alert their advertising departments if a potentially undesirable flow looms—say an airplane crash with a scheduled airline advertisement. Advertisers are wary of flows that might hurt sales; both broadcasters and advertisers want to avoid the appearance of collusion where none exists. This is not to say that all flows smoothly on television or that advertisers' strategies can be easily discerned. The September 24, 1996, broadcast on NBC of *Mad About You,* for example, contained a comic subplot on the difficulties of breaking coffee addiction, followed by a networkwide ad for coffee.

74. Williams, *Television,* 118.

75. Bill McKibben, *The Age of Missing Information* (New York: Random House, 1992), 213.

76. A. J. Liebling, *The Press* [1946–1964], 2d. ed. (New York: Pantheon, 1975), 1.

77. Antonio Gramsci, *Selections from the Prison Notebooks [1929–1935],* ed. and trans. Quintin Hoare and Geoffrey Nowell Smith (New York: International, 1971), 419.

78. Browne, "Political Economy of the Television (Super) Text," 180.

79. This includes experiments in advertiser-supported satire of its products on shows it sponsors. See Savan, "Your Show of Shills."

80. Coca-Cola supplemented its TV bottle-cap contest with a special *Friends* Web page ("www.dietcoke/friends") that required participants to register their e-mail addresses. Random winners of free bottles of Diet Coke were asked to register their mailing addresses. Laurie Petersen, "Coke, NBC Make Friends," *Direct* (February 1996): 87; on-line, Lexis-Nexis, May 15, 1996. The company also hosted *Friends* parties on 50 U.S. college campuses February 22, 1996. "New Age Drink Sales Are Losing Some Momentum," *Chain Drug Review,* February 12, 1996, 28; on-line, Lexis-Nexis, May 15, 1996.

81. Barbara Wickens, "Rethinking the Commercial," *Maclean's,* January 15, 1996, 6; on-line, Lexis-Nexis, May 15, 1996.

82. For an application of these ideas to children's viewing, see Jodi D. Jacobson and Ellin K. Scholnick, "Children's Understanding of Television: A Theory of Mind Perspective," a paper delivered at the Jean Piaget Society Symposium, Philadelphia, June 1996. Hsueh Yeh called this source to our attention.

83. Jennifer Daryl Slack, "The Theory and Method of Articulation in Cultural Studies," in *Stuart Hall: Critical Dialogues in Cultural Studies,* ed. David Morley and Kuan-Hsing Chen (London: Routledge, 1996), 114.

84. T. J. Jackson Lears, "The Concept of Cultural Hegemony: Problems and Possibilities," *American Historical Review* 90, no. 3 (1985): 569.

85. Daniel C. Hallin, *We Keep America on Top of the World: Television Journalism and the Public Sphere* (London: Routledge, 1994), 12.

86. Larry Grossberg, *We Gotta Get out of This Place: Popular Conservatism and Postmodern Culture* (New York: Routledge, 1992), 244–245. For a history and critique of this position, see Colin Sparks, "Stuart Hall, Cultural Studies, and Marxism," in Morley and Chen, *Stuart Hall,* 71–101. See also John Rosenthal, "Who Practices Hegemony?: Class Division and the Subject of Politics," *Cultural Critique* 9 (Spring 1988): 25–52, for a compelling argument that class as a category envisioned by radical

thought has not been and should not be "analytically equal." He argues that the importance of class has been widely denied in the United States and that unlike gender and race, categories that objectified people in the interests of the powerful, class as a category developed "from below," by its working-class subjects and their allies. In the next chapter, we consider connections between the social roles of consumer and worker in the generation of elite wealth. These are critical to the environmental politics of television. For a journalistic survey of centrist discussions of class in U.S. politics, see Jason DeParle, "Class Is No Longer a Four-Letter Word," *New York Times Magazine*, March 17, 1996, 41 ff. Perhaps the most important U.S. anticapitalist treatment can be found in Harry Braverman, *Labor and Monopoly Capital: The Degradation of Work in the Twentieth Century* (New York: Monthly Review, 1974).

87. Stuart Hall, "Introduction: Who Needs Identity?" in *Questions of Cultural Identity*, ed. Stuart Hall and Paul du Gay (London: Sage, 1996), 4.

88. Ibid., 6.

89. Ibid., 3.

90. Robert Goldman and Stephen Papson, in their detailed critique of bogus environmental advertising, argue that corporations not only seek to deflect environmentalist critique, but they hope such marketing "relegitimates consumption . . . by alleviating the guilt associated with overconsumption by creating a distinction between good consumption and bad consumption." *Sign Wars*, 187–188. Yet this strategy may well be double edged. At what point will ads for refill Tide devalue the throwaway version?

91. Rosenthal, "Who Practices Hegemony?" 48; emphasis omitted.

92. Ernesto Laclau and Chantal Mouffe, *Hegemony and Socialist Strategy: Towards a Radical Democratic Politics* (London: Verso, 1985), 176–179.

93. Larry Grossberg, "Identity and Cultural Studies: Is That All There Is?" in Hall and du Gay, *Questions of Cultural Identity*, 88.

94. Kobena Mercer, "Back to My Routes: A Postscript to the 80s," in "Critical Decade: Black British Photography in the 80s" (special issue), ed. David Bailey and Stuart Hall, *Ten-8* 20, no. 3 (1992): 33; Feuer, *Seeing through the Eighties*, 16. This is not to devalue the drive of otherwise disempowered people to create spaces where they can be as much or more subjects of meaning as objects of others' definitions. John Fiske's distinction between two ways of thinking about an intersection of power—as a "locale," organized from the grassroots, and as a "station," organized by elites for grassroots control—seems helpful in this context. See his *Power Plays, Power Works* (London: Verso, 1993). But it is to stress the importance of participation in developing social movements over even the most sophisticated form of solitary consumption.

95. Herbert Marcuse, *An Essay on Liberation* (Boston: Beacon, 1969), 91.

Seven. From Consumers to Activists

1. The literature on global warming continues to grow as the problem intensifies, and there are scientists, not all of them corporate employees or free-market ideologues, who question the danger of the phenomenon. The information in this paragraph comes from a particularly helpful summary, William K. Stevens, "Experts Doubt a Greenhouse Gas Can Be Curbed," *New York Times* (national ed.), November 3, 1997, 1, 8. See also the *Times's* special section on global warming of December 1, 1997.

2. Keith Bradsher, "Auto Makers Plan Cuts in Emissions of Sport Vehicles," *New York Times*, January 6, 1998; on-line, Lexis-Nexis, January 14, 1998. "Anybody who has concerns about the environment can set them aside," Ford's president of worldwide operations, Jacques Nasser, told Bradsher. On January 9, 1998, perhaps worried about sales of such vehicles among affluent buyers with Greenish sensibilities, Ford took out a full-page ad in the *Times* (sec. A, 11) headlined "Every 1999 Sport Utility Vehicle We Sell Will Be Cleaner." Claiming it is Ford's "commitment to doing its part to save

the environment," the ad included a small green-colored leaf in its graphic design but mentioned nothing about global warming or that Ford's pickup trucks would remain unchanged. "There's a lot of green behind the blue Ford oval," it said.

3. Keith Bradsher has written several articles on the costs and hazards of sport utility vehicles and light trucks. See, e.g., his "Trucks, Darlings of Drivers, Are Favored by the Law, Too," *New York Times* (national ed.), November 30, 1997, 1, 22–23, and "Further Problems of Safety Found for Light Trucks," *New York Times,* December 12, 1997; on-line, Lexis-Nexis, January 14, 1998. *Road to Ruin,* a 1998 video by Robin Andersen and Paper Tiger Television (www.papertiger.org) offers an incisive and entertaining look at the marketing of sport utility vehicles. See also Andersen's "Sport Utilities: Vehicles of Cultural Mythology," in *Critical Studies in Media Commercialism,* ed. Robin Andersen and Lance Strate (New York: Oxford University Press, in press).

4. Homi Babha, "The Postcolonial and the Postmodern: The Question of Agency" [1992], in *The Location of Culture* (London: Routledge, 1994), 172.

5. See Carl Boggs, *Gramsci's Marxism* (London: Pluto Press, 1976).

6. See Michael Omi and Howard Winant, *Racial Formation in the United States: From the 1960s to the 1990s* (New York: Routledge, 1994).

7. See Joseph Turow, *Breaking Up America: Advertisers and the New Media World* (Chicago: University of Chicago Press, 1997). Turow attributes the concept of "image tribes" to Don Peppers and Marsha Rogers, *The One to One Future* (New York: Doubleday, 1993). The concept of "gated communities" of consumers is Turow's.

8. Murray Bookchin, "The Left That Was: A Personal Reflection" [1991], in *Social Anarchism or Lifestyle Anarchism: An Unbridgeable Chasm* (Edinburgh, Scotland: AK Press, 1995), 67.

9. Ella Shohat and Robert Stam, *Unthinking Eurocentrism: Multiculturalism and the Media* (London: Routledge, 1994), 48.

10. Chuck Kleinhans, "Cultural Appropriation and Subcultural Expression: The Dialectics of Cooptation and Resistance," Northwestern University Center for the Humanities, November 14, 1994. Also at http://www.rtvf.nwu.edu/studies/people/kleinhans/cult_and_subcult.html. The paper offers not only an accessible overview but also a good bibliography. We have written several pieces on this topic: Mike Budd, Robert M. Entman, and Clay Steinman, "The Affirmative Character of U.S. Cultural Studies," *Critical Studies in Mass Communication* 7 (June 1990): 169–184 (Kleinhans includes a valuable critique of portions of our argument); Mike Budd and Clay Steinman, "Cultural Studies and the Politics of Encoding Research," in *Communication Yearbook* 15, ed. Stanley Deetz (Newbury Park, Calif.: Sage, 1992), 251–262; Mike Budd and Clay Steinman, "Television, Cultural Studies, and the 'Blind Spot' Debate in Critical Communications Research," in *Television Studies: Textual Analysis,* ed. Gary Burns and Robert J. Thompson (New York: Praeger, 1989), 9–20; and Clay Steinman, "Audience Research and the Wish for Science," in *Political Communication Research: Approaches, Studies, Assessments,* ed. David Paletz (Norwood, N.J.: Ablex, 1996), 2: 225–235. Several recent articles and books have taken up the topic explicitly. See below for a short list.

11. Kleinhans, "Cultural Appropriation," 7.

12. See bell hooks, "Madonna: Plantation Mistress or Soul Sister?" in *Black Looks: Race and Representation* (Boston: South End Press, 1992), 145–156. Kleinhans also quotes Essex Hemphill, "To Be Real," in *Ceremonies: Prose and Poetry* (New York: Penguin-Plume, 1992), 114: In a video dominated by images of African American and Puerto Rican men, "the litany of names [Madonna] calls in the song as representative of style and attitude deliberately excludes Blacks and Puerto Ricans."

13. One need only go to academic media studies conferences or read a range of graduate and undergraduate papers to see that what started out as a political project has for

many students without progressive politics understandably ended up as a new method for celebrating their affection for artifacts of consumer culture. As the editors of the *Baffler* put it succinctly in their critique of a decade of academic cultural criticism, "When the subject was everyday life only one interpretation held their interest: that the noble consumer used the dross with which he or she was bombarded to fashion little talismans of rebellion and subversion. And with that polite little moué, a hundred-year legacy [of radical social critique] was abandoned when we needed it most." Thomas Frank and Matt Weiland, eds., *Commodify Your Dissent: The Business of Culture in the New Gilded Age* (New York: Norton, 1997), 14. This cannot reasonably be blamed on either the theory or its major practitioners. Rather, it has to do with what cultural studies has been saying all along: people use texts in ways based on their frames of reference. One way academics critique political economy reproduces a frame of reference, red-baiting, with a pedigree almost as long as the 20th century. They make political economy a bad object of Marxism. For an uncharacteristically shrill example, see James W. Carey, "Abolishing the Old Spirit World," *Critical Studies in Mass Communication* 12 (March 1995): 87.

14. Oscar H. Gandy Jr. has put it well: "A social categories perspective that assumes that common social experience generates common tastes, preferences, values, commitments, rationales, and so forth, seems doomed to perpetual challenge (if not falsification) in the face of compelling evidence of diversity within as well as between categories." "Introduction to Colloquy," *Critical Studies in Mass Communication* 12 (March 1995): 61.

15. This is a complex argument that we can only introduce. See Judith Mayne, *Cinema and Spectatorship* (London: Routledge, 1993). For other analyses, see Martin Allor, "Relocating the Site of the Audience," *Critical Studies in Mass Communication* 5 (1988): 217–233; Shaun Moores, "Texts, Readers, and Contexts of Reading: Developments in the Study of Media Audiences." *Media, Culture, and Society* 12 (1990): 9–29; and relevant portions of Ien Ang, *Desperately Seeking the Audience* (London: Routledge, 1991) and *Living Room Wars: Rethinking Media Audiences for a Postmodern World* (London: Routledge, 1996); James Hay, Lawrence Grossberg, and Ellen Wartella, eds., *The Audience and Its Landscape* (Boulder, Colo.: Westview, 1996); David Morley, *Television, Audiences, and Cultural Studies* (London: Routledge, 1992); and Robert Stam, Robert Burgoyne, and Sandy Flitterman-Lewis, *New Vocabularies in Film Semiotics: Structuralism, Post-Structuralism, and Beyond* (London: Routledge, 1992).

16. Mayne, *Cinema and Spectatorship*, 158; Ang, *Desperately Seeking the Audience;* and Rick Maxwell, "The Image Is Gold—Value, the Audience Commodity, and Fetishism," *Journal of Film and Video* 43 (1991): 29–45.

17. See Vincent Mosco, *The Political Economy of Communication: Rethinking and Renewal* (London: Sage, 1996).

18. Dallas Smythe, "Communications: Blind Spot of Western Marxism," *Canadian Journal of Political and Social Theory* 1, no. 3 (1977): 1.

19. "With all these labor-saving innovations [refrigerators, laundry machines, vacuum cleaners, microwaves, ready-made clothes, and processed foods], no labor has been saved. Instead, housework expanded to fill the available time. Norms of cleanliness rose. Standards of mothering grew more rigorous. Cooking and baking became more complicated." Juliet Schor, *The Overworked American: The Unexpected Decline of Leisure* (New York: Basic Books, 1991), 8. Also see Arlie Russell Hochschild, *The Time Bind: When Work Becomes Home and Home Becomes Work* (New York: Metropolitan Books, 1997).

20. Schor, *Overworked American,* 1–5, 7, 8–9.

21. Lawrence Wallack and Lori Dorfman, "Media Advocacy: A Strategy for Advancing Policy and Promoting Health," *Health Education Quarterly* 23, no. 3 (1996): 293–317.

22. Herbert Marcuse, "Ecology and the Critique of Modern Society" [1979], *Capitalism, Nature, Socialism* 3, no. 3 (1992): 33.

23. Joel Kovel, "Commentaries: II," *Capitalism, Nature, Socialism* 3, no. 3 (1992): 42.

24. See, for example, Karen J. Warren, ed., *Ecological Feminism* (London: Routledge, 1994).

25. Marcuse, "Ecology and the Critique of Modern Society," 36.

26. Jim Motavalli, "Enough!" *E Magazine* (March/April 1996): 28–35. See also the excellent video *Affluenza,* shown on many public television stations. It is available for $24.95 plus 4.50 shipping and handling from its makers, public station KCTS-TV, 4612 Union Bay Place, N.E., Seattle, WA 98105, or call 1-800-937-5387. A sequel, *Escape from Affluenza,* is also available.

27. Joe Dominguez and Vicki Robin, *Your Money or Your Life: Transforming Your Relationship with Money and Achieving Financial Independence* (New York: Penguin, 1992); Duane Elgin, *Voluntary Simplicity: Toward a Way of Life That Is Outwardly Simple, Inwardly Rich,* rev. ed. (New York: Morrow, 1993).

28. *Adbusters* (Autumn 1997): 48–52.

29. Ann De Vaney, ed., *Watching Channel One: The Convergence of Students, Technology, and Private Business* (Albany: State University of New York Press, 1994).

30. *TV-Free America's 1997 TV-Turnoff Organizer's Kit.*

31. Remarks by Elizabeth Thoman at the Media Literacy Group, Founding Convention, Cultural Environment Movement, March 1996.

32. Frances Moore Lappé and Paul Martin Du Bois, *The Quickening of America: Rebuilding Our Nation, Remaking Our Lives* (San Francisco: Jossey-Bass, 1994), 109.

33. Ibid., 131.

34. Shohat and Stam, *Unthinking Eurocentrism,* 35.

35. 1997–1998 Media Education Foundation Catalog.

36. Mark Dowie, *Losing Ground: American Environmentalism at the Close of the Twentieth Century* (Cambridge: MIT Press, 1996).

37. Don Fitz, "Who Are the Greens?" *Synthesis/Regeneration* 14 (Fall 1997): inside front cover.

Index

(Page numbers in italics refer to illustrations and charts)

About the Authors

MIKE BUDD is professor of communication and director of the Film and Video Program at Florida Atlantic University. He received his B.A. in English from the University of Kansas and his Ph.D. in communication studies, specializing in film, from the University of Iowa. He has written about television and film for the *Journal of Communication, Critical Studies in Mass Communication, Cinema Journal, Jump Cut, Cultural Critique,* and other journals. His edited book *The Cabinet of Dr. Caligari: Texts, Contexts, Histories* was published by Rutgers University Press in 1990, and his audio essay can be heard on the restored version of *Caligari* released on laserdisc in 1996 and on DVD in 1997 by Image Entertainment.

STEVE CRAIG is professor and chair of the Department of Radio, Television, and Film at the University of North Texas. He holds a B.S. in broadcasting and an M.A. in journalism and communications from the University of Florida and a Ph.D. in mass communications from Florida State. During his 20-year career in university teaching, he has also served on the faculties of the University of Maine and Florida Atlantic University. In addition, he has worked professionally in radio, television, and newspapers. His articles on the media have appeared in *Journalism Quarterly, Journal of Broadcasting and Electronic Media, Journal of Communication,* and others. He is the editor of the anthology *Men, Masculinity, and the Media* (Sage, 1992).

CLAY STEINMAN is professor and chair of communication studies and a member of the steering committee of the Comparative North American Studies Program at Macalester College in Saint Paul, Minnesota. He holds a bachelor's degree in history from Duke University, a master's degree in journalism from Columbia University, and a master's degree and a doctorate in cinema studies from New York University. He has written for several anthologies and such journals as *Critical Studies in Mass Communication, Cultural Critique, Journal of Film and Video,* and *Jump Cut.* A former journalist, he won a Distinguished Teacher Award at Florida Atlantic University in Boca Raton, Florida.

One of the world's foremost communication scholars, **GEORGE GERBNER** is currently Bell Atlantic Professor of Telecommunication at Temple University. He was professor and dean of the Annenberg School of Communication at the University of Pennsylvania from 1964 through 1989 and is a founder of the Cultural Environment Movement, an international media reform coalition dedicated to fairness, equity, and diversity in media.